The
100 Best
Small Art Towns
in America

2nd Edition

Where to Discover
Creative Communities, Fresh Air,
and Affordable Living

John Villani

John Muir Publications
Santa Fe, New Mexico

Second edition. First printing June 1996.

Library of Congress Cataloging-in-Publication Data

Villani, John
    The 100 best small art towns in America : where to find creative communities, fresh air, and
      affordable living / John Villani. — 2nd ed.
      p. cm.
   Includes index.
   ISBN 1-56261-275-1 (pbk.)
   1. Art patronage—United States. 2. Artist colonies—United States. 3. Cities and towns—United
States—Ratings. 4. United States—Description and travel. I. Title.
   [NX503.V55 1996]
   700'.973—dc20   96-13558
                                                            CIP

Editors: Nancy Gillan, Chris Hayhurst, Heidi Utz, Elizabeth Wolf
Production: Janine Lehmann, Nikki Rooker
Cover art: Tony D'Agostino
Map: Michael Bain
Design: Cowgirls Design, Marilyn Hager
Typesetter: Marilyn Hager
Printer: Quebecor Printing

Distributed to the book trade by
Publishers Group West
Emeryville, California

For Andree, Joseph, and Serge

Life's greatest rewards are reserved for its most creative individuals.
—Maria Thompson

Contents

Forewords

John Villani has created a wonderful resource for all of us interested in hunting the treasures of the American small community. In every corner of our nation, towns survive and thrive because of the local ingenuity, stunning natural resources, unique cultural traditions, and wonderful stubborn resolve. This book is loaded not only with examples of great places to go and things to see, but also with the promise of people to meet.

Other important insights come clear upon reading this book. For example, the arts are seen as a truly valuable economic contributor to the financial well-being of small towns and rural America. Whether tourism, or the jobs created by local arts institutions, or the cultural quality of life that attracts new business to a community, it is clear that the arts and other cultural activities are a solid partner in helping to sustain a healthy American economy. The profiles in this book support through pictures and stories the research findings of the National Assembly of Local Arts Agencies. Our studies at NALAA show the nonprofit arts in the United States to be a $36.8 billion industry supporting 1.3 million jobs and returning $3.4 billion to the federal government in taxes, not to mention returns at the local and state levels. It is wonderful to see these national statistics illustrated by towns like Northampton, Massachusetts, and Eureka, California.

There are other factors that come through as I read this book and think about the people and arts organizations that I have come to know in many of these towns across the country. I continue to be impressed by what the leadership of one or a handful of people can accomplish. The inspiration of a few dedicated visionaries can indeed make a town a better place to live.

Another point illustrated by the communities profiled in these pages is flexibility and creativity. There is no cookie-cutter arts and cultural community; each town is different from the next. These small towns have demonstrated a real sensitivity to local need and local arts resources. In the process each created a unique cultural identity. We seek out this uniqueness. It makes us want to spend time in these places, with these people.

It is gratifying for me to see how many local arts agencies play a role in shaping the small communities found in the following pages. The 3,800 local arts agencies in America, whether called arts councils or city arts commissions or the Mayor's Office of Cultural Affairs, seem to be making an important contribution to quality of life, community development, social problem solving, economic impact, and cultural growth. These are good things. The 100-plus small communities in this book exemplify these good things, and I am delighted that John Villani has taken the time to give us this valuable road map to the great small art towns of our nation.

Robert Lynch
President and CEO
National Assembly of Local Arts Agencies

In his refreshing and encouraging work, John Villani has identified, quantified, and described another 106 small art towns that have realized the multifaceted benefits of locally based and professionally guided arts projects. The company that I direct, the Missoula Children's Theatre, annually visits hundreds of communities that won't make it into John's book—places that, for the most part, cannot afford to give their children access to the broad-based arts programming available in many of the small towns he has profiled.

We live in a highly competitive era. Youngsters are introduced at an early age to the critical realities of our success-oriented society. From academics to athletics, children are pressured to achieve. At the same time, some people view the arts as a frill, a luxury, an extracurricular activity that runs a distant second to sports. MCT approaches children with a full awareness of these conditions and strives to use participation in the arts as a vehicle to develop the lifeskills and self-esteem necessary to equip kids to meet the challenges of our competitive times.

Our MCT Tour Project is based on week-long residencies wherein two actor/directors develop and produce a full-scale children's musical production, using 50 cast members selected from the local community. This year alone, we'll be staging Tour Projects in more than 600 communities from one corner of the continent to the other. When a child is cast in or becomes a crew member of an MCT play, he or she is guided by our actor/directors in developing emotional stability, teamwork, physical stamina, confidence, social interaction, and goal-oriented discipline.

Our impact on a community isn't limited to what we can do for the local children. When MCT sets up a residency in a small town, a sense of excitement spreads through the entire community. Suddenly, in a place where there was little interest in the arts, kids, adults, teachers, business leaders, grandparents, and politicians sit up to take notice of the small miracles taking place within the confines of MCT's rehearsal space. In other words, what we have been able to do in many of these small towns is to raise the community's awareness of its talented inner-self.

In the 25 years that I've operated MCT, I've had the opportunity to watch many small towns develop into precisely the sorts of great art communities that John focuses on in his book. If you had told me ten years ago that places like Scottsbluff, Nebraska, or Dillon, Montana, would one day be thriving small art towns, I'd have wondered whether you knew the difference between grease paint and gear lubricant. But these communities and hundreds of others across the U.S. and Canada have indeed become leaders in the locally-based cultural renaissance that has turned many depressed towns into the jeweled centers of America's small-town arts explosion.

And that's why a book like *The 100 Best Small Art Towns in America* is important: it acknowledges an amazing shift, a groundswell of creative ingenuity and civic pride in the arts that we at MCT see in small towns across the continent from one end of the year to the other. These are success stories in which we all can be enormously proud, and I take a special sense of pride in knowing that MCT played an important role in helping many of these unique communities become part of *The 100 Best Small Art Towns in America*.

Jim Caron
Founder and Executive Director
Missoula Children's Theatre

Introduction

Toss a dart at a map of North America and chances are it will land someplace where small towns are the focal point of people's lives. From eastern Washington to the panhandle of Florida, the countryside is a mosaic of rural communities that are safe, solid, and secure. But many of these small towns lack any sort of cultural life. This book identifies towns in the United States and Canada that combine the benefits of rural living with the stimulation only a culturally aware community could provide. In other words, they are not boring places to live!

The longing that many urbanites feel toward the notion of moving to a small town and leaving all their metropolitan worries behind must be tempered with a dose of reality: what the heck are you going to do there—besides have an amazing garden? My point is this: why bother moving to a small, affordable town if the only action taking place on Friday nights involves a can of beer and a jukebox? Wouldn't small-town life be much more interesting if there were opening receptions for exhibitions at art galleries, or live theater performances taking place at the restored art deco theater, or chamber music presentations at the arts center? The good news is that in many places across the U.S. and Canada, this type of artistic revival is precisely what local folks can take advantage of—and they don't have to leave home to do so.

Although the cultural action found in the towns covered in this book does not pass for the arts-avalanche taking place in a metro area like Vancouver, there are a growing number of small communities that serve up some truly first-rate arts programming. If you seek a life wherein a large city's bombardment of cultural activities is replaced by a small town's more narrow range of events, then let this book be your guide. You'll find wonderful communities where local residents can maintain their connection to the nation's cultural mainstream, yet still enjoy a small-town life. These are places that will welcome you and your family with open arms, places that hold the promise of a better life.

In many of the profiled towns, economic revival has gone hand-in-hand with cultural revival. Throughout the book you will encounter communities that once knew prosperity, but in more recent years fell on tough economic times when their (fill in the blank: mining, agriculture, manufacturing, fishing, or forestry) industries crashed and burned. Fortunately, artists, actors, musicians, gallery owners, and arts entrepreneurs noticed these towns' near-vacant infrastructures and began moving in, investing their meager financial resources and unlimited enthusiasm in an effort to make miracles happen. A decade later these same towns resemble a scene stolen from a Frank Capra movie. Downtown storefronts are filled, local working folks bring their children to the towns' new arts centers to see puppet shows on weekend afternoons, coffee bars have sprung up on side streets, old mansions have been converted into bed-and-breakfast inns, and annual summer arts festivals have become wildly popular community reunions.

Two types of towns are profiled in this book. The first offer residents fantastic access to the arts—communities where the arts action is geared toward the people who live there. The second are the towns that have benefited from the 1990s phenomenon of cultural tourism—the sort of economic upsurge that takes place when tourists visit for the express purpose of sampling art galleries, music performances, theater festivals, concerts, and dance presentations.

As culturally hip Americans and Canadians become more mobile in their quests to find places to visit, they are tiring of attraction-based tourism oriented toward theme parks, go-cart rides, ice cream parlors, and T-shirt shops. Instead they want authenticity and originality. Coupled with an adventurous spirit willing to trek off the beaten path, these wants define the reader who appreciates this book as an important arts-locating resource: the individual who knows great art when she finds it and who can make smart buying decisions when she discovers it in a thoroughly unexpected place.

Cultural tourism is the powerful economic engine driving resurgent small art towns from Alaska to Florida. It's a force that supports not only artists, theaters, and arts-related businesses, but also restaurants, nightclubs, brew pubs, and hotels. Cultural tourists search out artists in out-of-the-way places because they know that many have moved to smaller communities after establishing themselves in metro-area galleries, theaters, and concert halls. Today it's entirely possible for artists to live in small towns, while pursuing national and international careers in nearby urban centers. For this reason the serious art lover traveling in the splendor of the countryside knows better than to pass up a small-town gallery or crafts center.

Entrepreneurial spirit and the dedication of thousands of professionals to promoting the arts are key components in many of the places profiled in this book. Local arts administrators pour their hearts and souls into both enriching the cultural lives of their neighbors and educating their community's children on the tremendous benefits that flow from exposure to, appreciation of, and participation in the arts. Theater directors, conductors, dance instructors, art teachers, arts underwriters, gallery owners, curators, and the artists themselves work to make their communities a better place to live, and they deserve our support.

As this book is published, an important national debate is taking place over the issue of the government's role in supporting the arts with tax dollars. In many of the profiled towns, the government has provided the crucial investments needed to lead the communities to economic rebirth and surprising prosperity. Theater restoration, art center construction, historic district renovation, and art-education programs in local schools are just a few of the myriad ways in which aptly applied government funds have created success stories. Because there is no paradigm detailing how a small town can resurrect its economy based on the growth of cultural tourism, it is important to make clear the connection between an art town's economic growth and the continued commitment of government funding. Local, state, and federal governments must understand that funding for the arts is an economic development expenditure as much as it is a cultural expenditure, that in this final decade of the century many of America's rural communities have found economic as well as community strength in their successes. Arts equals jobs—let's never forget it!

My sincere thanks to the many dedicated arts professionals who have been so very gener-ous with their recommendations and information. Without their help this book couldn't have been written. Thanks as well to Denise Kusel, Maria Elena Alvarez, Phyllis Kapp, NALAA, Laura Loyacono, Rachel Rosen, Marta Boswell, Mark Cramer, Dan Anthony, Glenna Goodacre, Karyn Robinson, Michael Carroll, Tonya Turner, Jack Parsons, Manya Winsted, Nancy Cook, Ann Evans, Helen Alexander, and Janie Salinas.

John Villani
Santa Fe, New Mexico
March 1996

The Best Small Art Towns

BRITISH COLUMBIA

Banff

Chemainus
Salt Spring
Island

Nelson

ALBERTA

SASKATCHEWAN

MANITOBA

Anacortes
Coupeville

Metaline
Falls

Bigfork
Sandpoint

Olympia

WA

Walla
Walla

Moscow

Newport

Helena

ND

OR

Joseph

MT

Dillon

Ashland

ID

Sheridan

SD

Eureka

WY

Mitchell

Scottsbluff

Virginia City
Carson City

Springville

Loveland

NE

NV

UT

CO

Mariposa

Moab

Salida

Lawrence
Salina

KS

Telluride

Durango

CA

Raton

Taos

Guthrie

Madrid

OK

AZ

NM

Albany

TX

Bisbee

Alpine

Kerrville

Round Top

AK

Lahaina

HI

Rockport

Homer

Ketchikan

ONTARIO

QUEBEC

Baie-St.-Paul

St. Jean-Port Joli

NEW BRUNSWICK

ME

New York Mills

MN

Hancock

La Pointe

Johnson

Burlington

Woodstock

VT

Amery

NY

NH

Deer Isle
Belfast
Lewiston

WI

Fish Creek

Middlebury

MA

Newburyport
Peterborough
Northampton

Lanesboro

Galena

MI

Alfred

Corning

CT

RI

Nantucket

Spencer

Cedar Falls

IA

Jamestown

PA

Easton

Westerly

Shelburne Falls
Litchfield

IL

IN

OH

Carnegie

NJ

Peekskill

Quincy

Lancaster

MD

DE

Red Bank

Arrow Rock

MO

New Harmony

Columbus

Elkins

Berkeley Springs

Cape May
Lewes
Rehoboth Beach
Easton

Hannibal

Berea

KY

WV

VA

Abingdon

Salisbury
Fredericksburg
Charlottesville

Fayetteville

Blowing Rock

TN

Asheville

Woodbury

NC

Salisbury

AR

Oxford

SC

Hot Springs

Clarksdale

AL

GA

Beaufort

MS

Brunswick

LA

Panama City

FL

New Smyrna Beach

Small Art Towns

in the

United States

Homer, Alaska

Location

Hip, happening little Homer—Alaska's most artsy community—is so far removed from the rest of civilization that the widely used nickname for this art town is "the end of the road." Well, that suits Homer's artists just fine. They live here for the region's splendor, solitude, and salmon. So if these aren't your thing, slap on your mukluks and drive four hours northeast to Anchorage.

Great Outdoors

In the face of Alaska's incredible beauty, the human presence isn't just diminished, it is negligible (unless one decides to dump 10 million gallons of crude oil as his calling card). Homerans' favorite method of consorting with mother nature comes from the business end of a fishing rod, which turns out to be a perfect way to greet local celebrities: the halibut and salmon. Homer's at the far end of the Sterling Highway, a road traveling through some of the world's most breathtaking scenery along the Kenai Peninsula. The Peninsula features the Kenai National Wildlife Refuge and the Kenai Fjords National Park—two places rich with campgrounds, hiking trails, wildlife, and mosquitoes the size of Cobra choppers. City campgrounds can be found along the Homer Spit, as well as in the campsite park above town. Kachemak State Park, a great place for everything from clamming to back-country hiking to glacier skiing, is less than ten minutes away.

Lifestyle

To live here, you have to work like hell in the summer and hold on like mad in the winter. Alaska's powerful summer economic boom comes courtesy of the cruise ship business and the annual salmon and halibut runs. No matter who you are or where you live, in this part of the world you're either subsisting on the tourist industry or plucking valuable fish from the ocean waters. Homer's artists are absolutely wild about the town's annual flood of cultural tourists from all over the world who consistently bolster the town's economy.

In these parts, anyone who wants a spectacular view can have one, with average small-home prices in the $125,000 range, somewhat less if you're willing to live across the bay in Halibut Cove.

Arts education is taken seriously by the local schools, though funding cutbacks have prevented residents and teachers from reaching their goals for school art programs. Locals are employed as artists-in-residence, and the school district imports native Alaskan artists for craft and fine art residencies. While the local arts agency lacks a facility in which to offer many adult or kids' art classes (though the Homer Council on the Arts' summer pottery program for kids and adults is popular and highly regarded), Kenai Peninsula College has several. The college's winter foreign film festival is very popular with the local arts community, and the historically oriented Pratt Museum has winter exhibitions, including a student art exhibit, a juried regional show, and solo shows of work by top Alaskan artists.

Arts Scene

Homer's visual arts scene comprises commercial galleries and an artists' cooperative space called the Bunnell Street Gallery. Once a trading post, today their small space is used for rotating member exhibitions. Seating up to 75, it also hosts occasional classical and folk music performances. The commercial galleries do so well in the summer, that some close for the winter when their owners flee to Maui. Ptarmigan Arts, Picture Alaska, Art Shop Gallery and the Sea Lyon are considered the town's best places for art sales. Homer artists face the challenge of wedging their way into one of these spaces while also maintaining a presence in the town's many summer arts festivals.

Because of Homer's isolation, residents take the performing arts to heart. Winter dance, theater, and musical performances at Homer High's 400-seat Mariner Theatre are usually sold-out weeks in advance. Homer's community theater group, the Reduced Shakespeare Company, presents a few winter productions in its 90-seat Pier One Theatre home, and has an ambitious schedule of summer theater productions continuing through September. The arts council produces Homer's classical concert program, a five-performance series showcasing touring musicians, as well as the town's annual Nutcracker and regular literary readings.

Alternatives

Most of Homer's restaurants and cafés exhibit the work of local artists. The best are Café Cups, Two Sisters Bakery, and Latitude 59. Café Cups hosts poetry and literary readings through the winter, as does Latitude 59, which also presents folk and jazz musicians.

Art Perspectives

Contemporary ceramicist Annette Bellamy notes that in Homer, artists have to make money while the midnight sun shines. "Summers are incredible—people from all over the world, lots of sales, lots of things to do. It's difficult to handle, because it's so busy and there's so much daylight. Artists here don't feel out of touch, because there's so much different work being created. We all like to travel, and some come here after having lived all over the world."

Details

Population: 4,000

Important Arts Events: Spring Art Festival in April, Community Theater summer season at Pier One Theatre, Summer Street Fair in July, Concert on the Lawn in August, Seafood Festival in September

Must-See Art Galleries: Art Shop Gallery, Bunnell Street Gallery, Norman Lowell Studio Gallery, Picture Alaska Gallery, Pratt Museum

Local Arts Agency: Homer Council on the Arts
P.O. Box 1764
Homer, AK 99603
907/235-4288

Natural Foods Store: Smokey Bay Cooperative

National Public Radio: KBBI - 890 AM

Bookstore: The Bookstore

Chamber of Commerce: P.O. Box 541
Homer, AK 99603
907/235-7740

Ketchikan, Alaska

Location

The 15,000 residents of Ketchikan live on the far southeastern tip of Alaska, just west of the British Columbia border. Winters here aren't just cold . . . they're very wet and cold. The nearby Misty Fjords National Monument gets 150 inches of rain each year, so pack your hip waders for a trip to this town.

Great Outdoors

Ketchikan's island location in the middle of Alaska's Tongass National Forest contributes to the popularity of sportfishing as a favorite way to while away an afternoon. The surrounding region is filled with campgrounds and wilderness areas as well. Nearby Misty Fjords National Monument, when not shrouded in clouds, attracts tourists to its soaring peaks, cascading rivers, and many hiking trails. Deer Mountain Trail starts at the edge of town in City Park and works its way to the top of a 3000-foot peak. Although the area's islands are connected to each other by the state ferry system, many locals have their own planes to get from one place to another.

Lifestyle

Parts of Ketchikan's downtown have started to take on the appearance of a strip mall due to the growth of gift shops and souvenir stores that cater to cruise ship visitors, but a dedicated group of historic preservationists and cultural tourism advocates are working to prevent a complete takeover of the area. While the town has prospered from the cruise ship business (Smaller homes here sell for $125,000.), its challenge is to better promote the quality and uniqueness of the local arts and crafts trade.

Ketchikan is surrounded by one of the nation's richest tribal arts traditions—the totem carving arts of the Tlingit and Haida Indians. Several internationally prominent Native Alaskan carvers call the Ketchikan region home, including Tlingit master artist Israel Shotridge, who maintains his studio, classroom, and gallery space in Ketchikan. The Totem Heritage Center, operated by the town's museum department, is a repository of nearly three dozen historically significant totem poles. It is also one of the nation's most prestigious centers for traditional Northwest Coast arts education. Nearby Totem Bight State Historic Park is home to more than a dozen totem poles, while Saxman Village, a short drive south of town, has the state's largest collection of standing totems.

Local schools participate in the state art council's and the local arts agency's artist-in-residence program, but the summer fine arts camps in Sitka and Fairbanks offer the only arts education opportunity for kids outside of basic school programs. Adults can enroll in art classes at the town's University of Alaska Southeast branch.

Arts Scene

Ketchikan's Native Alaskan arts scene is centered around the Totem Heritage Center's exhibitions and the Cape Fox Corporation's programs at the Saxman Tribal House and arts center, a facility dedicated to both the performing and visual arts of this region's tribal artists. Shotridge Studio and Cultural Center also stages occasional exhibitions of Native Alaskan art. Ketchikan's nonprofit arts space, the Main Street Gallery (operated by the arts council), runs an ambitious year-round exhibition calendar featuring local work. The town's commercial galleries carry work by local and regional artists, with the Scanlon Gallery, Bell's Gallery, Soho Coho Gallery, and Beauty & the Bead being the most active. Tongass Historical Museum has a visual arts exhibition space used for some well-executed regional, statewide, and national visual arts shows. No Ketchikan artist misses an opportunity to exhibit work at the annual Ketchikan Blueberry Arts Festival, an arts council event with nearly 100 artists' booths, food, music, and tens of thousands of art buyers.

Performing arts are outstanding in Ketchikan, with the First City Players running a five-play season through the winter months in their Main Street Theatre. The theater is also the site of the art council's wildly popular foreign film series. The arts council produces its First Nighter Series, which features classical, ethnic, and pop music touring acts at the high school auditorium, the Saxman Tribal House, and the Ted Ferry Civic Center. Ketchikan Theater Ballet is active year-round but also operates a summer ballet camp, usually performing in its own recital space but occasionally using the high school for larger productions. Local classical musicians present their programs at the Main Street Theatre and one of the town's churches. Ketchikan's literary community holds regular readings at Parnassus Books.

Alternatives

Most Ketchikan restaurants are still caught up in their velvet Elvis stage, but there are two local places showing and selling local art: Five Star Café and Westmark Cape Fox Lodge.

Art Perspectives

Kate Berntson, a watercolor artist, says local sales are surprisingly strong. "The art council's annual art fairs are great ways to sell and to meet tourists who commission work you can do over the winter. Ketchikan's got an enthusiastic group that strongly supports the arts. In the past few years a steady stream of artists have been moving in, and it's been great to have their input and different perspectives."

Details

Population: 14,000

Important Arts Events: Festival of the North in February, King Salmon Derby in May, Alaska Blueberry Festival in August

Must-See Art Galleries: Alaska Eagle Arts, Bell's Gallery, Main Street Gallery, Scanlon Gallery, Shotridge Studios, Soho Coho, Tongass Historical Museum, Totem Heritage Center

Local Arts Agency: Ketchikan Area Arts & Humanities Council
338 Main Street
Ketchikan, AK 99901
907/225-2211

Natural Foods Store: Sunrider

National Public Radio: KRBD - 105.9 FM

Bookstore: Parnassus Books

Chamber of Commerce: P.O. Box 5957
Ketchikan, AK 99901
907/225-3184

Bisbee, Arizona

Location

Located in southern Arizona's Mule Mountains, Bisbee was built by generations of European and Mexican craftsmen and the money generated by copper mining. Today it is home to nearly 6,800 residents, many of whom are self-employed artists, authors, and business owners. Bisbee's closest big city is Tucson, a two-hour drive northwest. Its closest beach is less than a five-hour drive into Mexico.

Great Outdoors

While the rugged hillsides surrounding Bisbee (elev. 5,700 ft.) are dry as a bone, the nearby Huachuca Mountains, a half-hour's drive west, are thickly forested. The 8,000- and 9,000-foot peaks are part of the Coronado National Forest, which nearly stretches from the Mexican border to the suburbs of Tucson. The Huachucas boast one of North America's highest concentrations of hummingbirds, and for a good part of the year, Bisbee and its countryside become a birder's paradise. The Huachuca's Ramsey Canyon Preserve is home to mountain lions, monarch butterflies, black bears, javelinas, and gray fox, which is why the canyon is part of the Nature Conservancy's national system of natural refuges. Nearly 200 migratory species make their way through the area during fall and spring, spending part of their time at the 40-mile San Pedro Riparian National Conservation Area, a 58,000-acre bird watching and hiking paradise. Coronado National Monument, a short drive west of Bisbee in the foothills of the Huachucas, is a 5,000-acre wildlife and native plant preserve named after the Spanish conquistador who explored the Southwest almost 500 years ago looking for the Seven Cities of Gold. Chiricahua Monument, which has campgrounds, hiking trails, and a visitors' center, is a short drive north of Bisbee.

The region's landscape is one of the harshest environments in North America, but its high desert beauty is glorious. And the moderating effect of Bisbee's elevation allows the town to escape the extremes of Arizona's midsummer heat. It is not uncommon for temperatures here to be 10 or even 20 degrees cooler than in Tuscon's low desert furnace.

Lifestyle

Bisbee was born as an arts community when its prevailing copper mining industry dried up and moved away in the 1970s. That devastating economic blow ended an era that began in the late 1800s and had brought prosperity to this small community. Dozens of turn-of-the-century architectural treasures still stand in Old Bisbee, many in the same condition as when they were rebuilt after a devastating fire nearly a century ago. When the mines closed in 1975, Bisbee's small homes went begging for buyers, and what once could be snapped up for $5,000, today costs at least ten times that amount . . . and even more if the place is on the sunny side of Tombstone Canyon and has a view. An average-sized home in good condition runs in the $75,000 range, and it's getting more expensive with each passing year.

The Queen Mine, one of those left behind when the mining companies left town, is a tourist attraction today where people pay for the privilege of riding a rail car down into the

47-degree dampness of a copper miner's 9 to 5 prison. Every now and again there's talk of reopening one of these mines because they're still owned by a mining company, but so far nothing's come of the exploratory holes occasionally sunk into Bisbee's soil. The Bisbee Mining and Historical Museum borders downtown's Main Street on one side and the Copper Queen Hotel, a spectacular 1902 structure that's still a hotel, bar, and restaurant, on the other side. Main Street winds uphill from Old Bisbee's downtown, becoming Tombstone Canyon Road by the time it hits the "Copper Miner", a statue of a muscular man mounted on a pedestal along the roadside.

Local art education programs have been hurt by school funding cutbacks, but the Bisbee Arts Coalition attempts to take up some of the slack by funding an artist-in-residence program in the local schools. Some artists volunteer their time to teach an occasional art class. The Bisbee Repertory Theatre runs a kids' summer theater, music, and writing camp, and Dance Arts is Bisbee's private dance academy.

Arts Scene

Bisbee has a lot in common with the small art town of Hot Springs in that both communities were, until recently, extremely inexpensive places for commercial and residential property— places that attracted artists and other creative individuals. Both have now become popular, and their real estate values have become much more expensive as cultural tourists have made investments of their own in the communities. In Bisbee's case, the town was loaded with homes that had been lived in by mining families: a mix of some Victorians, but mostly much plainer and more modest working-class homes.

For years the arts scene was very quiet and geared toward entertainment for the locals, while the town's visual artists scraped by on meager local sales. Bisbee was quiet and outside the tourist path. Just a few years ago things started picking up, and the arts scene is now a sur- prisingly prosperous one. Many artists are able to make a respectable part of their annual income from selling into the local market. The Bisbee Gallery Association has nearly two dozen members, most of whom operate visual arts and fine craft exhibition spaces in Old Bisbee's historic downtown. The Bisbee Arts Coalition raises money through community-wide arts events to fund not only its artist-in-residence program but also to award grants to the Bisbee Repertory Theater and the Fiber Arts Festival, to publish the town's arts events calen- dar, and to conduct grant-writing workshops for local arts groups. The Bisbee Council on the Arts and Humanities maintains the mining museum and partially funds the Bisbee Belles Choral Group and the Rotary Chorus, working with the Bisbee Foundation. The Central School Project is a nonprofit group that owns and operates Bisbee's historic downtown Central School building, which has been turned into a vibrant, three-story complex of studios, audito- rium, and nonprofit organization offices.

Bisbee's nonprofit visual art exhibitions are primarily staged at the Central School's gallery, which is open to local artists willing to hang, publicize, and gallery-sit their own shows. The Central School Project also presents four annual exhibitions of its own, one being an exhibition for the project's 35 artist members and guest artist members. The Bisbee Convention Center, which is housed in an art-deco structure across from the mining museum, maintains a nonprofit exhibition space, and the Old Baptist Church Showcase Theater, which serves as the home of the Bisbee Rep, rotates nonprofit exhibitions through its lobby gallery space during each production's run.

Bisbee's commercial gallery scene is getting stronger, in part because of the large number of sophisticated artists who have been attracted into town and in part because more and more cultural tourists are venturing into Bisbee to check it out. The work that's selling is largely created by local and regional artists, with the range running from Southwestern landscapes by Arizona and New Mexico artists to contemporary crafts, fine photography, Native American fine crafts and jewelry, and contemporary paintings. The big change in the commercial galleries is the increase in the price of art being sold here. Where you once found prints and paintings selling for $500 or much less, there are now sales being made in the $2,000 range (though there's still lots of $500 and under art being exhibited), which is quite a leap in the space of three short years. Fortunately, much of that increase is flowing directly to Bisbee artists, a group whose own level of creative skill has risen along with the town's reputation as a must-stop on the Southwest's cultural tourism circuit.

On the performing arts end of things, Bisbee is already doing well, and the future looks bright. The Bisbee Repertory Theatre is a new company that's presenting six productions annually in the Old Baptist Church Showcase Theater, a 150-seat converted church along Main Street in Old Bisbee. The company's tastes run from melodrama to comedy to heavy drama, and it's been able to tap into the town's healthy tourist business as a way to fill seats during its year-round season. The town's comedy theater company, B.T.V., presents spoofs of Bisbee's current political and social events in nearby Lowell at the Erie Street Theater. Theatre Degree Zero is dedicated to experimental work and new plays and uses the 120-seat auditorium at the Central School for its performances. Central School's auditorium is also used for occasional performing arts programs in dance and music, monthly readings presented by Borderline Poetry Theatre, and the September–May International Film Series presented by Cochise College.

The town's classical music series is For the Love of Music, an October–May series of performances by regional music professionals from Tucson, Phoenix and sometimes Los Angeles, who perform at the Bisbee Women's Club, a 150-seat auditorium on Quality Hill overlooking Old Bisbee. For some reason, Bisbee always seems capable of turning out in numbers for live reggae performances at the Kilimanjaro Club, a converted Odd Fellows hall that is also the town's smoke-free dance space. Local bands play at several venues around town, including the slightly sleazy St. Elmo's Bar and the much spiffier Stock Exchange, both of which are located in Brewery Gulch, a part of town once famous for its cat houses and gambling joints. Two other bars, at the Copper Queen Hotel and the Bisbee Grand Hotel, also feature live music on weekends.

Alternatives

Most of Bisbee's restaurants exhibit the work of local artists, and many sell it straight off their walls with surprising frequency. Rotating shows are hung at the Copper Queen Hotel lobby, Café Roka, Iron Man Café, the High Desert Inn, Renaissance Café, Eighteen Steps, and Thunderbird's Table. One of the town's largest annual arts events is the Fiber Arts Festival, which takes place in November and serves as a showcase for Bisbee's fast-growing community of weavers, sewers, and clothing designers. The festival's activities include exhibitions at several of the Old Bisbee gallery spaces, a lecture/workshop by a top national fiber artist, and a fiber art fashion show at the Bisbee Women's Club.

Art Perspectives

Jane Hamilton, president of Bisbee Gallery Association says, "What's different about the art market of today is that we're having buyers show up now at times when we wouldn't normally have seen them. The new artists tend to be very good at what they do, and their work is more expensive than what's sold in the past, but even that kind of art is selling these days. And the galleries are becoming more professional in the way they deal with their artists and their clients. They're finding that by raising their standards they're getting good results."

Bates Lockhart, founder of the Bisbee Repertory Theater, notes, "There's a real interest in Bisbee for live theater, and there are talented people to fill the different roles as well as an audience that will get out there and buy tickets. We give away lots of free and reduced-price tickets to seniors and kids, because those are the local people we need to have coming through our doors. If we can become a sort of cultural center for the community, a place where musicians and dancers are able to come for performances and classes, we would be filling even more of Bisbee's needs."

Details

Population: 7,000

Important Arts Events: Bisbee Poetry Festival in August, Fiber Arts Festival in November

Must-See Art Galleries: Bellasai Gallery, Bisbee Fiber Arts Cooperative Gallery, Bisbee's Finest Gallery, Central School Project, Coyotillo Gallery, Firehouse Gallery of Fine Art, Hunting Crow, Jane Hamilton Fine Art, Johnson Gallery, Meridian Gallery, Molly Ramolla Gallery, Mountain Meadow Gallery, Richard Byrd Gallery, Subway Gallery, Write On Paper

Local Arts Agency: Bisbee Arts Coalition
118 Arizona Street
Bisbee, AZ 85603
520/432-4866

Natural Foods Store: Bisbee Food Co-op

Farmer's Market: Weekend mornings at the traffic circle

National Public Radio: KUAT - 90.5 FM

Bookstores: About Books-About Bisbee, Atalanta Books, Eureka Books

Chamber of Commerce:
P.O. Box BA
Bisbee AZ 85603
520/432-5421

Fayetteville, Arkansas

Location

In Arkansas' spectacular northwest corner, the Ozark Mountains fold in and out of lakes, rivers, agricultural valleys, and small backwoods communities. Fayetteville, home of the University of Arkansas, is a town of 45,000 residents located about a two-hour drive east of Tulsa.

Great Outdoors

Beaver Lake, a 28,000-acre outdoor recreation magnet, is a year-round canoers' paradise, as well as a seasonal destination for water skiing, sailing, sportfishing, and duck hunting. Those not wishing to make the 20-minute drive can visit Lake Fayetteville and its surrounding park. The Ozark Mountains are one of the nation's premier white-water rafting resources and also hold a canoeing trail system. During much of the year, easy access to beautiful rivers, lakes, and streams is just a short drive away. Devil's Den State Park, 30 minutes south of town, combines its many campgrounds and lakeside cabins with one of the state's favorite hiking areas. If salt water is more to your liking, Galveston's Gulf Coast beaches are just a day's drive south.

Lifestyle

As a university town, Fayetteville has a lot in common with small art towns like Charlottesville, Lawrence, and Moscow. These communities have managed to integrate both their campus and local arts scenes to come up with an exciting hybrid. Wal-Mart and Tyson's Corporations, both headquartered in the region, are major Fayetteville arts underwriters.

Until a few years ago, the town's arts scene was almost exclusively a campus affair of theater and music department offerings. Local visionaries decided that the town really needed a multimillion-dollar performing and visual arts/arts education center. Fayetteville looks with pride to the spanking new Walton Arts Center, a state-of-the-art, 1,200-seat performance space with an adjacent 240-seat black-box theater. The facility also comprises a small amphitheater, arts organization offices, classrooms, demonstration studios, and a library. To its credit, the Walton Arts Center puts much of its energies and funding toward education, an admirable effort that takes up the slack from regional school programs. Area schoolkids are treated to everything from performances to lectures, classes to summer art camp. Students at every level can participate in matinees, special events, and visual/performing arts training and appreciation classes year-round. The center trains teachers to integrate arts education into the school curriculum and attracts other adults for its series of classes.

Arts Scene

The Walton Arts Center has three nonprofit visual arts exhibition spaces: the Markham Gallery, the Main Lobby Gallery, and the Just Off Center Gallery. Markham is the largest, presenting mostly regional work by painters and fine crafts artists, plus some touring national exhibitions and Native American shows. The contemporary Main Lobby and Just Off Center Galleries each rotate six annual exhibitions of primarily one-artist shows.

On the University of Arkansas campus, the Fine Arts Center gallery displays touring national shows as well as faculty and student work, while the Kittrell Gallery exhibits student and art department faculty work exclusively. The Ozarks are one of America's leading fine crafts regions, and many of the area's best artisans exhibit at both the Arkansas Craft Guild Gallery and the Enigma Gallery. Indian Paintbrush Gallery, in nearby Siloam Springs, features a strong group of Arkansas painters, while the Fayetteville Art Association exhibits member work at Miss Phydella's Art Gallery in town.

Fayetteville's performing arts scene is centered around the Walton. The center presents four to six monthly performances of its own, while serving as home to the U of A's fine arts performance series. The Walton's acts cover classical, folk, ethnic, and jazz music, as well as one-night stands of touring Broadway shows. The university's series brings contemporary dance, classical, and pop music into town, while the school's theater and music departments use the two on-campus venues for their own productions. The North Arkansas Symphony stages its winter season at the Walton Center and tours the region for a series of summer outdoor pops concerts. During summer the symphony presents a month-long festival series of chamber, orchestral, and pop music, and organizes a youth symphony orchestra as well.

Being a college town means that Fayetteville can support an alternative music and theater scene. Ozark Stage Works, an experimental company, uses the Walton's black box for its four annual productions of new material. Some local bands make their living playing at such places as the 36 Club and George's Majestic Lounge.

Alternatives

Arsaga's Expresso Café is Fayetteville's most popular alternative to the gallery scene, exhibiting monthly shows of contemporary work by local artists. Popular hangouts in town include the Ozark Brewery, Emerald Coast Coffee House, Jose's Mexican Café, and the Dickson Street Grill.

Art Perspectives

Susan Jones of the Walton Arts Center says, "Our landscape is breathtaking, there's a beautiful lake, and hundreds of artists in every field. This community promotes and appreciates what our artists do."

Details

Population: 42,000

Important Arts Events: Concerts in the Park in summer, Arkansas Music Festival in July, Autumnfest in October

Must-See Art Galleries: Arkansas Craft Gallery, Fine Arts Center Gallery, Joy Pratt Markham Gallery, Just Off Center Gallery, Kittrell Gallery, Main Lobby Gallery, Miss Phydella's Art Gallery

Local Arts Agency: Walton Arts Center P.O. Box 3547

Fayetteville, AR 72702
501/443-9216

Natural Food Store: The Ozark Natural Foods Co-op

Farmer's Market: Tuesday, Thursday, and Saturday mornings at City Square

National Public Radio: KUAF - 91.3 FM

Bookstore: Hays and Sanders

Chamber of Commerce: P.O. Box 4216 Fayetteville, AR 72702 501/521-1710

Hot Springs, Arkansas

Location

The small town of Hot Springs, a fast-growing community with big-time arts ambitions, sits in west-central Arkansas an hour southwest of Little Rock. Tucked into a river valley and surrounded by Ouachita National Forest's rugged terrain, Hot Springs is best known for its wild past as a gambling mecca and its more sedate present as President Clinton's boyhood home. If the town's artists, musicians, and arts administrators have their way, though, Hot Springs could become a hot spot for the national and international art worlds.

Great Outdoors

True to its name, Hot Springs does indeed have water, pushed to the surface by ancient springs beneath the town. West of town is Lake Ouachita, a sprawling outdoor recreation treasure, attracting not only sailors, jetskiers, and houseboaters, but also a steady influx of recent Hot Springs immigrants from the West and East, whose lifelong dream has been to live in a waterfront home.

Lake Ouachita is so crammed with wide-mouth bass that the idea of dropping a line into the lake is irresistible. The lake is warm and clear during most of the year, and early morning waterskiing in mid-April isn't unusual. You can find campgrounds, state parks, hiking trails, fishing holes, mountain biking trails, and freshwater springs throughout Ouachita National Forest. Ouachita's verdant hillsides are pockmarked with natural mountain springs. It's no coincidence that the region is home to one of the nation's largest producers of mountain bottled water.

In town, the Hot Springs National Park Visitors Center sits along a scenic stretch of Central Avenue known as Bathouse Row. Huge spa buildings built during the early part of the century hark back to a time when Hot Springs was one of the nation's most prominent healing centers. The park covers 5,500 acres, with 47 natural thermal springs that supply the Hot Springs Health Spa, Buckstaff Bathhouse, and Arlington Hotel Bathhouse. The Park also features 30 miles of hiking trails leading into Ouachita Mountain back-country regions and campgrounds.

An hour's drive west of Hot Springs takes you into the untamed natural beauty of Ouachita River country, one of the South's most popular canoeing stretches.

Lifestyle

Over the past few years, real estate sales have boomed in Hot Springs. Artists who bought their downtown, three-story gallery buildings for dirt-cheap prices four years ago have watched their investments double, triple, even quadruple. Every commercial storefront on Central Avenue is now filled. Tawdry topless joints and seedy bars have been run out of town, their locations taken over by art galleries, sophisticated restaurants, and specialized boutiques. Downtown renovations are moving ahead at lightning speed, and the community is optimistic.

The uplifting impact of an expanding cultural tourism economy in Hot Springs is the main reason for this renaissance. Hot Springs once had an economy founded on backroom casinos, brothels, bookies, and bootleggers. But in the early part of the century, it depended on the dollars of visitors who poured into the town for its healing waters and therapeutic treatments. The tourist infrastructure remains in surprisingly good condition, attracting artists, musicians, and other professionals who have far-reaching ideas of how the community can prosper in the tourist trade.

Hot Springs is still shabby in some quarters—the result of several decades of neglect when the community's economy was scraping by in the '60s, '70s, and '80s. But the town retains its historic architectural legacy, attracting the right kinds of people to restore everything to its original glory. Homes around Hot Springs range widely in value, with houses 10 miles from Central Avenue selling for around $60,000 and lakefront property going for $150,000 and up.

One of the more interesting aspects of Hot Springs is the way town opinion on tourism has changed. For years, visitors came to Hot Springs to ride go-carts and listen to country music. This attraction-based tourism failed to boost downtown Hot Springs' real estate values. But ever since artists arrived in Hot Springs, the value of downtown real estate has skyrocketed. Business leaders have been quick to realize that their best shot at a prosperous future is directly related to the health and continued growth of Hot Springs as an arts center. They realize that by investing today in performing arts facilities, art education centers, and historic building renovations, Hot Springs can attract a better quality of tourist. Don't be surprised if the community's rapid ascent to prominence in the art world attracts corporate ventures and the types of businesses that have made such places as the small art towns of Sandpoint, New York Mills, Durango, and Northampton so grateful for cultural tourism's powerful economic impact.

Arts Scene

It all started in the late 1980s with two art galleries. At the time, Hot Springs had lots of cheap space in dilapidated downtown buildings, along with a potential only a handful of people realized. Today, new galleries are added each year to the current mix of nearly a dozen commercial visual arts exhibition spaces in the downtown area. What's more interesting is that the original galleries still prosper, exhibiting and selling a challenging range of art.

As unlikely as it might seem, the town's visual arts focus has built on the presence and exhibition of work by contemporary Italian painters and sculptors. An Italian artist, Benini, was one of the town's first gallery owners. Malinda Herr-Chambliss, a gallery owner committed to exhibiting the work of Italian contemporary artists, was another early arrival on the Central Avenue arts scene. Since then, Hot Springs has attracted other Italian artists who have moved their studios and homes here. An Italian from New York opened a Northern Italian restaurant that also hosts traveling exhibitions by Italian artists.

Hot Springs galleries also exhibit regional and local work, covering everything from young artists fresh out of the University of Arkansas arts department, to established players on the Memphis, Dallas, and New Orleans arts scenes, all the way up to national masters. Hot Springs has a non-profit gallery exhibiting the traditional work of its art league members, and will acquire a large exhibition space inside the convention center being built at one end of the downtown district. Two local restaurants, the Thai food Lotus Restaurant and the Northern Italian sophisticated atmosphere of Belli Arti Restraunte, exhibit rotating shows of visual work by local artists.

Hot Springs galleries have publicized their existence to the rest of the region by sponsoring monthly "Gallery Walks," coordinated by the newly established Arkansas Celebration of the Arts. Art Walks not only brings new exhibitions into Hot Springs, it also sponsors a performing arts festival, a classical music series, poetry readings by top national poets, and a children's performing arts program.

While the Arkansas Celebration of the Arts has introduced the performing arts to Hot Springs, the newly organized Hot Springs Music Festival has carved out a place on the nation's classical music map. The Festival is a 22-concert, two-week event that includes classical music performances throughout the historic downtown district. Organized by relocated Philadelphia conductor Richard Rosenberg and his wife Laura, Hot Springs Music Festival brings more than two dozen established national music professionals into town for performances. These visiting experts also teach 75 young musicians, guiding them as they move into positions in the music world.

Only two community theater groups are active in Hot Springs, but theater could blossom after the expansion and renovation of the convention center's 1,200-seat performing arts hall. The new facility could become a major stop on the nation's touring performing arts circuit, pulling in top theater, dance, and music companies. If the Clinton Cultural Campus project turns the old Hot Springs High School into an arts education, administration, and performance facility, this small art town might become an American version of the Banff Centre for the Arts.

Another local performing arts organization that has gotten off to a hopeful start is the Hot Springs Documentary Film Festival. In just four years, the festival has become the nation's preeminent event in the documentary film genre, bringing more than 100 screenings of three dozen award-winning works into Hot Springs for a week-long event. The festival is purchasing a permanent home in downtown Hot Springs' historic Malco Theatre, a 450-seat movie house that could become as successful as the great Oscar Regent Theater in the small art town of Cedar Falls.

Alternatives

While Hot Springs has attracted top national and international artists to make their homes and studios in the town, it has yet to address the need for public works of art. French sculptor Jeanfo, creator of monumental works exhibited in the U.S., Canada, and Europe, has no publicly exhibited works in Hot Springs—and he's just one of many local talents available for public art projects.

Art Perspectives

"In a place like Hot Springs an artist can take chances, and doesn't have the same sorts of pressures an artist living in a large city has to deal with," says Richard Rosenberg, conductor and co-founder of the Hot Springs Music Festival. "When you go somewhere where there's no precedent, you're free to reinvent the wheel, which is a challenge that interests me. Hot Springs is the kind of place that is incredibly supportive of people like Laura and me—they want us here, and we want to be here."

Linda Palmer, owner of Palmer's Gallery 800 comments, "The amazing thing about Hot Springs is its art market. We're pulling in collectors from five states, people who appreciate new and different ideas in art. A few years ago, nobody could have predicted what's happened in Hot Springs, but somehow the word has gotten out. Collectors who like certain kinds of work have started finding their way here. I think our community and our art market is still in its infancy."

Malinda Herr-Chambliss, gallery owner, says, "What the Rosenbergs are doing for Hot Springs' performing arts is exactly what the galleries here are trying to do for its visual arts. The Clinton Cultural Campus project will attract opera instructors, photographers, drama professionals, and many more other artists into town. The second floor of the center could be devoted to music education because, after all, the President himself is a saxophone player. Even our hospital has collected over 500 original works of art that it exhibits in patient rooms."

Italian artist, Benini: "What Hot Springs needs is a gallery exhibiting Latin American contemporary artists and African American artists—and a first-rate sushi chef."

Details

Population: 34,000

Important Arts Events: Hot Springs Music Festival in June, Hot Springs Documentary Film Festival in November, Arkansas Celebration of the Arts in November, Hot Springs Monthly Gallery Walk

Must-See Art Galleries: American Art Gallery, Contemporanea Fine Arts, Herr-Chambliss Fine Arts, Palmer's Gallery 800, The Art Foundation

Local Arts Agency: Arts Cooperative Team 211 Exchange

Hot Springs, AR 71901
501/321-0234

Natural Foods Store: The Country Store

Farmer's Market: Saturday mornings in Hill Wheatley Plaza

National Public Radio: KUAR - 89.1 FM

Bookstores: Golden Leaves, Lambert's Bookstore

Chamber of Commerce: P.O. Box 6090 Hot Springs, AR 71902
501/321-1700

Eureka, California

Location

California's north coast extends from the art town of Mendocino and nearby Point Arena clear up to the Oregon border, bounded to the east by coastal mountain ranges and to the west by the storm-tossed waters of the Pacific. Five hours north of San Francisco, pervasively green Eureka occupies a nearly oceanfront location on Humboldt Bay. While scattered remnants of both its logging industry and fishing fleet still exist, these economies have taken hard hits in recent years. The downturn, however, has an up-side. A very forward-thinking group of arts activists, artists, actors, and musicians have moved into Eureka and turned it into a very different place than it was just ten years ago.

Great Outdoors

The town's 28,600 residents live within reach of some of the most spectacular natural wonders America offers. Historically this region was supported by forestry, especially the cutting of redwoods. But while many of the most magnificent trees fell to loggers' blades, the region today has several parks devoted to preserving and appreciating what remains. The most prominent of these is Redwoods National Park, a World Heritage Site with old-growth redwoods strung along 40 miles of coastline less than an hour north of town. The park is home to the world's tallest tree, a redwood more than 350 feet tall, standing side-by-side with thousands of others merely 250 feet tall. Humboldt Redwoods State Park, a short drive south of Eureka, is famous for its 31-mile Avenue of the Giants, a drive through the middle of a 51,000-acre, old-growth redwood forest. Nearby Grizzly Creek Redwoods State Park has a similar wealth of beauty but is much less crowded on summer weekends. Redwoods thrive on tremendous amounts of moisture, and this region's climate gives them what they need, with monthly rainfall averaging nearly five inches for the year's cooler seasons.

As you head inland from Eureka, the landscape is dominated by 6,000- to 8,000-foot mountain peaks towering over parks, wilderness areas, back-country hiking trails, and trout streams. Six Rivers National Forest's 1 million acres cover much of that mountainous terrain, where the forest service maintains a dozen campgrounds. The closest downhill skiing is about four hours away, but cross-country skiers and winter sports lovers can find lots of places closer to Eureka.

Along this section of the coast, the Pacific's waters are cold year-round, and a dip in the ocean water is usually just that. Locals can enjoy the water, if only from a distance, from the sand dunes of several state parks and beaches. One of the most popular is the 14,000-acre old growth preserve at Prairie Creek Redwoods State Park, but there are also Patrick's Point, Trinidad State Beach, and Humboldt Lagoons State Park, with their spectacular coastal hiking trails, campsites, and beaches. In Eureka itself is the 52-acre Sequoia Park and Zoo, as well as Fort Humboldt State Historical Park. Nearby Arcata, located on the north end of Humboldt Bay, is home to a 154-acre wildlife sanctuary right at the edge of the town's business district. Surf casting, clam digging, and driving ATVs on ocean dunes are popular year-round.

Lifestyle

As is the case with many of the small towns discussed in this book, Eureka's reputation as an arts town started to grow when the community's economic foundations began shifting. As efforts to revive the fishing and forestry industries failed, the writing on Eureka's wall became clearer and clearer: something else had to be done. Several of the necessary art town components were already in place. Humboldt State University in Arcata had for years been graduating visual arts and music majors who often decided to stay in town. A number of local residents had moved to the North Coast after having spent much of their lives in the Bay Area and Los Angeles. Small businesses such as vegetarian cafés, head shops, and craft stores had been here since the '60s.

The town's turnaround came when the municipal government launched its Century III project to preserve Eureka's historic, but then-shabby, downtown. Shortly thereafter the community's 49-block central business district was officially designated Eureka's Cultural Arts Resource District, an effort jointly overseen by the Eureka Main Street program, the Humboldt Arts Council, the Eureka Redevelopment Agency, and the Eureka Arts and Culture Commission. Working together, these groups have used the arts to revive the economy of the Old Town district. Their efforts have been abetted by a Live/Work Ordinance allowing district artists to convert their second-story commercial studios into living spaces. A restoration program has returned commercial storefronts to their original beauty, and a muralist-in-residence program has completed nearly a dozen murals in the Old Town area. A phantom art gallery project, modeled after a successful venture in Tucson, has brought short-term art shows into vacant storefronts, attracting permanent tenants to several buildings.

In all, the success of Eureka's Cultural Arts District program has been dramatic. Not only has the district's appearance improved, but several art galleries, crafts shops, restaurants, and cafés have moved into the area, bringing daytime foot traffic and even a nightlife of sorts. Artists are moving in as well—both those who exhibit and sell their work in Eureka, and others who market their work elsewhere—and a new generation of entrepreneurs have joined them, making this community's arts-based economic development project one of America's greatest small-town success stories.

Building on that success, the Eureka arts organizations are working together to plan and construct a performing arts complex and an art museum that will also serve as the town's convention facility. This project will give Eureka a modern 850-seat theater, a 250-seat black-box rehearsal space, and a museum-quality visual arts showcase for national touring shows. It will dramatically impact the town's arts scene and could bring Eureka national renown for the scope of its performing arts.

One of the most interesting Cultural Arts District proposals to fly off the drawing board is the development of an arts incubator project inside one of Old Town's vacant industrial buildings—a project that replicates the phenomenally successful Torpedo Factory arts center in Alexandria, Virginia. The Torpedo Factory has resulted in some incredible successes for its artists, neighboring property owners, and the city of Alexandria, which has reaped a fortune in taxes from the increased revenue of area businesses.

Art education programs in Eureka's schools are well-funded, innovative, and comprehensive. Local arts organizations such as the Humboldt Arts Council and the Ink People have complimentary programs aimed at Eureka's youth. The arts council focuses on bringing fine art, lectures, and video presentations into the schools. It also sponsors an in-school literary program, an at-risk kids' mural program, and an annual exhibition of youth art in the phantom galleries. The Ink People, a nonprofit arts center housed in a turn-of-the-century schoolhouse, coordinates Eureka's artists-in-residence program, using local artists for projects within the schools' integrated arts curriculum. The Ink People also offers an extensive program of kids' art classes, as does nearby Humboldt State University's Academy of Art for Children, one of the country's top schools for arts educators. Many of the region's performing arts organizations offer kids' classes, both as after-school programs and as more serious training programs to introduce kids to performing arts career possibilities.

Arts Scene

Eureka's primary nonprofit exhibition spaces are run by the Humboldt Arts Council, the Ink People Center for the Arts, and the Redwood Art Association. The art council's exhibition space and offices are inside the renovated Carnegie Library. Its shows range from master works of its permanent collection to regional invitationals and local one-artist shows. The Ink People's exhibits have a contemporary slant, drawing from its 450-member artists and holding national invitationals such as its highly acclaimed annual masks exhibition, *Maskibition*. Exhibitions take place inside a renovated 6,000-square-foot, two-story schoolhouse complex. Eureka's oldest visual arts organization, Redwood Art Association, exhibits the work of its many accomplished members in the Humboldt Cultural Center, an Old Town visual arts gallery. The association's exhibits are known for works using traditional imagery.

Eureka's commercial gallery scene has its share of comings and goings. Ten galleries actively exhibit local and regional visual art and fine crafts. The town also has a highly successful alternative art project that rotates hundreds of artists' work through 65 commercial businesses around the region. The impact of the visual arts in this area can't be overestimated. Many of Humboldt County's smaller communities have their own nonprofit art centers and commercial galleries showing the work of the region's many fine artists. Ferndale, Arcata, Blue Lake, Garberville, and Fortuna can all stand on their own as small art towns.

The Eureka area's performing arts powerhouse is CenterArts, a Humboldt State University organization bringing top performing artists to the school's 800-seat Van Duzer Theatre. CenterArts offers both amazing quality and breathtaking diversity, ranging from rock to classical, from jazz to ethnic, from gospel to Baroque, and from folk to contemporary dance. This truly first-rate organization would turn heads in any metropolitan area.

Eureka has three theater companies: North Coast Repertory, Plays in Progress/World Premier Theatre, and the Humboldt Light Opera Company. Atop Eureka's brewpub you'll find World Premier Theatre, presenting recent works and an annual new plays festival during its ten-month season. The repertory theater's 200-seat Old Town playhouse is the setting for its nine-month, five-production season. In nearby communities, choose from the Ferndale Repertory Theatre, Blue Lake's professional Dell'Arte School of Physical Theatre, and a summer Shakespeare festival in Garberville. The region's contemporary dance company is Dancenter, in Arcata, presenting classical and ethnic dance instruction for all ages.

Musical offerings are similarly plentiful. The Eureka Symphony performs its winter season at venues around town, while the Humboldt Community Concert Association's touring classical soloists and chamber orchestras play in area churches. College of the Redwoods, a two-year school, presents its own program of touring classical music groups in the college's Forum Theater. In summer months the arts council presents a series of free outdoor musical performances at Sequoia Park and Adorni Center Amphitheater. Eureka also has an alternative music scene, with nightclubs such as Club West, the Eureka Inn, and Hotel Carter presenting jazz, rock, and reggae. In the college town of Arcata, bands play at Humboldt Brewery, Jambalaya, and Café Mokka.

Alternatives

Looking for an alternative? Start with the Cultural Arts District's phantom galleries, work through the list of 65 businesses participating in Eureka's alternative gallery program, then stop in for a meal at New Lazio's, Folie Douce, Eureka Baking Company, Humboldt Bay Coffee Company, Los Bagels, or the Sea Grill, and Eureka! You've found it.

Art Perspectives

Libby Maynard, director of the Ink People Center for the Arts, relates, "We're about emerging artists, emerging organizations, and emerging programs. Our motto is 'community development through the arts.' We work to have our local artists challenged by the competition that's created nationally. Our 'alternative gallery' program is very successful at getting local artists sales."

Painter Joan Gold notes, "Eureka's become a much more sophisticated place to live. There are art organizations with different, exciting visions, and I feel like I'm always able to get something out of attending the exhibitions here."

Painter Jim McVicker adds, "Tourists are coming into Eureka to buy art, and that's something new. There's a positive, supportive feeling among the artists here, and there are lots of ways the arts organizations help artists get their work out into places where it can be shown."

Details

Population: 28,600

Important Arts Events: Humboldt International Film Festival and Redwood Coast Dixieland Jazz Festival in March, World Championship Great Arcata to Ferndale Cross Country Kinetic Sculpture Race (a.k.a. the Triathlon of the Art World) in May, Mad River Festival and WoodFair in July, Reggae on the River in August

Must-See Art Galleries: Ambiance Gallery, Arcata Storefront Gallery, Art Center, Hotel Carter Gallery, Humboldt Arts Council Gallery, Humboldt Cultural Center Gallery, Humboldt's Finest, Ink People Center for the Arts Gallery, Old Town Art Gallery, Truchas Gallery

Local Arts Agency: Humboldt Arts Council
214 East Street
Eureka, CA 95501
707/442-0278

Natural Food Stores: Eureka Natural Foods, North Coast Co-op, Wildberries

Farmer's Market: Tuesday and Thursday mornings on the plaza in Old Town, Eureka

National Public Radio: KHSU - 90.5 FM

Bookstores: The Booklegger, Eureka Books, Sit & Sip Awhile, Thompson House Books

Chamber of Commerce: 2112 Broadway
Eureka, CA 95501
707/442-3738

Mariposa, California

Location

One of Yosemite National Park's gateways takes you right through the community of Mariposa. A gold-rush town of about 2,500, Mariposa has managed to maintain its historic authenticity amidst a gorgeous setting framed by towering peaks. The Bay Area is a four-hour drive from here, while L.A. is six hours to the south.

Great Outdoors

A huge piece of Yosemite National Park forms the eastern edge of Mariposa County, making the park a major local employer and providing residents with easy access to one of the jewels of the park system. Though crowded during summer, for most of the year Yosemite is a quiet, secluded place filled with back-country hiking trails, premier rock climbing sites at Half Dome and El Capitan, and Bridalveil Falls, Hetch Hetchy Reservoir, and Mirror Lake. Mariposa sits at the edge of two national forests, Stanislaus and Sierra, both of which are filled with state and regional parks, streams, lakes, and wilderness trails. Millerton Lake, an hour's drive south, is a sailboarder's dream. In nearby Snelling are Lake McClure and Lake McSwain, while Santa Cruz's beach and boardwalk are a three-hour drive west. Several ski areas are within easy reach of town, the closest one at Yosemite's Badger Pass, is just 30 minutes away.

Lifestyle

Artists here learn how to deal with the seasonal cycles a resort area. Winters are quiet, mostly sunny stretches of time ideally suited to concentrating on work, while in summer the name of the game becomes selling. Housing is affordable by California standards; for $150,000, you can find a home with a bit of land and maybe even a view of one of the 10,000-foot peaks to the east. This historic little town has gone to great lengths to preserve its architectural integrity, and most developers have elected to build down the valley at Oakhurst. Mariposans seeking access to movie theaters, malls, and pizza parlors need only drive down a rugged, twisting road.

Being so close to Yosemite, Mariposa has more than its share of employment options for a town of its size—with Park Service positions at the top of the list. Also coveted are jobs with the many outdoor recreation companies, guiding tourists on horseback, river rafting, bicycle, rock climbing, and fishing trips. Other common choices are restaurant and hotel employment.

Mariposa's schools have hooked up with the Mariposa County Arts Council for an artist-in-residence program at the elementary school level, but for older kids, the arts education programs are still in the "art-cart" and music-class era. During the summer months the arts council runs its art camp, an extensive series of art classes in six regional schools. Though geared toward kids, the program is also sprinkled with adult classes in media such as basket-making, acrylic painting, leather crafts, and jewelry.

Arts Scene

Mariposa's visual artists can make a good part of their yearly income from summer's flood of tourists, but the challenge is in getting their art displayed in one of the park's hotel gift shop/galleries. That may change as tourists are lured by Mariposa's aggressive promotional campaign touting the town as *the* place to grab lunch and fill up before entering Yosemite.

The arts council has opened its own exhibition space in Mariposa's folksy business district, and an artists' cooperative exhibition space is located at the Sierra Artists Gallery. Both are selling local work in surprising numbers as culturally motivated tourists discover that Mariposa is a great place to find affordable, inventive works of art. There is a thriving Native American artist community in the region; however, these artists find more of a market for their traditional fine crafts and turquoise-and-silver jewelry than for their contemporary work.

Performing arts in Mariposa are limited to high school plays and some bar music; thus the Oakhurst community theater is a popular diversion. The community supports several very fine historical museums: the California State Mining & Mineral Museum, the Mariposa County History Center & Museum, and the Northern Mariposa County History Center in nearby Coulterville.

Alternatives

Some local restaurants exhibit the work of local artists. Among the best are the Sawmill Restaurant, High Country Health Food, and Goldie's.

Art Perspectives

According to William Fontana, a painter living in Yosemite Park, "Our art catches people by surprise, and I think the reason it's so good is the freedom you feel from living here. I have the best art studio in the world, just 50 yards from the Merced River and a short walk to all the park's great sights."

Potter Connie Collins agrees, "I'm always impressed by the quality of the art made here, so it's no surprise that many artists are doing quite well from local sales. Artists here have a strong sense of community and are connected to each other through the art council's programs."

Details

Population: 2,000

Important Arts Events: Gold Rush Days in May, Music on the Green during the summer, Holiday Arts & Crafts Fair in December

Must-See Art Galleries: Mariposa County Arts Council Gallery, Sierra Artists Gallery, Yosemite Valley Art Activities Center

Local Arts Agency: Mariposa County Arts Council
P.O. Box 2134
Mariposa, CA 95338
209/966-3155

Natural Foods Store: High Country Health Food

Farmer's Market: Sundays at Darrah schoolhouse

National Public Radio: KVPR - 89.3 FM

Bookstore: The Book Connection

Chamber of Commerce: P.O. Box 425
Mariposa, CA 95338
209/966-2465

Durango, Colorado

Location

Southwest Colorado is a land where three dominant geographical features intersect: the broad, parched badlands of the Colorado Plateau; the beauty of the San Juan Mountains' 14,000-foot peaks; and the desert wonderland of the Four Corners region, home of Monument Valley and Mesa Verde National Park. From Durango, it's a five-hour drive to Albuquerque. Phoenix is almost closer then Denver, which is seven hours across the Rocky Mountains.

Great Outdoors

More than any other art town in the Southwest, Durango's combination of mountains, rivers, and deserts make it an ideal setting for every kind of outdoors activity imaginable. The town's 13,000 residents are liable to head outdoors at the slightest provocation, whether it's a winter blizzard that sends them to Purgatory Mountain (one of Colorado's best ski areas, less than an hour north of Durango), or a summer heat wave that pushes them into the San Juan Mountains on the backs of their mountain bikes. Spring thaws make Animas River an ideal white-water rafting destination, and glorious autumn days are perfect for soaking tired bodies in 100-degree thermal pools at Trimble Hot Springs.

Durango has also become an important stop on the national mountain biking circuit, hosting the world championships a few years back. Bikers from around the country arrive to sample the San Juan National Forest's rugged terrain, heading either to or from the art town of Moab, a three-hour drive away. Many of the nation's top mountain bikers live in Durango, and some of the hottest racing bikes are crafted in small shops on the outskirts of town. Major mountain biking events held here include the Iron Horse Classic (a race against a steam train), the Durango Century Classic, and World Mountain Bike Week at Purgatory ski resort. Several great mountain bike rides start right at the edge of downtown, heading into the foothills of the narrow Animas River valley.

The Animas River—or El Rio de las Animas Perdidas ("River of Lost Souls")—cuts through the center of Durango as it winds its way from the base of the San Juans toward the San Juan River and the Grand Canyon. The Animas features white-water rafting of national reputation, and one stretch through town is a kayaking slalom course. In fact, some of the Southwest's top white-water events are held just a few minutes' from downtown.

Vallecito Lake, just a half-hour drive east from Durango, is the town's favorite place for windsurfing, canoeing, lake fishing, and camping. The landscape surrounding Durango includes three-million-acre San Juan National Forest—a huge expanse of mountains and valleys stretching nearly to the small art town of Telluride. The national forest is filled with everything you'd expect from the Rocky Mountains: dozens of campgrounds, untouched wilderness, raging rivers, and mountain views.

One of the best ways to get a feel for the forest is to take a day trip on the Durango & Silverton Narrow Gauge Railroad, a turn-of-the-century steam railroad that travels between Durango and the former mining town of Silverton. The train rolls along tracks that at times look as though they have been wired into the sides of the cliffs along the Animas River. The tracks also run through beautiful meadows like the ones surrounding Blue Lake Ranch.

Durango's southern flank is bordered by the Southern Ute Reservation and the Mountain Ute Reservation, the home of Native Americans who once controlled most of what is now Colorado and Utah. The Anasazi Indians constructed an amazing complex of cliffside villages that are preserved inside Mesa Verde National Park, less than an hour west of Durango. As one of the crown jewels of the National Park system, Mesa Verde is an inspiring and awesome place—the homeland of a civilization that left because of drought a millennium ago. Today the Ute tribes are right at the forefront of the nation's casino-building craze. Sky Ute Lodge & Casino, a half hour drive south of Durango, is an interesting place to view authentic Native American fine arts and traditional crafts.

Lifestyle

Like many other Western mountain towns, Durango got its start because it was near gold and silver mines. Its turn-of-the-century mining boom was responsible for much of the downtown's National Historic District, which is lined with two-and three-story brick buildings that look as beautiful as they did when Teddy Roosevelt was President. Of course, mines need trains to haul ore in one direction and miners in the other. One of the reasons why Durango is such a popular tourism spot is because the railroad never quit running. Every afternoon, when the Durango & Silverton Narrow Gauge completes its daily runs and drops off its passengers downtown, hundreds of tourists hit the town's stores, factory outlets, and art galleries, pumping needed dollars into the local economy.

For Durango, prosperity has come with a price tag. Downtown parking during the summer is so tight that Durango might only be a year away from turning the entire downtown area into a valet parking zone. Also bad are the unconscionable rent increases imposed by landlords, most of whom are newcomers or live outside the area. Durango's real estate values ($150,000 and rising) have priced many local families out of the market. Today, it's common for people who work in town to live in one of the surrounding communities.

Still, Durango is a wonderful place for artists, mostly because it's an easy drive into the art gallery wonderlands of Santa Fe, Taos, Aspen, and Beaver Creek. Unfortunately, living here requires a two-income household where both wage-earners are earning significantly more than minimum wage. The town has done a great job of promoting itself as a stopover on the Southwest's tourism circuit, pulling in visitors from Santa Fe and Moab, which might be why Durango has such great restaurants, art galleries, and clothing stores. Cultural tourism has made a substantial contribution to Durango's prosperity.

Durango benefits greatly as the home of Fort Lewis College, a four-year school that is part of the state college system. The school has strong music and art departments, and turns out more than its share of first-rate teachers in the town's local school system. A few years ago the college's arts programs suffered a setback when heavy snows caused the roof of the performing arts center to collapse. A new 600-seat performing arts center will be completed in 1997, which could dramatically improve Durango's access to big-name performing artists.

Durango's schools have decent programs in arts education. The arts center has formed a partnership with the local school district aimed at funding artist-in-residence programs, with a long-term goal of creating an integrated arts curriculum. A series of after-school and weekend classes are also in the works. The community's performing arts organizations have programs designed to teach kids about performance, several artists who specialize in private art classes for kids, and a children's dance academy called "Over the Rainbow." The town has two historical museums: Animas Museum (Durango and Western history) and the Grand Motorcar & Piano Collection.

Arts Scene

Durango's most prominent and most active nonprofit visual arts exhibition space is operated by Durango Arts Center, located on Main Street in historic downtown. The gallery exhibits nearly 20 shows spotlighting local artists with a decided emphasis on contemporary work. Occasionally, the center brings touring exhibitions into Durango. Through the gallery shop, the center sells the region's most professionally executed art work, similar to the way the Holter Museum of Art handles artists in Helena, Montana. The town's other prominent nonprofit exhibition space is the Fort Lewis College Fine Arts Gallery, which exhibits mostly faculty and student art. The gallery is scheduled for relocation to the school's new performing arts center when that facility is completed.

Over the past several years, Durango has developed a surprisingly healthy gallery scene as more cultural tourists visit southern Colorado. There are more than a dozen commercial galleries downtown and another commercial space in nearby Hermosa. Not all these galleries exhibit work by Durango artists, but several take local arts seriously and have resisted the urge to turn themselves into watered-down versions of galleries in Taos and Santa Fe. One example of fine local art is produced by Durango's jewelry makers who sell their work across the continent.

The performing arts in Durango have taken their share of hits in recent years, but artists and organizations have managed to survive. With the new performance center at Fort Lewis College, the Alexander Murray Series of classical music will no longer be confined to Roshong Recital Hall, and the San Juan Symphony (composed largely of faculty members) will move from the Miller Middle School Auditorium. The college will also present a series of its own, which could bring touring musicians, contemporary dance companies, theater, and ethnic dance to Durango. Durango Arts Center is another presenting organization, even though its performance space seats only a couple of hundred audience members. It does an outstanding job of presenting groups such as the Animas Chamber Players as well as children's theater and jazz performances.

"Music in the Mountains" in late July is Durango's most notable classical music festival, an event that puts together an orchestra from musical organizations around the Southwest. It also invites nationally known soloists for a series of performances at the Purgatory ski lodge, and presents several programs in regional communities, including a children's concert Rotary Park. Two other organizations that routinely present musical performances are the Four Corners Jazz Foundation, which brings acts into town for shows at the Strater Hotel's Diamond Circle Theater, and the Durango Society of Cultural and Performing Arts, which uses the same stage for contemporary folk music, blues, reggae, and jazz.

Durango's student population supports a vibrant night scene. With the help of curious tourists and locals who enjoy a night on the town, places such as Chelsea's London Pub, Farquahrt's, The Steaming Bean, Edgewater Lounge, and Pelican's Nest keep Durango's musicians employed.

Durango's theater scene is currently in a state of change. The college's drama department performs at its own facility, bringing in guest directors for its various series. But the Durango

Repertory Theater Company, a 15-year-old community theater group, recently lost the lease on its performance space in the historic district to a landlord who would like to see the building become Durango's new T-shirt mall. Time and again, community theater companies in small art towns have realized that the best strategy for planning their secure future is by purchasing a building or becoming a tenant in a municipally operated performing arts center. It remains to be seen whether local artists can persuade the city to put a performing arts center on the planning agenda.

Alternatives

Many of Durango's restaurants and coffee bars show work created by local artists, but the most popular places to exhibit art are The Steaming Bean, Season's Grill, Lola's Place, and Mama's Boy.

Art Perspectives

Lawrence Nass, a classical and adult-contemporary pianist says, "Durango is a tough place to start a career as a musician, but it's an enjoyable place to live. If you look hard enough, you can find room to do what you need to do. It is supportive of the arts—teaching piano is an important source of my revenue. I do year-round concerts in places like Telluride, Moab, and Aspen. Hopefully, with the new performing arts center opening, we'll start to see a stronger calendar of touring performing arts. We certainly have the kinds of people here who can support it."

Details

Population: 13,000

Important Arts Events: Art in the Park in August, Bluegrass Festival in April, Spring Gallery Walk in June, Music in the Mountains in July, Main Avenue Arts Festival in August

Must-See Art Galleries: Durango Arts Center, Fort Lewis College Fine Arts Gallery, Gallery Ultima, Hermosa Fine Arts Gallery, Termar Gallery, Toh-Atin Gallery

Local Arts Agency: Durango Arts Center 835 Main St. Durango, CO 81301 970/259-2606

Natural Foods Stores: Durango Natural Foods and Nature's Oasis

Farmers Market: Saturday mornings in Bayfield

National Public Radio: KSUT - 89.5 FM

Bookstores: Maria's Bookshop, The Bookcase, The Southwest Book Trader

Chamber of Commerce: P.O. Box 2587 Durango, CO 81302 970/247-0312

Loveland, Colorado

Location

America's sculpture capital, Loveland is slightly more than an hour's drive north of Denver. This community of 43,000 sits at the western edge of the Great Plains and the eastern edge of the Rocky Mountains' Front Range, providing the year-round inspiration of mountain views.

Great Outdoors

Boyd Lake, a large freshwater recreation magnet a few minutes' drive east of Loveland, is the town's favorite place for water-skiing, sailing, and bass fishing. The west side of Loveland climbs into the Rocky Mountains, near Rocky Mountain National Park. Some 60 miles to the southwest, Loveland Basin ski area is invariably Colorado's first to open its lifts—usually in late October. The national park is an outdoor dream—hiking trails by the hundreds, backcountry campgrounds, trout streams—and what's not in the national park can be found in the Roosevelt National Forest's millions of surrounding acres.

Lifestyle

Loveland exemplifies what a small town can accomplish when it coordinates its time and talents to use the arts to redefine its future. The town has sent a clear message that its priorities are on building its arts scene and attracting cultural tourism. Its success has attracted the attention of art communities around the West. Places such as Joseph, Bigfork, and Springville all look to Loveland in directing their own efforts to use the arts as economic-development drivers.

The arrival of a single artist who established a bronze foundry in the early 1980s, casting his own work and that of a few other friends, led the change. In those days Loveland was a hidden treasure where homes and downtown studio spaces could be had for a song (try whistling $125,000 today), so many of these sculptors moved into Loveland to be near their foundry. In time, Loveland's reputation spread throughout the world of realist sculptors whose bronzes sell in Santa Fe, Aspen, Sun Valley, Scottsdale, and Park City galleries.

Today, Loveland is home to hundreds of sculptors, enlargers, casters, welders, craters, and pedestal makers. Nearly a hundred other artists (painters, glassblowers, ceramists, weavers) have moved into town to take advantage of Loveland's unique critical mass of creativity. It's become a great place for those who want to live in a community of artists. The influx has generated an economic renaissance in Loveland. As real estate prices have rebounded, downtown storefronts have been completely restored and rented out, and the community has developed a strong reputation as a "must-stop" on the regional cultural tourism circuit.

A highly successful summer sculpture festival and a percent-for-the-arts program have united to fund the installation of nearly 80 public sculptures all over Loveland, from school campuses to senior centers, government offices, and the town's main streets. Everywhere you turn, Loveland's art hits you squarely between the eyes. The Loveland High Plains Art Council, a local sculptors' group, has used some of the money from its annual Sculpture in the Park exhibition to fund the installation of public sculpture throughout a lakefront park, and in just over ten years more than 40 bronzes have been permanently installed in Benson Park.

Arts Scene

The Loveland Museum/Gallery is this community's municipal museum; the 4,000-square-foot gallery is used for a wide range of rotating shows, from masterworks by local sculptors to touring fine-crafts exhibitions and one-artist paintings shows by Colorado artists. The museum/gallery also coordinates a lecture series, an art education program for local kids, literary readings, and studio demonstrations by visiting artists. Loveland's commercial gallery scene has developed momentum and a wonderful reputation over the past several years, creating many jobs and business opportunities for the town. Ten galleries are scattered around Loveland's unpretentious downtown area, and each year others are added to the mix.

Loveland's performing arts scene is geographically desirable for Colorado State University's first-rate performance series, which brings top names in classical, jazz, theater, and contemporary dance to nearby Ft. Collins. Loveland's own chamber orchestra presents an energetic series of classical music programs at the First Christian Church and in some private homes. It also conducts a young artists competition with cash awards for schoolkids. Loveland Civic Music Association's concert series, at Roberta Price Civic Auditorium, presents five productions through the autumn and winter months. August through May is Loveland Community Theater's six-play season. One of the most promising developments on the town's performing-arts front is the renovation of downtown's Rialto Theatre; when completed it will host most of the town's performing-arts events.

Alternatives

In this small art town, sculpture is everywhere you look—from the insides of restaurants to peoples' homes to the downtown streets to the town's parks.

Art Perspectives

As Mike Langhoff of the Loveland Community Theater says, "One of the new facilities being built here is a natural amphitheater, which will give us a performance area right on the lake. The renovated Rialto will be too small a stage for what we do, so we can't use it."

Details

Population: 43,000

Important Arts Events: Governor's Invitational Art Exhibition in April, Sculpture in the Park in August

Must-See Art Galleries: Benson Park public sculpture, Columbine Gallery, Demott Gallery, Gallery East, Loveland Gallery/Museum

Local Arts Agency: Loveland High Plains Art Council
125 East 7th Street
Loveland, CO 80537
970/663-2940

Natural Foods Store: Cabin Country

Farmers Market: Saturday mornings at Fifth and Lincoln

National Public Radio: KUNC - 91.5 FM

Bookstore: Footnote Books

Chamber of Commerce: P.O. Box 7058
Loveland, CO 80537
970/667-6311

Salida, Colorado

Location

Colorado's Arkansas River Valley is laced with alpine streams that channel crystal-clear, glacier-cold snow melt from dozens of towering Rocky Mountain peaks. Salida and its 5,300 residents are nestled near the entrance to this spectacular valley. The Arkansas River, a premier white-water river, cuts right through the middle of town.

Great Outdoors

The Arkansas River was one of the first white-water rivers to attract the attention that has led this sport to become a favorite pursuit across the country. Your watersport choices are rafting with a group of friends or handling the river on your own in a dart-shaped kayak. Either way, you're surrounded by massive peaks of the Rocky Mountains and a deep blue, seemingly endless sky. This part of the state also has fantastic fishing.

If action off the raging waters is more your speed, jump on Salida's other fun-time highways, hundreds of miles of mountain biking trails that wind up and over the Sangre de Cristo's 14,000-foot peaks. Four-wheeling on abandoned logging roads is another summertime favorite, and this part of Colorado is rich with back-country jeep trails that are perfect for three-day camping trips along rugged mountain roads.

Monarch Pass, less than a 30-minute drive from Salida, is the town's closest ski area, while Crested Butte is just another hour or so west. Wilderness areas are within an easy hike of Salida, and Great Sand Dunes National Monument, as unusual a place as you'll find on the continent, is an hour's drive south of Salida on the east side of the San Luis Valley.

Lifestyle

Once a tough little town filled with miners, gamblers, and Gibson girls, the Salida of today is finding a new salvation in its pursuit of cultural tourism. The town is prospering from this change, as evidenced by the $125,000 price tag for an average-sized residence. In fact, some artists are wondering if maybe they've gone far enough. But for now, Salida's quite happy to be attracting artists from places like Denver, Santa Fe, and even Durango, who want the quality of life this small community affords its residents. Salida's action is not yet year-round. Rather, summers are busy, make-hay-while-the-sun-shines sorts of months, and winter is the time to lure skiers heading to and from Monarch Pass. Spring and fall can be very quiet times that are great for working on art but lousy for making a living.

Being in a small district, Salida schools are financially constrained from doing too much in the way of art education programs, but there is some instruction in music and the visual arts. An artist-in-residence program recently started in the elementary schools is being expanded to the middle and high school levels. The local artists' group, Art of the Rockies Association, has developed a summer program for kids that holds classes in the town's funky arts center, the Salida Steam Plant (once the town's electricity source).

Arts Scene

Visual arts exhibitions take place in two nonprofit spaces, the Salida Steam Plant and the Chaffee County Courthouse just up the road in Buena Vista. The Steam Plant is a work-in-progress—its renovation dollars have trickled down in dribs and drabs. When the renovation is complete, Salida will have the sort of combined visual arts exhibition space/performing arts hall/arts education and studio facility that other towns of its size can only dream of.

The Steam Plant currently exhibits local visual arts both as one-artist shows and group exhibits by members of Art of the Rockies. Salida's commercial galleries scene is nothing short of outstanding and is one of the main reasons the town has developed such a healthy cultural tourism economy. A dozen galleries line the tiny downtown streets, and in the past few years those galleries have attracted new restaurants and B&Bs into Salida, making the town a sterling example of how cultural tourism can positively impact all sectors of a community.

Salida's performing arts are in great shape, thanks to the Steam Plant's energetic summer subscription series that brings in Rocky Mountain regional performing artists. An exciting "Salida-Aspen Concert Series" presents several performances showcasing Aspen Music festival performers during the summer in the Salida High School auditorium. Dancer Barbara Baker, a ballet professional, instructs children at her downtown dance studio and also presents dance performances at the Steam Plant Theater. An informal classical music group, the Alpine Orchestra, presents occasional concerts in Salida and Buena Vista.

Alternatives

Many of Salida's restaurants exhibit the work of local artists, including Il Vicino, Laughing Ladies, and First Street Café.

Art Perspectives

Gallery owner Michael Boyd says, "Originally, you could buy a house or a commercial space very inexpensively, but that's changed in the past few years. We're still attracting artists, though. They come here for the mountain ambiance, the seclusion, and the rivers."

Details

Population: 5,300

Important Arts Events: Salida Art Walk (30 gallery and business exhibitions) in June, Art in the Park in July, Art of the Rockies member show in July, Buena Vista Gallery Walk in July, Downtown Saturday Nights in August, September, and October

Must-See Art Galleries: Clay Basket, Courthouse Gallery, Fresh Ideas Gallery, Michael Boyd Studio, Palace Hotel and Gallery, Salida Steam Plant

Local Arts Agency:
Salida Steam Plant
P.O. Box 758
Salida, CO 81201

Natural Foods Stores: Honey Bear, Pantry Natural Foods

National Public Radio: KUNC - 89.9 FM

Bookstores: Crooked Hearts, First Street Books

Chamber of Commerce: 406 W. Hwy. 50
Salida, CO 81201
719/539-2068

Telluride, Colorado

Location

Colorado's southwest corner is a breathtakingly beautiful part of the Rocky Mountain West. Telluride sits at the end of a box canyon, surrounded by the 13,000-foot peaks of the San Juan mountains. The closest city of any size is the town of Durango, a three-hour looping drive south.

Great Outdoors

Telluride lives up to its reputation as one of the world's top ski destinations. The lifts carry skiers up and over several amazing ridges and start at the edge of the downtown streets, as do cross-country trails and miles of groomed snowmobile tracks. The town is surrounded by the wilderness areas of Uncompahgre National Forest, where trout streams, waterfalls, wildlife, and astounding natural beauty await back-country hikers. The incredible beauty of Mesa Verde National Park, site of an ancient Indian civilization, is just two hours from Telluride.

Lifestyle

Not long ago Telluride was an off-the-beaten-path hangout favored by hippies and ski bums. Thanks in large part to the local airport expansion, however, it has been discovered by real estate speculators, second-home owners, and urban refugees. While Telluride still has plenty of down-to-earth artists and business owners, the community's quotient of "Am-I-a-Cowboy/Cowgirl-Yet?" types has skyrocketed—as have housing prices. The median price of an "affordable" home has risen into the $160,000 range.

Telluride's schools have done a great job of using the arts as an important educational component. The town's government has recently funded a "Gifted and Talented" program aimed at addressing the needs of kids showing talent in the arts. "Bridging the Gap" is the Telluride schools' successful artist-in-residence program.

The Ah Haa School for the Arts, a nonprofit art education center in Telluride, employs local artists and performers in its innovative, year-round series of art classes geared for beginning to expert artists and covering an amazing range of artistic disciplines. Ah Haa's summer kids' programs are fantastic and give Telluride's young people lots of ways to channel their creative energies. Telluride Academy, another of the town's nonprofit education centers, emphasizes outdoor recreation in its programs, but also stages a summer children's education series covering drama, dance, and music.

Arts Scene

Though it lacks a community visual arts center, Telluride nonetheless manages to support a growing visual arts scene through the sheer marketing power of its many commercial art galleries. The most prominent nonprofit exhibition space is at Ah Haa School, used for everything from one-artist local exhibitions to group shows by visiting faculty to regional invitationals. Local commercial galleries tend to exhibit as many Santa Fe artists as they do Colorado artists, in many instances opting to mimic Santa Fe's success rather than working to develop Telluride artists' reputations. This situation may change for the better as more accomplished artists move into the region.

In terms of quality and range, Telluride's performing arts scene rivals that of communities a hundred times its size. The renovated Sheridan Opera House, a 240-seat theater built in 1913, is Telluride's performing arts center. It serves as a winter home for the Telluride Repertory (which holds a new plays festival with readings by national playwrights in February), the Telluride Choral Society, and the Telluride Dance Gallery (a contemporary dance school that's presently working to bring a metropolitan area dance company into Telluride for a summer residency program). The Sheridan is also used for a wonderfully programmed film series covering foreign, first release, and revival movies.

Unlike some ski resort towns, Telluride enjoys year-round tourism thanks to its summer arts schedule. When it comes to summer arts festivals, Telluride takes a back seat to nobody. From the internationally regarded Telluride Music Festival to the Telluride Bluegrass Festival, summers bring dozens of great events—the Telluride Jazz Celebration, the Telluride Film Festival, and the Native American Writers' Forum, to name a few. The Telluride Chamber Music Festival's two-week August stint at the Sheridan pulls in top classical musicians from across the West. The Rep moves outdoors for a Shakespeare production at the town park's Shellman stage each summer.

Two nightclubs, Fly Me to the Moon and One World Café, keep Telluride's night music scene hopping with touring national and regional acts. The Peaks, a local resort, presents a strong calendar of national folk, blues, and world musicians.

Alternatives

Local artists' work sells well through the monthly exhibitions at Steaming Bean, The Ice House, Floradora, and Between the Covers Bookstore & Coffeehouse.

Art Perspectives

Art Goodtimes of the Telluride Art Council says, "The town's arts commission kicks in big bucks to help make things happen around here, and a lot of that money goes into advertising. To make an event work in Telluride you've got to pull people in from far away."

Details

Population: 1,200

Important Arts Events: Celebration Arts in July, Telluride Mushroom Festival in August

Must-See Art Galleries: Ah Haa Gallery, Elinoff-Cote Gallery, Golden West Galleries, Lucas Gallery, Telluride Gallery of Fine Art

Local Arts Agency: Telluride Council for the Arts and Humanities
P.O. Box 152
Telluride, CO 814335
970/728-3930

Natural Foods Store: The Natural Source

Farmer's Market: Saturday mornings at Society Turn

National Public Radio: KOTO - 91.7 FM

Bookstores: Between the Covers, Bookworks

Chamber of Commerce: P.O. Box 653
Telluride CO 81435
970/668-0376

Litchfield, Connecticut

Location

The northwest corner of Connecticut is the most New Englandesque part of the state. Called the Litchfield Hills, the region is packed with small villages, white clapboard churches, charming town squares, and country stores. It's all beautiful, and the small art town of Litchfield stands out as particularly blessed for having retained its historic architectural legacy. This community of 8,500 residents is an hour's drive from Hartford and two hours from New York City.

Great Outdoors

Tucked into this scenic part of the state are a stretch of tall hills sheltering several ski areas. If conditions are right, local folks can be on the slopes of Mohawk ski area in less than a half-hour. Spring runoff on the Housatonic River provides white-water that's best run in a canoe. Topsmead State Forest has biking, hiking, and riding trails, as does the state park at Mt. Tom. While local road traffic tends to clog during autumn foliage season, the region is basically quiet. The White Memorial Conservation Center Foundation opens its 4,000 acres to runners, riders, cross-country skiers, and campers, while still managing to preserve its pristine natural legacy. Just a few miles from Litchfield center is Bantam Lake, a summer recreational hangout.

Lifestyle

If ever there was a small town that addressed the creative potential of its young people, it's Litchfield. The school system seems to get anything it wants and has integrated an arts education program into its curriculum. Litchfield Performing Arts, the community's exemplary local arts agency, has tapped into the full range of state, local, and private foundation assistance available for bolstering children's creative-arts programs. While Connecticut is an expensive place to live—with eye-popping taxes, steep housing (an average of $150,000), and costly services—what you get in exchange is a high quality of life. The streets are immaculate, local parks are well-tended, homeowners take great pride in their properties, and the community's sense of warmth extends into the watching-out-for-each-other realm—Litchfield is one of the safest towns in New England.

Arts Scene

It was 15 years ago that Vita West Muir pushed back the living room furniture in her Litchfield home to stage classical music concerts on Sunday afternoons. Since then, she has labored tirelessly to realize her vision of enhancing life with the performing arts. Today she's at the helm of Litchfield Performing Arts, an organization bringing top-name performers into Litchfield and its surrounding communities for an eight-month mainstage series that could hold its own in any metropolitan area. The venues range from Litchfield's 500-seat First Congregational Church, to the renovated Thomaston Opera House, to the Warner Theatre in Torrington (an art deco masterpiece), to the Johnson Art Center at the Forman School. The Warner is also home to the Nutmeg Ballet, the state's premier training school for dance. In addition to luring chamber music, dance, classical music, and theater acts into town, the organization uses ArtsAid funds to bring those artists to local schools. Another program, Project Poetry Live!, brings poets and dancers to area schools. The biennial Simone Belsky Music Award competition in October attracts major pianists from across the nation. LPA's Litchfield Jazz Fest (in August, at White Memorial) attracts world-class artists.

Local artists say they sell lots of work to weekend visitors from the New York area through the town's fine art galleries. Many mid-career artists who have established gallery connections in major markets have been moving into the Litchfield area lately, making studio visits especially worthwhile for collectors. The main outdoor art sales weekend is Gallery on the Green in June, which takes place in conjunction with the Litchfield Hills Road Race, drawing huge crowds to the town's center. Both a summer concert series on the Town Green and the Holiday House Tour represent major sales opportunities for regional fine crafts artists.

Alternatives

There's a tradition of weekend tourism in Litchfield, so the town's restaurants are fairly sophisticated. West Street Grill is the area's most popular dining spot as well as a great place for local art sales. The County Seat is another place worth checking out for local art. The Toll Gate Hill Inn is Litchfield's best spot for live music.

Art Perspectives

Pam Stockamore, a painter and Litchfield native, says the community's visual arts profile is subtle but powerful. "I think we've got the best of both worlds here," she says. "You can find huge studio space in the area for reasonable rates, it's a quiet place to work, and you can sell into the local market. I've had so many art dealers come through my studio, it would make your head spin—and they found me just by walking through the galleries. Since I've moved back into town, I've had my work picked up by galleries in New York, Los Angeles, New Orleans, and Zurich."

Details

Population: 8,500

Important Arts Events: Gallery on the Green in June, Litchfield Performing Arts concert series from October to May, Litchfield Jazz Fest in August, Simone Belsky Music Award Competition in October (biennial)

Must-See Art Galleries: Litchfield Art Guild, P.S. Gallery, Risley Gallery, Wolcott Library Gallery, Her Sister's Gallery, Litchfield Art Museum

Local Arts Agency: Litchfield Performing Arts

P.O. Box 69
Litchfield, CT 06759
860/567-4162

Natural Foods Store: Country Life

Farmer's Market: Saturday mornings on Route 202, west of Litchfield

National Public Radio: WPKT - 90.5 FM

Bookstores: Barnidge & McEnroe, The John Steele Bookshop

Chamber of Commerce: P.O. Box 59 Torrington, CT 06790
860/482-6586

Rehoboth Beach, Delaware

Location

Like many other self-sustaining arts communities across America, the oceanfront resort town of Rehoboth Beach proves once again that location is everything. The town is neatly sandwiched between two naturally beautiful areas: the 4,000-acre Cape Henlopen State Park to the north and the Delaware Seashore State Park to the south. Washington, D.C., Philadelphia, and Baltimore are each just a two-hour drive away.

Great Outdoors

This tiny art community is far enough south to receive little of winter's frigid blasts, and spring rolls into town like clockwork in late March. The tourists begin their descent on Memorial Day, bolstering Rehoboth Beach's population of 1,300 year-rounders into a tanned tidal wave of nearly 40,000. Returning to their desks after Labor Day, the beachgoers miss out on the town's reliably warm and sunny autumn. Winter sports are a half-day's drive away in West Virginia or Pennsylvania, unless you count long walks on a deserted beach as winter recreation—and most who live here do.

Lifestyle

This community has been under the development gun since the early 1980s, and subdivisions now stretch all the way around Rehoboth Bay, giving thousands of weekenders more places to party. The town is shoulder-to-shoulder from late May to early September, but the good news is that the madness doesn't last forever and the beach crowd spends money on everything in sight. Ugly, multistory condos line the boardwalk at Rehoboth Beach, and homes have become so expensive that local residents have to look long and hard—not to mention far from the water's edge—to find a place under $150,000. The way to survive summers is to join in the fun on weekdays, stay close to home on weekends, sell your work at the summer art fairs, and mark off the weekends till Labor Day.

The town's schools have a progressive attitude toward making arts education part of the regular curriculum, and art and music instruction exist at all levels in the local schools. During the summer there's a children's theater group at a local church hall as well as the Rehoboth Art League kids' programs ranging from theater and storytelling to painting and pottery classes.

Arts Scene

This is a great place for visual art and artists, with more than a dozen galleries, a five-month calendar of festivals and art fairs, and many Rehoboth Art League classes and exhibitions. The area's visitors are increasingly supportive of the community's painters and craft artists, and it's common for sales of more expensive art works to take place at the league's sales gallery.

The RAL's gallery, classrooms, studios, and sculpture garden are on the eighteenth-century Henlopen Acres Farm within Rehoboth Beach's city limits. The league uses the Homestead mansion as a gallery, the Chambers studio as both classroom and theater for its art film series and community theater company, and its pottery studio for instruction in ceramic arts. RAL's classes take place from May through September, with lectures, touring exhibits, and music performances coming through town. The big event on Rehoboth Beach's visual arts calendar is the RAL's Annual Members' Outdoor Exhibition, which fills the league's grounds each August with painters, sculptors, and craft artists from across the region. The weekend prior to the RAL's bash, you'll find art of a different sort at the Best Body on the Beach Contest.

The main performing arts event of the year is the Jazz Festival Weekend in October, a multivenue affair that takes place in the town's nightclubs, convention hall, and Bay Center. During the summer, theater comes to Henlopen Acres, and the Possum Point Players community theater group stages plays at the high school auditorium. Rehoboth Beach still needs a medium-sized performing arts venue, not only to house the local community theater company, but also to host classical music programs, children's theater, recitals, and dance programs. For the moment, the town's arts strength lies in its visual arts, and it should build upon that strength to broaden the scope of its community performing art programs.

Alternatives

Finding a place to dance to live music is easy in Rehoboth Beach, especially during the warmer months. Winters are somewhat slow. There's a lot of local art on the walls of the town's cafes and restaurants, and places like The Back Porch, Blue Moon, Dream Café, Sidney's Side Street, and Planet X are known for selling and showing work created by local artists.

Art Perspectives

Joanne DeFiore, a calligrapher and illustrator, sells her work in both the fine and commercial arts markets. "You can make a living selling to this town's tourist market," she says, "but your work has to capture a sense of the place. Rehoboth has become such a good art market that we could use larger spaces for exhibitions, especially for putting contemporary art into a better context. I think we're heading toward becoming a year-round art market, which means word's getting out about the great art you can find here."

Details

Population: 1,300

Important Arts Events: RAL Member's Exhibition in July, Best Body on the Beach Competition in July, RAL Art & Craft Outdoor Exhibition in August, Jazz Festival Weekend in October

Must-See Art Galleries: Cochran Gallery at RAL, Homestead Gallery at RAL, Nassau Gallery, Seashore Galleries

Local Arts Agency: Rehoboth Art League 12 Dodds Lane

Rehoboth Beach, DE 19971
302/227-8408

Natural Foods Store: Peter Rabbit's

Farmer's Market: Roadside stands outside town

National Public Radio: WSCL - 89.5 FM

Bookstore: Browse About Books

Chamber of Commerce: 501 Rehoboth Avenue
Rehoboth Beach, DE 19971
302/227-2233

Lewes, Delaware

Location

Situated between the Prime Hook National Wildlife Refuge to its north and Cape Henlopen State Park to its south, the 2,500 residents of Lewes have the Atlantic Ocean in front of them, great beaches to either side, and a ferry that runs ten trips daily to Cape May and back. Baltimore, Philadelphia, and Washington, D.C. are about two hours away, except on summer Fridays and Sundays, when traffic can be tied up for miles.

Great Outdoors

Living here has its advantages: access to sailing and windsurfing, deep-sea and surf fishing at your front door, and an uncrowded spot on the beach. Lewes also has its share of wildlife, hosting some of the most prolific migratory bird breeding grounds in the East. Mackerel runs start in March, and Lewes fishers haul in tuna, swordfish, sea bass, and stripers, to name a few. If you don't feel like leaving town, you can cast a line into the Roosevelt Inlet at the end of Cedar Street. Cape Henlopen State Park's 4,000 acres include the Seaside Nature Center, an educational facility for local kids as well as a popular stop for birders. If you get tired of sitting on the beach, you can hop the ferry for a 70-minute ride to the many galleries of Victorian Cape May, New Jersey. Winter sports are a three-hour drive to Pennsylvania or West Virginia.

Lifestyle

Lewes lucked out years ago when it developed a reputation as a middle-class, blue-collar town. Never a spot for wealthy vacationers, the town was more of a home base for local school principals and deep-sea fishermen. Lewes also became a place where artists could afford to buy a home (average price: $115,000), live close to the spectacular beauty of Cape Henlopen and the Atlantic, yet still easily drive to the major city arts markets. The pace of things has picked up slightly in recent years, but Lewes is still a down-to-earth place where people can live normal lives untroubled by the summer invasions endured by other beach towns.

The first official town in Delaware, Lewes was settled by Dutchmen who landed here in 1631. History buffs will enjoy two small museums, dozens of historic homes, and Shipcarpenter Square, an 11-acre historic district filled with restored homes moved here from other sites throughout the state. Local folks get their share of the national media spotlight each November, when the town stages its Punkin' Chunkin' contest, a challenge that involves shooting pumpkins out of hydraulic howitzers.

Arts Scene

The arts scene here is a low-key, homegrown affair that got its start several years ago when funding was allocated to spruce up Lewes' downtown. The renovation attracted new business into town, some of which sold local arts and crafts. Visitors who previously had only driven through town to get to the ferry now began to park their cars, poke their heads into the shops, and purchase some of the local art.

During the summer, the University of Delaware stages its University by the Sea Summer Arts Festival, a weeklong series of musical performances (including some by the Delaware Symphony) with some visual arts exhibitions staged around town. At the same time, the annual Cape Henlopen Craft Fair offers fine craft artists one of the region's premier summer venues. Each fall and spring the Art Around Town tours combine elements of an open studio tour, a downtown art tour, and a craft show. Nearby Georgetown and Milford have very active community theaters. Occasionally, the University of Delaware stages theatrical or musical performances at the local high school, while the community chorale stages performances at local churches. Among the commercial galleries in downtown Lewes, the traditional Cape Artists Gallery at the New Devon Inn is the best place for foot traffic and sales.

Alternatives

Most of the Lewes restaurants sign up for one or two art exhibits during the Art Around Town festival, and many keep local art on their walls throughout the year. Jerry's American Café, The Buttery, and Kupchick's have a good track record for selling art from their walls. Local spots popular with Lewes' creative crowd include La Rosa Negra, Lingo's Rose & Crown, and Gilligan's.

Art Perspectives

Stained glass artist, Barbara Berl, finds that artists survive best in Lewes if they keep busy. "It's no picnic, but it can be done if you can find a way to work hard. Artists come here to get off the beaten track, and if they have some sort of a culture attack after arriving, then they leave town for a few days or for good... I'm always surprised when people walk into my gallery (Peninsula Collections) and plunk down $2,000 on a painting. I mean, that was something unheard of in Lewes just a few years ago, and if you told me then that it would be happening now, I'd have laughed in disbelief."

Details

Population: 2,500

Important Art Events: The Great Delaware Kite Festival in April, Art Around Town in May and November, the University by the Sea Summer Arts Festival in July

Must-See Art Galleries: The Cape Artists Gallery, Market Street Studio, Peninsula Collections, Preservation Forge Gallery

Local Arts Agency: Sussex County Arts Council
P.O. Box 221
Georgetown, DE 19947
(no phone)

Natural Foods Store: Gertie's Greengrocer

Farmer's Market: Roadside stands outside of town

National Public Radio: WSCL - 89.5 FM

Bookstore: Books by the Bay

Chamber of Commerce: P.O. Box 1
Lewes, DE 19958
302/645-8073

New Smyrna Beach, Florida

Location

The art town of New Smyrna Beach is on the Atlantic Coast south of Daytona Beach, about an hour's drive north of Orlando. The land of perpetual summer, Florida is practically uninhabitable from mid-June to mid-September, when the heat drives all but the hardy to northern climes. But for the 18,000 residents who call this town home, there's a refreshing amount of vitality here year-round.

Great Outdoors

Far from the crowded shorelines at Daytona and Cocoa Beach, New Smyrna offers local residents a much-appreciated family-oriented setting. On New Smyrna's southern doorstep is the Canaveral National Seashore, a place filled with quiet beach retreats as well as campgrounds, hiking trails, and migratory waterfowl. Adjoining the Canaveral Seashore is Merritt Island National Wildlife Refuge, which borders the Kennedy Spaceport. Spending time on the water is a way of life, and owning a fishing or sailboat is guaranteed to make you a lot of friends.

Lifestyle

This is the part of Florida to come to if you're 1) independently employed, 2) retired, or 3) want to raise a family in an affordable, safe setting. New Smyrna Beach homes are bargains at $75,000 for something in town, though proximity to the Intracoastal Waterway raises home prices exponentially. Children attend school on year-round schedules, which keeps them in an air-conditioned environment during the most blistering months. Arts education programs are topsy-turvy in New Smyrna, though the nationally famous Atlantic Center for the Arts and its year-round series of master artist residency programs is located on the outskirts of town. The town's school system has not yet modernized its arts education programs, so many local kids gain exposure to the arts through programs offered by the Atlantic Center at its downtown Harris House exhibition and education facility. From New Smyrna, it's an easy drive to Daytona's many nightclubs, restaurants, and Cinematique, a theater showing foreign films.

Arts Scene

Because it's so close to Daytona, much of New Smyrna's performing arts in the areas of drama, classical, and jazz music tend to focus around what's taking place at Daytona's arts center and at Bethune-Cookman College. New Smyrna does offer a popular 75-seat community theater, and the Atlantic Center's visiting faculty often include playwrights and choreographers who stage works-in-progress at the center's black-box theater, or outdoors in its amphitheater. Each year, performing arts festivals celebrate the cultural traditions of the area's large African American and Native American populations.

The Atlantic Center's 67 acres of studios, residence halls, and performance facilities are reserved only for teaching artists and students in its three-week seminars. But the Atlantic Center really established its reputation through the visual arts. It continues to attract the contemporary art world's top names in painting and sculpture to teach mid-career artists (and some who aren't quite there yet). The center was founded in 1977 by Doris Leeper, a painter and sculptor whose work is collected by some of the nation's top museums. Since 1982, its residencies have branched out to include the performing and literary arts. Students accepted here pay less than $1,000 for room, board, and three weeks of master artist classes. Expanded theater and visual art exhibition space is currently under construction, which will provide more opportunities for locals to participate in the center's performances and exhibits. The Atlantic Center has one of the best privately funded community art centers in the country, the Harris House, a very active visual arts exhibition and educational facility. The emphasis here is on local and regional arts and artists, with some of Florida's top names conducting daylong classes and lectures, evening poetry readings, children's art programs, group and one-artist shows, and an arts and humanities lecture series.

Alternatives

Like most small art towns, New Smyrna Beach has its share of arts festivals, but the Images Art Festival in March has an interesting twist: most all of the work is contemporary, and the 175 artists drawn here from across the country are far from the sort found at most art festivals. The Euro Café is a locally owned restaurant exhibiting the work of area artists.

Art Perspectives

Trish Thompson, one of the region's most prominent painters, believes that New Smyrna's charms lie in its sleepy ways. "Nothing ever happens here. There's no movie theater, no beach festivals, no college kids on spring break, and all of that delights me! One of the best things that's happened lately is that Doris Leeper is putting together an exhibition and sales space for New Smyrna's local artists. Now we've all got a new place to run into each other. The Atlantic Center is open to everyone in the community, and it's affordable. The people who come here for classes are from all over the world. It's an amazing place to have in a small town like this."

Details

Population: 18,000

Important Arts Events: Art Fiesta in February, Indian River Native American Festival in February, Images Art Festival in March, Jazz Festival in April

Must-See Art Galleries: Artists Workshop Gallery, Atlantic Center for the Arts Gallery, Arts on Douglas Gallery, Harris House Gallery

Local Arts Agency: Atlantic Center for the Arts
1414 Art Center Avenue

New Smyrna Beach, FL
904/427-6975

Natural Foods Store: Heath's

Farmer's Market: Saturday mornings in the downtown park

National Public Radio: WFME - 90.7 FM

Bookstore: Mandala Books

Chamber of Commerce: 115 Canal Street
New Smyrna Beach, FL
800/541-9621

Panama City, Florida

Location

Florida's Gulf Coast is home to some of the best beaches in the country. Among them are St. Andrews Point and St. Joseph's Peninsula, known for their vast expanses of granular, "sugar sand." Panama City's 36,000 residents are closer to Houston than they are to Miami; the nearest city is Tallahassee, about 100 miles east.

Great Outdoors

A swimsuit is all you'll need to wear here for about eight months of the year. (Actually, swimsuits are optional on some of the beaches.) All the seaside sports are at your doorstep, along with several boundary island state parks where you can pitch a tent and camp for a weekend. The state maintains several marked canoe trails within easy reach of Panama City, one of which starts at Florida Caverns, a series of limestone caverns and spring-fed swimming holes. Florida's ante-bellum past is a main attraction of the restored 1800s plantation homes dotting this part of the state.

Lifestyle

Every year, Panama City's beaches are invaded by the cheeseburger-and-paradise spring break crowd—50,000 to 75,000 high school and college students. For the rest of the year things are fairly calm in this part of the state, where the population's spread out enough that nobody feels crowded.

Some of the nation's most innovative planned community developments are happening at places like Seaside and Carillion Beach. These are developments where people can live, work, and shop within walking distance of their homes. Homes in Panama City are in the $60,000 range, and somewhat higher in the newer, planned communities.

The schools have full-time visual arts and music teachers, but the programs tend to bog down in battles over funding priorities. Panama City's performing and visual arts organizations have picked up the slack, offering after-school programs, subsidizing matinee shows so school kids can be bussed in for performances, coordinating touring artists' schedules to permit in-school workshops, and using state artist-in-residence dollars to place local artists in schools. Because there is such a range of energetic and well-funded organizations around town, children with specific arts interests are well-served.

Arts Scene

Panama City has a nice balance of the many performing and visual arts interests. Bay Arts Alliance operates a 2,500-seat, state-of-the-art venue that's used by many of the region's organizations and is home to the Alliance's yearly series which features dance, jazz, and touring Broadway musicals. The Panama City Music Association, which uses the Marina Civic Center, brings in its own classical music performers, touring opera, ballet, and Broadway road shows.

The Kaleidoscope Theater, a sophisticated community theater company, opens its doors to anyone with an interest in theater and presents a half-dozen or so annual productions in its 300-seat facility. Finally, the Martin Theatre, a restored, 469-seat art-deco palace, runs a full-tilt series of cultural gems ranging from shows by its own repertory company, to touring national music and dance acts, to innovative children's theater companies. Panama City is also home to the Northwest Florida Ballet, which performs in the Strausbaugh Dance Center.

Panama City's visual arts scene is outstanding for a community of its size, both in terms of commercial galleries and its nonprofit arts and exhibition center. The Visual Arts Center of Northwest Florida, housed in what was once the community's city hall and jail, is an energetic place with 2,500 square feet of exhibition space, an arts library, a classroom, and a lecture hall. The center runs year-round art education programs for school children and adults, and coordinates the region's artist-in-residency programs at public schools. Downtown Panama City is clustered with visual arts, photography, and fine craft galleries, as well as print shops. Sales are strong enough for some artists to make a living on the regional art fair circuit, while others such as nationally known Paul Brent are wired into the lucrative national print market.

Alternatives

Most of the town's café and restaurant owners hang local art on their walls. Panama Java is one of the best sales venues and a hangout for the town's creative crowd. The Hawk's Nest is another place for local art, as well as a venue for Panama City's musicians. During the summer months there's a free downtown concert series at McKenzie Park, and the town's annual jazz festival is in June.

Art Perspectives

Mary DeSieno, a mixed media artist, finds the town's arts scene inspirational. "There are so many artists living here. All of them are friendly and most share their contacts with each other. Panama City's a supportive place for an artist to live, a place where there are lots of art festivals, some good galleries, and lots of strong exhibitions. The artists' studio tours are very popular, with 1,200 people running from one place to another. One of the most positive things being done here are the art programs for kids, especially those at the Visual Arts Center."

Details

Population: 36,000

Important Arts Events: Artist Studio Tours in spring & fall, Panama City Festival of the Arts in May, Jazz & Heritage Festival in June.

Must-See Art Galleries: Bay Arts Alliance Gallery, Impressions Gallery at VAC, Lyn's Fine Art, Paul Brent Gallery

Local Arts Agency: Bay Arts Alliance P.O. Box 1153

Panama City, FL 32402 904/769-1217

Natural Foods Store: Olive Leaves

Farmer's Market: Farm stands throughout the region

National Public Radio: WKGC - 90.7 FM

Chamber of Commerce: 235 West 5th, Panama City, FL 32401 904/785-5206

Brunswick, Georgia

Location

The Golden Isles of coastal Georgia have everything from Spanish forts to fancy golf resorts, with the art town of Brunswick serving as one of the focal points for the area's diverse cultural interests. While Brunswick specializes in the performing arts, the nearby community of St. Simons Island is the region's visual arts center. The closest major city is Jacksonville, an hour's drive south.

Great Outdoors

The Turtle River runs past downtown Brunswick and leads to the Atlantic Ocean just a few miles east down the St. Simons Sound. The area's best beaches are on St. Simons and Jekyll Island, whose stunning historic district is a shaded neighborhood with enormous, turn-of-the-century residences. Jekyll's crown jewel is a sprawling Victorian mansion renovated by Brunswick architect Larry Evans. The region's Atlantic coastline is bordered by two of the nation's most treasured coastal wilderness areas—Cumberland Island National Seashore to the south and Wolf Island National Wilderness to the north. Both are great places for back-country camping, birding, and leaving the real world behind. A short drive west lands you in the Okefenokee Swamp, another wilderness area surrounded by several state parks.

Lifestyle

Brunswick's economy was built in several different stages, starting with agriculture in the early 1800s and moving on to forestry later in the century. Brunswick is still an important milling and shipping point for the region's southern pine forests. The past few decades haven't been particularly prosperous for the town, and St. Simon's Island has become the direct beneficiary of Brunswick's woes. As families relocated to this newer, more upscale part of the Golden Isles, local real estate values began to double those of Brunswick. Still, you can find a Brunswick Queen Anne or Victorian for well under $100,000, and it's likely to include fabulous turn-of-the-century woodwork. Older Brunswick is filled with historic neighborhoods, brick streets, small-town groceries, and towering churches. Brunswick's schools have adopted an impressive approach to integrating arts into student curricula, and full-time visual artists and drama instructors now work at each middle and high school. Elementary schoolers are served by the Golden Isles Arts and Humanities Association (GIAHA), whose comprehensive Artz 4 Kids program coordinates after-school drama, dance, literature, and visual arts classes.

Arts Scene

The region's premier performing arts venue is the Ritz Theatre, a restored vaudeville house in pretty downtown Brunswick. Operated by the GIAHA, the Ritz stages an annual performance series of drama, dance, and pop and ethnic music programs. Groups that use the 525-seat Ritz include the civic orchestra, the community concert group (which imports national touring acts), various chamber music ensembles, and the community theater. The Ritz also accommodates Brunswick's energetic humanities programming: author appearances, academic lectures, a writers' conference, and kids' programs. Jekyll Island's outdoor amphitheater is the summer home of a three-production musical theater series performing mainstream works. A popular community theater group, the Island Players, performs at the Casino Theatre on St. Simons. At the lighthouse park, GIAHA presents a summer outdoor jazz concert series.

Although the Ritz houses Brunswick's sole visual arts exhibition space, there are several commercial and noncommercial galleries on St. Simons Island, as well as a gallery on Jekyll Island. Much of the St. Simons gallery art is of the seascape variety, but you can find contemporary work in town and French Impressionism at the Left Bank Gallery. St. Simons' nonprofit Glynn Art Association offers art classes, drawing workshops, and an annual outdoor art festival. The Coastal Center for the Arts sponsors touring exhibits, one-artist shows by top local painters, year-round art classes, and an arts lecture series.

Alternatives

Downtown Brunswick's two popular restaurants, the Grapevine and the Royal Café, exhibit changing shows of work by local artists. On St. Simons you'll find Dressner's Café and J. Mac's, a popular jazz club. A gambling cruise ship docked at Brunswick's spiffy waterfront marina park is one of the town's latest additions.

Art Perspectives

Nancy Muldowney, printmaker and paper artist says, "Some of the artists come for the inspiration of living by the ocean, some find the activities here to be just about enough to keep life interesting. It's just a nice place to live, someplace where creative individuals can bring their energy and find it easy to get involved. Artists have a strong support system through the Coastal Center, the Glynn Art Association, and through things taking place at the Ritz. . . . There are monthly get-togethers, groups of artists who meet for lunch, people who tell you what shows to do, things like that. One of the challenges in this area is to get our younger people more interested in the arts, to see them both as a way to make a living, and as the kind of tools that help you to deal creatively with life's problems."

Details

Population: 17,000

Important Arts Events: Harborfest in May, Georgia Coastal Artists Annual Summer Show in July, Sea Island Festival in August, Catfish Festival in September, Glynn Art Association Festival in October

Must-See Art Galleries: Caprice-Wallin Gallery, Coastal Center for the Arts Galleries, Left Bank Gallery, Ritz Theatre Gallery, Venedig Gallery

Local Arts Agency: Golden Isles Arts and Humanities Association

1530 Newcastle Street
Brunswick, GA 31520
912/262-6934

Natural Foods Store: Happy Days

Farmer's Market: Waterfront Park every day during growing season

National Public Radio: WWIO - 89.1 FM

Bookstores: Bison Books, G.J. Ford Bookstore, The Book Shop

Chamber of Commerce: 4 Glynn Avenue
Brunswick, GA 31520
912/265-0620

Lahaina, Hawaii

Ranked #17

Location

The small art town of Lahaina is located on the west side of Maui, the second largest of the Hawaiian Islands. In the tropical splendor of a turn-of-the-century whaling village, 14,500 Lahainans live in a place that has become one of the most lucrative art markets in the nation.

Great Outdoors

From the streets of Lahaina to the 5,788-foot crest of nearby Puu Kukui in Kepaniwai Park, an astounding range of natural beauty makes this town an irresistible place for artists from the mainland. Beaches and state parks are everywhere, from Launiupoko on Lahaina's south to Wahikuli on its north. Maui receives a tremendous amount of rainfall, and the West Maui Mountains are one of the wettest places on earth, giving rise to some of the island's main agricultural products: sweet Maui onions and the tropical flowers high school sweethearts pin on prom dresses. (Coffee, sugar cane, and macadamia nuts are also grown here). South Maui is dominated by the 10,023-foot giant of Haleakala Mountain, part of the Haleakala National Park and the Haleakala Wilderness Area, a favorite place for back-country hiking, camping, and even sledding. In this part of the Pacific, winter sports usually mean choosing which color bathing suit you'll wear on the sailboat. But every so often, the 13,796-foot peak of Mauna Kea is blanketed with several yards of snow, at which point anyone who owns skis will hop an island-jumping flight to an unforgettable day on the slopes.

Lifestyle

Lahaina was once a whaling town that attracted some of the world's least-socialized characters as well as some of its most strident missionaries. Both cultures left behind their share of architectural legacies that survive today, making Lahaina a community of historic structures that exist side-by-side with a few hotels and resorts. The downtown Lahaina business district looks as if it were dropped onto the island straight from coastal Maine, and its historic beauty attracts tourists in search of a dose of non-glitzy reality. In addition to its funk and fun, visitors find such a strong artists' market that many Lahainans can survive by selling to tourists. The cost of living here is expensive, as it is elsewhere in the Hawaiian islands. Without land, a fixer-upper home costs around $100,000; with land, prices can reach stratospheric heights.

Lahaina's public schools do a good job of exposing their students to visual and performing arts. The state funds an artist-in-residence program, and the Lahaina Arts Society works closely with the school district to integrate arts into the school curriculum. The arts society offers a year-round schedule of visual art classes for both members and local children who wish to be exposed to the visual arts, especially Hawaiian art traditions. The society exhibits student art in the Old Jail Gallery and annually awards a college arts scholarship to one Lahaina child.

Arts Scene

Lahaina's arts scene revolves around activities at the arts society's two exhibition spaces: the

Banyan Tree Gallery and the Old Jail Gallery. The Banyan Tree's namesake was planted in 1873 behind what's now the town's old courthouse. It has grown to become the islands' largest banyan as well as the shade covering a thrice-weekly outdoor art market that's the sole source of income for dozens of Maui artists. The Old Jail Gallery, inside the old courthouse building, annually rotates two-dozen exhibits through its gallery space and hosts dozens of art classes and lectures. The town's commercial gallery scene has had its ups and downs of late, but despite some closings, lots of places still exhibit and sell local work. Village Gallery, Lahaina Galleries, and Madaline Michaels Gallery have weathered the economic storm in fine shape. Another prominent Maui arts society is Hui Noeau, a contemporary art group that holds classes and exhibitions on estate grounds in Makawao, a South Maui mountainside town.

Lahaina has one theater company, Theatre-Theatre Maui, that presents occasional shows at hotel ballrooms. The Lahaina Civic Auditorium is sometimes used for hula competitions, but aside from rock and jazz clubs such as the Hard Rock Café and Planet Hollywood, local performing arts are limited. Those willing to drive 45 minutes to Kahului can attend the major performing arts center used by touring classical musicians, theater companies, and modern dance troupes.

Alternatives

Almost all of Lahaina's restaurants and hotels exhibit the work of local artists, some of whom find selling in these venues quite lucrative.

Art Perspectives

Marian Freeman, an established Lahaina painter, notes that artists need to be realistic about life in Lahaina. "It's true that quite a few artists can make a living here, but its tough finding an affordable place to live and it's tough finding a gallery to sell your work. A lot of artists move out of Lahaina after they realize the reality of having to work that hard to survive."

Details

Population: 14,500

Important Arts Events: Lahaina Whalefest in March, Seabury Hall Crafts Fair in May, Friday Night is Art Festival in June, Maui Onion Festival in August, Halloween Mardi Gras in October

Must-See Art Galleries: Banyan Tree Gallery, Lahaina Galleries, Martin Lawrence Gallery, Old Jail Gallery, Sargent's Fine Art, Village Gallery

Local Arts Agency: Lahaina Arts Society 648 Wharf Street

Lahaina, HI 96761
808/661-3228

Natural Foods Store: Westside Natural Foods

Farmer's Market: Friday mornings in Lahaina Square

National Public Radio: KKUA - 90.7 FM

Bookstore: Tropic Provisions Bookstore and Coffee Shop

Chamber of Commerce: Maui Visitor's Bureau 808/244-3530

Moscow, Idaho

Location

The sparsely populated but rolling and fertile landscape of Idaho's Palouse is one of the nation's premier wheat-growing regions. Bounded by the Clearwater National Forest and Washington's share of the Palouse, Moscow and its 20,000 permanent residents live in a university community that attracts a large number of resident artists, musicians, and actors.

Great Outdoors

Moscow is within easy reach of national forest wilderness areas to its east and south, and the enormous Hells Canyon National Recreation Area and Seven Devils Mountains are about two hours south of town. Elk Creek Falls, an hour east of Moscow, is a favorite place for hiking, back-country camping, and some of Idaho's best trout fishing. In the summer months, Spring Valley Reservoir is the place to go for canoeing, sailing, and lakeside camping, while Dworshak Reservoir offers water-skiing and sailboarding. Cross-country skiing is winter's answer to outdoor recreation; for downhill skiing skip the two small areas close to Moscow and head for Schweitzer's slopes, a three-hour drive north in the small art town of Sandpoint.

Lifestyle

Moscow is home to the University of Idaho, a small but very highly regarded state university whose influence dominates this town's economy. Well-paid teachers and administrators have kept Moscow's neighborhood homes in gorgeous condition. The prime area for Victorian and other turn-of-the-century homes is Moscow's Fort Russell Historical District, just a few blocks from the community's historic downtown. Homes in this neighborhood sell in the $250,000 range, but just a short drive away you can find average-sized homes for $80,000 or so. The Fort Russell District is also where you'll find the McConnell Mansion, a sprawling Victorian that once was home to Idaho's governor and is now an historical museum.

Art education programs at local schools are both comprehensive and well-funded, with artist-in-residence programs using local artists. Students from the University of Idaho and the University of Washington, which is 15 miles away in Pullman, support the flourishing bar and music scene. Places like John's Alley, The Beanery, and Moscow Social Club book local bands.

Moscow has a lock on the Palouse's best arts festivals and community-wide blowouts, including the Lionel Hampton Jazz Festival in February, the Mardi Gras in March, the Renaissance Faire in May, and Rendezvous in the Park in July.

Arts Scene

The University of Idaho's Prichard Gallery in downtown Moscow is the community's foremost nonprofit visual arts exhibition space. On the college campus, Ridenbaugh Gallery exhibits works by the art faculty and graduate students, while the Student Union Building's gallery wall rotates shows by the college's art undergrads and faculty. Washington State University's Museum of Art is a large, well-funded institution programming monthly exhibits in several of its galleries. The museum emphasizes contemporary work, but there are regular shows featuring fine crafts, Native American/Alaskan art, and some touring historical exhibitions. The area's commercial galleries are where local artists have their best exhibition prospects. Gallery West, Inner Vision, Northwest Showcase, and ArtFrames are Moscow's galleries, while For Art's Sake and Nica Gallery are the leading exhibition spaces in Pullman.

The Lionel Hampton Jazz Festival is Moscow's national claim to fame. This comprehensive, week-long winter bash takes place at several University of Idaho venues, including the Lionel Hampton School of Music Recital Hall, the 500-seat Hartung Theatre, and the town's several nightclubs. The festival brings to town the best names in jazz, not only for performances, but also for jazz clinics presented by a young musicians national jazz band competition taking place at the music school earlier the same week. The Auditorium Chamber Music Series brings touring classical acts to the University of Idaho Auditorium, and the Washington-Idaho Symphony, comprised largely of the region's college music faculty, performs throughout the Palouse.

Moscow is also the home of Festival Dance, a presenter organization bringing ethnic, contemporary, and classical dance companies into the area for its seven-month season. Idaho Repertory Theatre's summer season at Hartung performs four plays during its month-long run, focusing on new, challenging material, while the university's theater department's five-month winter season brings a mix of old and new work onto the Hartung stage.

Alternatives

Many of Moscow's visual and fine crafts artists do quite well at the area's summer art fairs, and during the winter months places such as The Beanery, Main Street Deli, and Key Bank are important alternative venues.

Art Perspectives:

Mary Blyth of the Moscow Art Commission says, "Our school district's programs for kids are one of the best things going. Money may be limited but the programs are getting stronger each year. Moscow is pro-art and pro-artist, and there's wide cooperation from all corners of the community to do whatever it takes to support the arts."

Details

Population: 20,000

Important Arts Events: Lionel Hampton Jazz Festival in February, Renaissance Faire in May, Rendezvous in the Park in July, Palouseafest in August

Must-See Art Galleries: Gallery West, Inner Vision, Northwest Showcase, Prichard Gallery, Ridenbaugh Gallery, WSU Museum of Art

Local Arts Agency: Moscow Arts Commission P.O. Box 9203 Moscow, ID 83843 208/883-7036

Natural Foods Stores: The Moscow Co-op, Pilgrims Natural Foods

Farmer's Market: Saturday mornings at Friendship Square

National Public Radio: KRFA - 91.7 FM

Bookstores: Bookpeople, University Bookstore, Inner Vision

Chamber of Commerce: P.O. Box 8936 Moscow ID 83843 208/882-1800

Sandpoint, Idaho

Location

The 43-mile-long Lake Pend Oreille sits squarely in the middle of Idaho's Panhandle, a narrow strip of land separating Washington, British Columbia, and Montana. Truly one of the most picturesque landscapes in America, the small art town of Sandpoint, population 6,000, is just 80 miles from Spokane, home of Gonzaga University and the Bulldog Tavern.

Great Outdoors

Sandpoint is ideally positioned to take advantage of the panhandle's summer and winter tourist seasons. Once home to a World War II naval training center, Lake Pend Oreille is one of the Northwest's most popular sportfishing destinations, yielding massive kokanee salmon and Kamloops, rainbow, cutthroat, and Dolly Varden trout. The lake's many marinas, public beaches, campgrounds, and resorts make it one busy place to enjoy the capricious weather that passes for a Northwest summer. Come winter, Sandpoint's own first-rate downhill ski resort, Schweitzer Mountain, attracts huge crowds of skiers from the surrounding states and provinces. The entire Panhandle region is filled with state parks, national forests, outdoor recreation sites, snowmobile trails, back-country wilderness, and hiking trails. Old logging roads provide an ideal setting for cross-country skiing in the winter and for mountain biking in the warmer months.

Lifestyle

Sandpoint was created as a result of the area's mining and logging industries. While the miners have moved elsewhere, forest products still account for one-fifth of the regional economy, and 18-wheelers hauling old-growth timber are a common sight. A mass of relocated Californians employ much of the local workforce in construction. An average-sized house costs about $115,000, but many less expensive homes can be found in the outlying areas.

Local schools take the standard visual art and music class approach. The local arts agency, Pend Oreille Arts Council, coordinates an artist-in-residence program using local artists in Sandpoint's schools. Sandpoint Art Works, a nonprofit organization, offers mostly adult art education classes, with a few children's programs as well. The Fiddlers' Hatchery is Sandpoint's Suzuki-method violin instructional program, and its summer schedule also boasts performance and touring for young musicians. Another local organization that works to supplement the school district's programs is the Performing Arts & Humanities of Sandpoint, which organizes children's (and some adult) programs in voice, drama, dance, and visual arts. The organization presents winter and spring performances featuring the work of local kids and adults.

Arts Scene

The Pend Oreille Arts Council operates its own nonprofit exhibition space in the lobby of Sandpoint's Panhandle State Bank, featuring local artists in its solo and invitational shows. Each summer the council sponsors Artwalk, rotating three consecutive shows through each of 14 galleries and businesses between Memorial Day and Labor Day. Artwalk artists are drawn from Idaho, Washington, and British Columbia. Sandpoint's six commercial galleries exhibit mostly regional work that includes art glass, fine crafts, bronze sculpture, paintings, and monoprints, with Seattle area artists strongly represented.

The Festival at Sandpoint is a month's worth of fantastic shows that feature everything from Spokane Symphony classical to Jamaican reggae, Nashville country-and-western to Hollywood pop. The Festival's artistic director, maestro Gunther Schuller, has developed a musical masterpiece that could hold its own in any metropolitan setting. The Festival sponsors nearly two dozen performances on its mainstage at Memorial Field, plus a series of new works concerts in Spokane, on the Pend Oreille lakefront, and at the Schweitzer Mountain Resort. In addition to its regular season, the Festival operates a three-week Schweitzer Institute of Music at the ski resort. The institute attracts 60 of the nation's premier young classical musicians to Sandpoint for intensive programs in conducting, composition, and progressive jazz performance. The institute's musicians perform in a series of intimate concerts toward the end of their studies. During the rest of the year, the arts council stages *It's Happening in Sandpoint*, a showcase for eight national acts ranging from ballet to ethnic dance to light opera. The shows take place at Sandpoint's historic Panida theater, a 575-seat facility also used for an extensive film program, independently produced rock, country, chorale, and benefit concerts, and kids' theater. It's also home to Unicorn Theatre Players, Sandpoint's longstanding community theater organization, which stages four productions each year.

Alternatives

The most active alternative exhibition sites in Sandpoint are the Edgewater Resort, Gregory's, and Java Adagio.

Art Perspectives

According to Ginny Robideaux of the Pendoreille Art Council, "We live in staggering natural beauty, and we'd love to have more artists moving in. But Sandpoint's not an easy place for an artist to make a living. I call it a 'tough paradise,' because so many people just aren't able to hang on and they end up leaving here, disillusioned."

Details

Population: 6,000

Important Arts Events: Kite festival in April, Sunday Evening Concerts-on-the-Lawn in July, The Festival at Sandpoint in July & August, the annual Arts & Crafts Fair in August

Must-See Art Galleries: Eklektos Gallery, Lyman Gallery, Panhandle Art Glass, POAC Gallery, Selkirk Gallery

Local Arts Agency: Pend Oreille Arts Council
P.O. Box 1694
Sandpoint, ID 83864
208/263-6139

Natural Foods Stores: Greentree Naturals, The Enchanted Kingdom

Farmer's Market: Saturday mornings at Farmin Park

National Public Radio: KPBX - 101.7 FM

Bookstores: Book Gallery, B.J.'s Books, Elfin Rhythm, Dolphin House, Vanderford's Books

Chamber of Commerce: P.O. Box 928
Sandpoint, ID 83864
208/263-2161

Galena, Illinois

Location

This fast-growing art town is nestled into northwest Illinois' thickly wooded hillsides, just a five-minute drive from the Mississippi River and ten miles from the Wisconsin state line. Chicago is less than a three-hour drive east, affecting this community of 3,600 both positively and negatively.

Great Outdoors

Galena's far enough north to be ringed by several cross-country ski areas, and there's even a downhill slope or two in the region. The main outdoor-recreation attraction is the Mississippi, hosting several marinas, riverside campgrounds (some privately owned), and sternwheeler gambling boats. Apple Canyon Lake, Lake Galena, and Apple River Canyon State Park are magnets for tourists who pour into this region during the summer months. From June through August locals head for Wisconsin's less crowded parks just a short drive north.

Lifestyle

Until about 15 years ago, Galena was a sleepy little town best known for its 100 or so decrepit Victorian homes. It proved the perfect climate for Chicago artists who wanted out of the city but needed occasional access to galleries, museums, and the Cubs. Homes selling for $20,000 needed lots of work, but artists were in a great position to restore them as well as open studios and galleries in Galena's many vacant downtown storefronts.

Today Galena is an example of what can happen when a town becomes a victim of its own success. Shortly after its discovery by savvy cultural tourists who bought some of the local work, a flood of publicity brought more attention than this tiny town needed, and soon things started changing. Real estate speculators from Chicago began to snap up downtown buildings and huge chunks of rural farmland. Retail store owners moved in downtown, opening souvenir shops selling T-shirts and imports. Busloads of tourists cruised into town on weekends, while factory outlets and second-rate antique shops proliferated. And average-sized homes in Galena's pretty neighborhoods have now reached well over $125,000.

Arts Scene

Despite ongoing problems arising from its rapid growth, Galena remains a good place for artists to live and work. It's best to try to sell into the Chicago market and land work in one of the better Galena galleries—or simply to market your work nationally and disregard what's happening locally. Artists can still connect with one another in Galena, even if they do so outside of the main tourist season. Visual artists can join the local, 100-member art guild or pursue activities at the Galena Arts & Recreation Center. A few galleries show work by the many fine craft artists who call Galena home when not traveling on the craft show circuit.

The performing arts are fairly well-represented in Galena, with the Main Street Players staging a six-month season in a 400-seat former opera house, Turner Hall. The company also performs at the Sinsinawa Mound Theatre on the grounds of a Dominican retreat center. Galena has its own dynamic classical music organization, the Galena Chamber Ensemble, which uses several vacationing musicians from the Chicago Symphony in its performances at Turner Hall. Two local actors of national fame present one-man shows in Galena: Jim Post, who has created an award-winning Mark Twain character, and W. Paul Greco, who stages a General Ulysses S. Grant show.

Alternatives
Local artists who wish to market to Galena's cultural tourist base exhibit their work at the Living Room jazz club, the Café Italia, Woodlands Restaurant, El Diablo, and the Lost Art Café.

Art Perspectives
Gary David, a sculptor and fine craftsman from the wilds of New York, says that Galena's strong local art market greatly influenced his decision to move here. "We've got something like $600 million being spent here in tourism-related businesses, and 150 shops in a five-block downtown. On Main Street you can just see Galena's prosperity. The artists who moved here in the 1960s and 1970s built Galena's reputation, and that's a reputation still attracting people, but the town is having some growing pains. Galena needs to concentrate its promotional efforts on building its reputation as an arts center, so that we can make sure the people attracted here are the kinds of buyers we need to keep this good thing going."

Details

Population: 3,600

Important Arts Events: Galena Arts Festival in July, Galena Country Fair in October, Nouveau Beaujolais Celebration in November

Must-See Art Galleries: Carl Johnson's Gallery, Galena Artists Guild Gallery, The Pottery

Local Arts Agency: Galena Artist Guild
P.O. Box 269
Galena, IL 61036
815/777-9341

Farmer's Market: Weekend mornings on Markethouse Square

National Public Radio: KUNI - 98.3 FM

Bookstores: Cover-to-Cover, Chapter & Verse

Chamber of Commerce: 101 Bouthillier Street
Galena, IL 61036
815/777-0203

Quincy, Illinois

Location

Just as the Mississippi River reaches the west-central part of Illinois, it makes a long, arching bend westward past the art town of Quincy. Always eager to promote the arts, the 39,000 residents of Quincy live in a town that boasts the nation's first community arts council, formed in the 1940s.

Great Outdoors

The presence of the river is such a strong influence that town organizations sometimes use the name "Quinsippi" in their titles. Flat farmlands dominate Quincy's countryside, which makes the nearby state parks at Siloam Springs, Illinois, and LaGrange, Missouri, important outdoor recreation destinations for those tired of floating on the river or fishing for "cat." Cannon Dam and Mark Twain Lake in nearby Missouri are the best places for water skiing and summer camping. The local government maintains more than two dozen community parks.

Lifestyle

Around the turn of the century, hundreds of entrepreneurs made huge fortunes in Quincy's manufacturing and shipping industries. Shortly thereafter, the town hit the economic skids as the region's business, agricultural, and transportation activity solidified around St. Louis, a two-hour drive south. What remained, however, was one of the nation's last great 1800s-style communities, a place where block after downtown block was loaded with architectural masterpieces, from Greek Revival homes to Gothic churches and Federal-style commercial buildings. Today, Quincy has more than 2,000 buildings listed on the National Register of Historic Places, and nearly every one of them has been lovingly restored. The fact that Quincy held onto this historic legacy rather than allow it to crumble into ruin is a testimony to the town's "we-can-do-it-ourselves" spirit—the same spirit that makes this such a great place for the arts.

Quincy's broad-based economy is solid, and the region's manufacturing, electronics, and agricultural employers are, for the most part, key underwriters of its arts scene. The town accommodates ten museums, mostly historic. There's a community college with an arts department as well as a four-year, liberal arts university operated by the Franciscans. But one of the major reasons artists find this a great place to call home is the incredibly low cost of living: $40,000 buys a three-bedroom home with a garage, front porch, and garden, while the turn-of-the-century beauties start at about twice that.

Arts Scene

Communities like Quincy are considered great art towns for one reason: accessibility. The Quincy Society of Fine Arts is the umbrella organization that keeps the town's four arts groups from bumping into each other. With a large annual budget, it has the financial muscle and the access to facilities it needs to keep everyone singing from the same sheet music.

Quincy's visual arts scene is centered around the Quincy Art Center, a restored carriage house that has just expanded to nearly 2,000 square feet of museum-level exhibition space. It also serves as an education center, with art classes for kids and adults, a studio facility, a print shop, a lecture hall, and a collection of Quincy and Midwestern regional art. The town's new convention center, Oakley-Lindsay, contains one of Quincy's important visual arts exhibition spaces. The others can be found at the local colleges: the Mabee Gallery at Culver-Stockton and the Brenner Library Gallery at Quincy University. The arts society administers an in-school arts education program that funds artist-in-residence programs, performing arts shows, and a teacher education program. Although a couple of commercial galleries in town show local and regional work, the challenge for visual artists here is to sell elsewhere.

Quincy has cultivated a vibrant performing arts scene, one accessible to all quarters of the community's diverse population. Quincy Community Theatre rolls out six annual productions at the Oakley-Lindsay. The Community Concert Band performs in the Morrison Theatre, as do the Quincy Symphony, the Muddy River Opera Company, and touring classical music acts presented by the Civic Music Association. Some of the town's historic churches host symphony and chorale performances, and Quincy University sponsors a film series that brings foreign and art films into town.

Alternatives

The Arts/Quincy Riverfest celebration in early October is one of the region's premier marketing opportunities for Quincy artists, as are the several art festivals held downriver in nearby Hannibal, Missouri. A few of the town's restaurants exhibit the work of local artists; of these, T.J.'s and The Pier are the most popular.

Art Perspectives

Carla Gordon, a Quincy art teacher and "spoons" musician, notes that the community's progress in the arts is one of Quincy's selling points. "Our new art center has really taken off in popularity, especially with kids who can walk there from most of the schools in town. Quincy's supportive of all the arts, but especially music. There's full-time instruction in the schools, and for kids who want to do more, there are lots of after-school programs."

Details

Population: 39,000

Important Arts Events: Bluegrass Music Festival in January, Mid-Mississippi Muddy Water Blues Bash in July, Arts/Quincy Riverfest in October

Must-See Art Galleries: Brenner Library Gallery, Creative Art Gallery, Inman's Gallery, Mabee Gallery, Quincy Art Center, Quincy Museum

Local Arts Agency: Quincy Society of Fine Arts
300 Civic Center Plaza

Quincy, IL 62301
217/222-3432

Natural Foods Store: Tri-State Nutrition Center

Farmer's Market: Saturday mornings in Washington Park

National Public Radio: WQUB - 90.3 FM

Bookstore: Copperfield's

Chamber of Commerce: 300 Civic Center Plaza
Quincy, IL 62301
217/222-7980

Columbus, Indiana

Location

The rolling green hills of south-central Indiana have, since the late 1800s, attracted some of the nation's best landscape painters. Columbus, a unique community of 36,000 residents, is about an hour's drive south of Indianapolis and a half-hour east of Bloomington, a college town with its own large art community.

Great Outdoors

Several of Indiana's best outdoor recreation areas are within an easy drive of Columbus, including Brown Country State Park, Lake Monroe, Hoosier National Forest, and the Driftwood River's Atterbury Fish and Wildlife Area. Columbus itself is ringed by large city parks and recreation areas. One of these, the Mill Race Park, serves as a key venue for the local arts council's performing arts series.

Lifestyle

Columbus is a small art town unlike any other. Home to a lively visual and performing arts scene, it is also a showcase of contemporary architectural design. The downtown is a study in contrasts: beautifully historic two-story buildings share city blocks with dramatic examples of architectural design by leaders such as Cesar Pelli, Eliel Saarinen, I. M. Pei, Robert Venturi, and Alexander Girard. Columbus' churches, libraries, municipal offices, and schools are all masterpieces of contemporary design, surrounded by landscapes configured by several of the nation's foremost landscape architects. There are more than 60 buildings in Columbus that were designed by leading national architects, and displayed among them are massive works of public art by Henry Moore, Richard Bauer, and Jean Tingley.

Columbus is home to several large international corporations, including the Cummins Engine Company. Cummins masterminded the town's first play for architectural fame back in the 1940s, and Columbus picked up the ball and ran. In the '60s urban redevelopment craze, the city's progressive government ripped up the shabbiest part of downtown and built The Commons, a two-block Cesar Pelli–designed indoor/outdoor structure. The Commons houses the town's courthouse, movie theaters, arts council offices, performing arts space, and the visual arts exhibition showcase, a 4,600-square-foot state-of-the-art outpost of the Indiana Museum of Art.

Several years ago, Columbus' three corporate leaders, Cummins, Arvin Industries, and Cosco, spearheaded an international corporate recruitment drive and landed Toyota, Onkyo, Reliance Electric, and a half-dozen other solid local employers—as well as two of the best sushi bars this side of Seattle. But even with everyone working, Columbus is still affordable and safe; average home prices start in the $60,000 range. The local schools are not only architectural masterpieces, they support a full range of far-reaching arts education programs.

Arts Scene

The Columbus branch of the Indianapolis Art Museum stages five exhibitions annually, shows that run the gamut from ethnic art to contemporary paintings to photography to mixed media shows of folk art, fine craft, and prints. ArtColumbus, the town's visual artists' organization, sponsors classes for its artists and operates Artifacts, a nonprofit, 900-square-foot gallery in The Commons. Another ArtColumbus venture is its surprisingly successful. Art in Public Places project, which rotates members' art in ten downtown Columbus exhibition venues such as cafés, bank lobbies, and corporate offices.

When it comes to performing arts, Columbus' activity is more what you would expect in a city ten times its size. Much of the action revolves around The Commons, where the Columbus Area Arts Council presents a performance series for families and kids, and an annual series of jazz, gospel, country, and bluegrass festivals. Friends of the Commons presents off-the-wall music and theater acts originating in Bloomington and Indianapolis. The Columbus Dance Workshop performs at local school auditoriums and presents touring contemporary dance troupes at The Commons. The Columbus, Indiana Philharmonic, which performs September through April at area high school auditoriums and at The Commons. During the summer months, an outdoor performance series brings national pop music acts to the Mill Race Park Amphitheatre, another in this town's string of architectural gems.

Alternatives

Positively 4th Street and the Columbus Bar are two of the most popular venues.

Art Perspectives

Pat Carothers, a painter, says that Columbus visual artists are just beginning to get the recognition they deserve. "Our art group has 90 members, and there are lots of artists who live here and don't belong to ArtColumbus, artists who pursue their careers on a national level. Since we've had a chance to show our work in the Artifacts Gallery, we're a lot more in the public eye, and we're getting a surge of interest from new members. "

Details

Population: 36,000

Important Arts Events: Fair on the Square in May, Chautauqua of the Arts in September, Ethnic Expo in October

Must-See Art Galleries: Artifacts Gallery, Columbus Gallery, Indianapolis Museum of Art

Local Arts Agency: Columbus Area Arts Council
302 Washington Street
Columbus, IN 47201
812/376-2539

Natural Foods Store: Blooming Foods in Bloomington

Farmer's Market: Farm stands throughout the region

National Public Radio: WFIU - 103.7 FM

Bookstore: Viewpoint Books

Chamber of Commerce: 500 Franklin Street
Columbus, IN 47201
812/379-4457

New Harmony, Indiana

Location

Historic, bucolic New Harmony sits on the Wabash River in the southwest corner of Indiana. This quiet and gracious community, less than an hour from Evansville, is an art town that keeps its present firmly grounded in its past.

Great Outdoors

The Wabash River is one of the Midwest's scenic treasures. Unspoiled by shoreline development until far north of New Harmony, it's a favorite place for houseboating, water skiing, and fishing. New Harmony is surrounded by gorgeous, well-tended farmlands, thick forests, and clear streams. Harmonie State Park, a sprawling recreational facility with campsites, bike trails, hiking trails, and a boat ramp on the Wabash, is just down the road from the town's business district. Hovey Lake Wildlife Area is an easy drive from town, and there's a beginner's ski area at Paoli Peak, a two-hour drive east.

Lifestyle

New Harmony, once known as "The Athens of the West," is a community bound by its enduring cultural legacy. When you drive into town, you'll see evidence of its rich past. Quiet streets shaded by towering trees are lined with nineteenth-century commercial structures, restored to their full glory. An opera house, quaint private homes, and old farmhouses have been turned into shops and historic exhibits. Homes are priced in the $50,000 range.

What's also intriguing about New Harmony is its past as a religious community. It was populated first by Utopians in 1814 and later by free-thinkers and intellectuals in 1825. Today the town celebrates and preserves its unique historic legacy through what's known as the New Harmony State Historic Site, a collection of residential structures and workshops that were used by these early settlers. The local presence of employees and faculty of the University of Southern Indiana, which oversees part of the state historic site, is one of the reasons New Harmony's schools are solid as a rock.

The descendants of the town's Utopian founders, although not residents of New Harmony, are still influential here. These descendants pulled in corporate and foundation support from several sources to hire prominent architects such as Philip Johnson and Richard Meier to design the town's church (The Roofless Church) and visitors center (The Athenaeum). They also commissioned artists Stephen deStaebler and Jacques Lipchitz to create public works of art in New Harmony, enhancing the town's beauty without detracting from the visual appeal of its historic structures. The Labyrinth, a European hedge-maze occupying several acres downtown, is a treasure from the past that looks as if it were designed in the 1990s. In the middle of the maze sits the Utopians' House of Meditation.

Arts Scene

In an art town of New Harmony's size, you might expect to see one small shop selling crafts and paintings, and maybe a one-shot community theater group. But New Harmony has much more. The New Harmony Gallery of Contemporary Art has 2,000 square feet of exhibition space dedicated to the works of Midwestern artists. The New Harmony Theatre presents its annual American Masters Festival in the 450-seat Murphy Auditorium and in the 150-seat Thrall's Opera House. There are two other visual art galleries in town, and all five of New Harmony's restaurants exhibit the work of Indiana artists. During the summer months, a performing arts series brings in chamber music groups, a local foundation runs a children's music camp, and Harmonie State Park hosts regular bluegrass and folk music concerts.

Alternatives

The Grapevine Bar, part of the Red Geranium restaurant, is a favorite place of local artists. Check out its well-stocked bookstore, filled with literature on art, regional travel, and local history. New Harmony Coffee & Tea Co. is a showcase for local artists interested in marketing their work.

Art Perspectives

Rodney Stockment, a fine crafts artist creating contemporary furniture, says New Harmony is a town filled with surprises. "I didn't expect to sell very well after I moved here from Pennsylvania, but it's been very surprising to see the kinds of people walking in here and buying my work. There are lots of urban people who come through New Harmony on weekend trips out to the country—people from St. Louis, Indianapolis, and Louisville who know fine craft and are able to make decisions about buying a fairly expensive piece of art.

"Coming here was a risk I was willing to take. Some of what New Harmony offers are things important to me: inexpensive living, large vegetable gardens, a group of friendly artists, and the daily contact I have with people who are part of America's working class. It's a very positive environment for living and working."

Details

Population: 850

Important Art Events: Golden Raintree Festival in June, Midsummer Night's Stroll in July, Kunstfest in September

Must-See Art Galleries: New Harmony Gallery of Contemporary Art

Farmer's Market: At the New Harmony Train Depot on weekends

National Public Radio: WNIN-88.1 FM

Bookstore: Red Geranium Bookstore

Chamber of Commerce: Historic New Harmony
P.O. Box 579
New Harmony, IN 47631
812/838-3639

Cedar Falls, Iowa

Location

This fabulous community possesses two crucial assets for a vibrant local arts scene: broad arts support by the town's businesses and residents, and the dynamic presence of a highly regarded university committed to the arts. Cedar Falls is in northeast Iowa, two hours from Des Moines.

Great Outdoors

The 23,000 full-time residents of Cedar Falls live within easy reach of several state parks, including Pine Lake and its summer watersports, Heery Woods and its hiking trails, and Union Grove with its bass fishing. George Wyth Park's 500 acres of biking and hiking trails lie on the outskirts of town. Cedar Falls itself has an extensive park system that includes a 260-acre nature center, fishing lakes, a golf course, and an indoor recreation center. The University of Northern Iowa's sprawling campus is right in town, with running trails, ball fields, and an indoor track.

Lifestyle

Residents have easy access to a full range of visual and performing arts. Cedar Falls is a prosperous town thanks to the university's large local payroll and the opportunities in nearby Waterloo, home to several large agricultural corporations. Real estate is affordable, and $100,000 homes are easy to find. Cedar Falls residents are infected with a positive, independent spirit that has led to success as the town takes on major arts-related projects. Foremost among these is the recent $1.2 million restoration of the 500-seat Oster Regent Theatre, a turn-of-the-century vaudeville house that now serves as the community's premier performance venue. The university is building its own performing arts center with a 1,800-seat theater backed by enough financial muscle to lure national acts into town.

Arts Scene

The visual arts in Cedar Falls unite at the Hearst Center for the Arts, an exhibition facility with two large gallery spaces, art-education classrooms, studio space, and a theater showing foreign films. Cedar Falls' schools hold a typical "college town" approach to arts education; local teachers commit time and expertise to enhance their curricula with the arts. Even so, children's weekend and weekday art-education programs at the Hearst are popular, especially for kids who have specific talents to develop. There's another major art exhibition space on the university campus, as well as a historical museum, both of which will be expanded inside the school's new performing arts center. Nearby Waterloo has an art museum with one of the nation's largest Grant Wood collections.

Cedar Falls' several historical museums are located in large, turn-of-the-century mansions, one of which is an art-deco masterpiece. The Ice House Museum, once the "coolest" place in this part of the state, now houses not ice, but ancient industrial gear, roadsters, and delivery trucks. The downtown area has several commercial gallery spaces dedicated to locally created art; most noteworthy is the Henry W. Myrtle Gallery, which displays fine crafts, paintings, wood sculpture, and fine jewelry.

The town's door-busting outdoor art event, the College Hill Arts Festival, lines downtown streets with artists' booths, performance stages, ethnic food booths, and beer company tents, turning Cedar Falls into one of the premier Midwestern crafts fair sites for a weekend.

Cedar Falls' performing arts are exemplary. The Oster Regent Theatre is a gem, busy every weekend with children's theater, local repertory theater, touring classical music, contemporary dance, and top names on the nation's contemporary folk circuit. Some savvy local promoters also work to keep the entertainment scene lively and intriguing. The Oster Regent is used regularly by the Waterloo/Cedar Falls Symphony Orchestra and also by the Old Creamery Theatre Company, an Amana-based equity company that comes into Cedar Falls twice annually for a week's worth of sold-out shows. The Oster Regent also produces a foreign film series. The university's drama and music department is one of Iowa's best. For years, Cedar Falls folks have turned out in droves for the performances at the campus' Strayer-Wood Theatre.

Alternatives
Cedar Falls is a hip college town. With 13,000 students, the town has the critical mass to support an alternative music scene. Contemporary folk and jazz are also popular. There are several bars that feature touring national acts and a bevy of coffeehouses that open their doors for music performance on weekends.

Art Perspectives
Gary Kelley, a nationally known painter with a studio on the second floor of a downtown historic building, says that Cedar Falls supports its artists. "Like any other place, this is a tough place to survive on the local market, but the university has lots of teaching jobs and the summer art festival sells lots of work. One of the best things about living here is the theater and music department at the university; I've seen a lot of outstanding performances there. Cedar Falls is getting to be a better place for the arts. There's a sense of pride about having so much talent in one small town. It's a very tolerant place to live."

Details
Population: 23,000, plus 13,000 college students

Important Arts Events: Cedar Basin Jazz Festival in June, College Hill Arts Festival in July, Cedar Falls Community Theatre season October to June

Must-See Art Galleries: Hearst Center for the Arts, Henry W. Myrtle Gallery, Heritage Galleries, Twin Oaks, UNI Gallery of Art, Waterloo Museum of Art

Local Arts Agency: College Hill Arts 515 Clay Street

Cedar Falls, IA 50613
319/266-7304

Natural Foods Store: Stella's

Farmer's Market: Saturday mornings in the downtown park

National Public Radio: KUNI - 90.9 FM

Bookstores: Bought Again Books, University Books

Chamber of Commerce: 10 Main Street Cedar Falls, IA 50613
319/266-3593

Spencer, Iowa

Location

The small art town of Spencer is in Iowa's northwest corner, a short drive south of the Minnesota border. Spencer's 12,000 residents freeze through howling winters from Halloween until Easter, which is why they're so enthusiastic about the arts—it keeps everyone sane. Des Moines is a four-hour drive southeast, where you can catch a flight to Cancun.

Great Outdoors

The town's biggest tourist attraction is its downtown community arts center, "Arts on Grand." But Spencer promotes itself as the gateway to Iowa's Great Lakes region, a 30-minute drive north and home to the area's most popular summer recreation. Ringed by state parks and loaded with marinas, hiking and bicycle trails, campgrounds, and resorts, the Great Lakes are among Iowa's premier freshwater bass fishing sites; they remain busy with hunters and fishermen right through duck season.

Lifestyle

Spencer was selected for this book largely because its hopes are hooked to the arts and cultural tourism as a way of improving the community's quality of life and bringing people into town. Spencer is quiet, friendly, and safe—and for $40,000 you can find a fixer-upper home on a neighborhood street close to one of Spencer's parks, recreation areas, wildlife reserves, or its public golf course. The region's agricultural industry is an economic giant, but the largest corporate employer is Great Lakes Airlines, and local experience has proven that pilots buy art.

The school system does employ art teachers, but hasn't made the leap into incorporating arts-based curricula. This has left the door open for Arts on Grand, which has made a point of bringing the entire realm of arts education into town in a big way. Touring and local artists come to Arts on Grand year-round to teach children's and adults' art education classes, which cover everything from nature photography at the Great Lakes migratory waterfowl refuges, to stained glass, papermaking, and watercolor.

Arts Scene

Spencer built itself into an arts town after the Spencer Area Arts Council took control of what was once the local movie house. Through sweat equity and privately raised funds, what is now Arts on Grand houses the arts council's administrative offices; through a recent expansion project it is also home to two large visual-arts exhibition spaces, a sales gallery that sells local artists' work, a modern pottery studio, and a classroom space that doubles as the town's lecture hall. The visual art exhibited here is not limited to northwest Iowa artists. Instead, Arts on Grand houses everything: regional museums' touring textiles exhibitions; regional invitationals; annual schoolchildren's art exhibitions; and one-artist shows by local artists and others from Des Moines, Iowa City, and Omaha. One of Arts on Grand's most popular projects is its "Films for the Cinematically Disadvantaged" series, which brings foreign and indie flicks into town for one-night showings on the facility's gallery walls.

With a wildlife art gallery in town and several galleries scattered around the Great Lakes, Spencer's artists have the opportunity to make part of their living from selling their work locally. The town's main arts festival takes place during the county fair, when the local arts council runs an exhibition and sales space known as the Art Tent.

Spencer has had its own community theater facility since 1982, and the Spencer Community Theatre's 266-seat downtown playhouse is filled to the rafters for each of their four annual productions (September–April). There's also a highly regarded summer repertory theater company in the lakeside resort of Okoboji. Spencer kids can sign up for the community theater's summer camp, which whips them into artistic shape then releases them onstage for a series of performances. During the school year, children with strong theater interests can continue their involvement by acting in one of the theater's regular-season performances. The Spencer Community Concert Association presents an annual program of about six classical music shows with touring national artists at the Spencer Middle School Auditorium.

Alternatives

Spencer's visual artists can exhibit their work at the Great Lakes region galleries—Storm Lake's Witter Gallery and Okoboji's Lakes Art Center are two of the best places for sales. Around Spencer, the Hanna Marie Inn shows local artists' work, as do the Boatmen's Bank and Mercantile Bank of Clay County. The Hotel, a restored early-1900s inn, is known for displaying the work of regional artists and for its successful sales. The Grand Tap is a local artist hangout.

Art Perspectives

Katie Plucker, a painter whose colored-pencil work has been featured in national art magazines, says Spencer isn't immune from run-of-the-mill art controversies. "Considering that the town promotes its arts, and that the downtown business community is a huge arts supporter, you would think local government would step up and provide us with the financial support we need to fund our projects. I'm not saying we should be supported by government, but from the small amounts of support they cast our way I know they could do better."

Details

Population: 11,000

Important Arts Events: Tent for the Arts at Clay County Fair in September, Spencer Community Theatre season from September to April, Spencer Area Concert Association season from September to May

Must-See Art Galleries: Arts on Grand Galleries, Great Outdoors Wildlife Gallery, Lakes Art Center, Witter Gallery

Local Arts Agency: Spencer Area Arts Council
408 North Grand Avenue

Spencer, IA 51301
712/262-4307

Natural Foods Store: Midwest Health Foods Plus

Farmers Market: Tuesday and Saturday mornings at the north end of town

National Public Radio: KUOO - 103.9 FM

Bookstore: Books 'n' Things

Chamber of Commerce: 122 West Fifth Street Spencer, IA 51301
712/262-5680

Lawrence, Kansas

Location

Halfway between Topeka and Kansas City is the art town/college town of Lawrence, a community of 73,000 full-time residents and 30,000 students attending "K.U."—the University of Kansas. Kansas City lies an hour east.

Great Outdoors

In places, the landscape here could fool you into thinking you're in Spokane, Chapel Hill, or Madison—it's hilly, wooded, and cut by rivers and streams. Right outside of town, the prairie starts rolling across the landscape in all directions. Clinton Lake, on the edge of town, has nearly 4,000 acres of water surface and plenty of campgrounds, nature trails, and beaches. Perry Lake, a short drive from Lawrence, is slightly larger. Duck hunting and bass fishing are the big outdoor draws, unless you want to count University of Kansas football. Everyone drives to Colorado at least once a winter for a ski trip, and a day's drive south will take you to Galveston's seawall.

Lifestyle

Prosperous, unpretentious, friendly, and multicultural (it was a stop on the Underground Railroad), Lawrence revels in a quality of life most communities can only dream about. Turn-of-the-century homes with line quiet streets within easy walking distance of a beautiful downtown and the campus. The university is the area's largest employer. Hallmark Cards is a distant second.

The K.U. presence is everywhere you look, but Lawrence is a town that stands on its own two feet when it comes to the arts. While the university arts scene is dynamic, broad, and well-funded, what makes Lawrence special is its perfect integration of the community's and the university's cultural programming. Lawrence benefits mightily from the wealth of talent employed in the university's music, arts, and theater departments. With the large student population comes a tremendous leveraging of economic power—a force strong enough to support an alternative music scene and many music shops.

Lawrence spares no effort or investment to make certain that education is as strong as it can be. The university faculty and staff families (i.e., voters) expect nothing less. So strong is the town's demand for more exhibitions, classes, and experimental theater, that the Lawrence Arts Center is building a $5 million addition to its converted Carnegie Library office-performance-education-exhibition space. Already home to one of the nation's premier arts-based preschool programs, the center runs an incredibly diverse, year-round series of classes aimed at all segments of Lawrence's population and offering instruction in the full range of arts. An emphasis is placed on kids' arts education through after-school, weekend, and summer classes.

Arts Scene

The Lawrence Art Center's Eastwood Gallery has everything from Lawrence Art League exhibitions and one-artist shows by major Midwestern regionalists to local invitationals. The university's enormous Spencer Museum of Art mounts multiple exhibitions ranging from historic to international contemporary, all the while rotating pieces from its permanent collection. K.U. also has its Natural History Museum and the Museum of Anthropology, which is known for its rotating exhibitions of Native American, African, Northwest Coast, and pre-Columbian art.

Each fall, through the combined efforts of the Museum of Anthropology and Lawrence's Haskell Indian Nations University, the town turns itself into one of the nation's most dynamic Native American art centers. The museum exhibits work by the nation's top Indian artists, (and other shows are held at the Spencer, the arts center, and the city library), while Haskell hosts a weekend outdoor market attracting nearly a hundred Native American artists and craftspeople and more than 10,000 cultural tourists.

The city of Lawrence gets into the act through its "percent-for-the-arts" program. These funds are used to purchase public sculpture by prominent national artists and to fund an annual sculpture show that lines downtown's Massachusetts Avenue with a dozen major works.

The performing arts programs at Lied Center, K.U.'s $14 million theater, bring major national and international acts into Lawrence several times each month. The university's theater department uses Murphy Hall for its school-year productions and a separate stage for its summer Shakespeare festival, its kids' theater, and its annual new plays festival. These venues are shared with the symphony orchestra, the chorale, and Lawrence's Chamber Players. The Lawrence Community Theatre, a 159-seat converted church, is home to six annual productions running from September to June (don't expect to see "The Music Man"). The art center is home to two very active theater companies, Seem-to-Be-Players and Prairie Wind Dancers.

Alternatives

Art is everywhere you turn in Lawrence—just take a look around town.

Art Perspectives

Ann Evans, director of the Lawrence Art Center, says, "We serve lots of children who need the creative opportunity to express themselves and to succeed. In the arts, you're not told that what you're doing is right or wrong . . . and that's the kind of acceptance all kids need."

Details

Population: 73,000

Important Arts Events: Art in the Park in May, Lawrence Indian Art Show and the Haskell Indian Art Market in September, Harvest of the Arts in October

Must-See Art Galleries: Eastwood Gallery, Phoenix Gallery, Free State Glass, Holt/Russell Gallery at Baker University, Kansas Union Gallery, Lawrence Arts Center, Lawrence Library Gallery, Lithography Workshop, Roy's Gallery, Spencer Museum of Art

Local Arts Agency: Lawrence Arts Center 200 West 9th

Lawrence, KS 66044
913/843-2787

Natural Foods Stores: Wild Oats, Community Mercantile

Farmers Market: Tuesday, Thursday, Saturday on Vermont Street

National Public Radio: KANU - 91.5 FM

Bookstores: Jayhawk Bookstore, Adventure Bookstore, Raven Bookstore

Chamber of Commerce:
734 Vermont St. # 101
Lawrence, KS 66044
913/865-4411

Salina, Kansas

Location

Standing in downtown Salina you're halfway from New York to L.A., and of course you're right in the middle of Kansas. This town of 43,000 has a healthy case of the self-reliance syndrome that has spawned many of the country's diverse local arts scenes. The closest city is Kansas City, a three-hour drive east.

Great Outdoors

Salina is situated in the rolling landscape of the Great Plains. Bass fishing on Milford Lake, an hour's drive east, is one of the most popular outdoor escapes. Closer to town, the lakes at Kanopolis State Park and Glen Elder State Park have nature trails, campgrounds, and marinas. Quivara National Waterfowl Refuge, a two-hour drive southwest of town, is another favorite among hikers and canoeists. Winters here are punctuated by blizzards that roll in off the High Plains every couple of weeks, turning Salina's many city parks into cross-country ski areas.

Lifestyle

Traditionally, Salina has been connected to the military one way or another, from the Buffalo Soldiers of the mid-1800s Indian Wars to the present Fort Riley, which employs a sizable part of the local work force in nearby Junction City. Today, the largest local employer is Tony's Pizza. The town's non-pizza manufacturing base is huge, producing everything from private planes to RVs. Homes are very affordable, with average-sized homes selling in the $55,000 range.

Local schools place a high priority on art education. Through the state-funded Art Infusion Program, the Salina Arts and Humanities Commission coordinates a comprehensive teacher training and art curriculum integration program. The Art Infusion approach includes classroom visits by local artists, as well as artist-in-residence programs and school performances by touring artists. Many of Salina's arts organizations have their own children's education programs, with groups such as the community theater, visual arts center, symphony orchestra, community access television, historical museum, and nature institute presenting programs in acting, music performance, and gallery tours.

Arts Scene

The pace of the visual arts scene is set by the Salina Art Center, a multi-use, 1,000-square-foot visual arts exhibition space and adjoining children's art-discovery area. The center exhibits contemporary art, especially touring national shows and exhibits on loan from other Kansas art institutions. Fine-craft exhibitions are handled by the historical Smoky Hill Museum, also home to one of the town's better galleries.

Bluestem Gallery is the community's artists' cooperative, exhibiting the work of a dozen local painters, sculptors, and fine crafts artists. Studio Two Gallery is shared by two local painters who sell their work and occasionally teach adult art classes. South of Salina, in the farming town of Lindsborg, is the Birger Sandzen Museum and Gallery, home to an outstanding collection of landscape paintings by Birger Sandzen, a seminal painter of the American West and longtime art instructor at Lindsborg's Bethany College. The most popular arts event in Salina is the annual Smoky Hill River Festival, a multi-stage performing arts celebration with over 100 artists' sales booths.

Salina's most prominent performing arts group is the Salina Community Theatre. From September through June, the organization stages five productions in its 300-seat playhouse. The theater also presents a children's and family series during the winter months featuring touring theater companies. During the summer, one of the town's theater pros runs a youth theater school that treats kids to the annual Institute for Creative Arts play. Kansas Wesleyan University's drama department is another active force in Salina's theater scene, presenting student productions in the school's Fitzpatrick Auditorium.

Musically, the town has both the Salina Symphony and the organization's youth symphony performing in the Sams Chapel on the KWU campus. Salina Chorale also uses the Sams Chapel, while in nearby Lindsborg the college's Presser Hall offers an outstanding slate of classical music events, from top-name touring national acts to recitals by touring soloists. Art á la Carte is Salina's free downtown spring and fall music performance series, while That's Entertainment brings rock and country groups to Oakdale Park during the summer. The Joseph Holmes Chicago Dance Theatre conducts an annual two-week contemporary dance residency, which mixes masters classes, performances, lectures, and in-school classes all over town.

Alternatives

Gutierrez Restaurant is extraordinarily supportive of Salina's arts scene, exhibiting the work of local artists as well as hosting an annual poetry series that attracts leading poets from across the nation. The Coffee Gallery also exhibits local artists' work.

Art Perspectives

Martha Rhea, executive director of the Salina Arts and Humanities Commission, says, "We're serving a wide part of north-central and west-central Kansas, so our programming is regional in scope. Our downtown Fox Theater is empty and needs rehabilitation. Last year's Smoky Hill River Festival drew 90,000 in three days! It's an important show for Kansas artists."

Details

Population: 43,000

Important Arts Events: Spring Poetry Reading Series in April and May, Bygone Days in May, Smoky Hill River Festival in June

Must-See Art Galleries: Bluestem Gallery, Birger Sandzen Museum and Gallery, Salina Art Center, Smoky Hill Museum Gallery, Studio Two

Local Arts Agency: Salina Arts and Humanities Commission P.O. Box 2181

Salina, KS 67402 913/826-7410

Natural Foods Store: Nature Place

Farmer's Market: Fruit and vegetable stands are hard to miss

National Public Radio: KHCD - 89.5 FM

Bookstore: Downtown News & Books

Chamber of Commerce: P.O. Box 586 Salina, KS 67401 913/827-9310

Berea, Kentucky

Location

The eastern end of Kentucky has some of the poorest communities in the nation, but the college-and-crafts town of Berea is an exception. An hour's drive south of Lexington, this town of 10,000 residents is surrounded by fertile farmland, spring-fed streams, and forested, rolling hillsides.

Great Outdoors

The lightly populated terrain around Berea is short on state and national parks, forcing outdoor sports lovers to West Virginia for skiing and to Tennessee for serious hiking. Within an hour's drive are several lakes in the Daniel Boone National Forest. Winters here are brief, but even a light snowfall can bring Berea to a grinding halt. Spring arrives early, the growing season stretches into Halloween, and mosquito repellent is de rigueur the entire summer.

Lifestyle

One of the most successful cultural tourism stories in the nation, Berea owes its identity as an arts town to the influence of Berea College. The four-year, tuition-free institution puts many of its students to work creating traditional Kentucky crafts, which are sold to raise funds that keep the college operating. Today, the college's endowment provides a financial cushion, so craft sales aren't the life-or-death proposition they were in the past. Nevertheless, many Berea College students can whip together a broom as easily as they can handle a pop quiz. The college is also Berea's largest employer, and the local school system is filled with teachers who either have been trained at Berea College or have spouses employed there. Average homes in the tree-lined neighborhoods sell in the $60,000 range. Inexpensive farmland is available less than ten minutes from town. Berea is within easy reach of Richmond, another cultural magnet with a reputation as a music and theater town.

Arts Scene

Fine crafts are Berea's claim to fame. Some of the craft pros in town are graduates of Berea College, while others have moved into town to take advantage of two important assets: the presence and expertise of fellow artists and the financial opportunities derived from the community's healthy cultural tourism economy. Unlike other places in the mid-South, Berea hasn't been destroyed by fast-buck commercial ventures such as outlet malls and go-cart tracks. This town realizes that preserving what it already has is the best bet for keeping its lifestyle intact. And whenever the scent of commercialism starts fouling Berea's historic air, you can bet the college will throw its financial and political clout on the side of preserving the town's pristine character.

The college creates and sells traditional Appalachian crafts and furniture through several of its businesses, including a historic hotel, a history museum, a planetarium, and three galleries/gift shops for student arts and crafts. It operates retail stores in Lexington and Louisville, where students learn how to run a profitable business. The college also offers performing arts, ranging from student theater to touring classical and jazz music groups.

Within easy walking distance of the college is Old Town, a section of Berea that's home to many of the town's galleries, open artists' studios, and fine crafts shops. A few visual arts galleries dedicated to paintings and sculpture do well enough in Berea to survive, but fine craft objects sell best. Concentrated into a five-block area along with restaurants and cafés, the Old Town area draws hundreds of thousands of tourists annually, helping hundreds of Berea artists and craftspeople make a living without leaving their hometown.

Alternatives

This is a quieter college town than you'd expect; it doesn't have a raucous bar scene or the frat rows that plague some small communities. Berea College students are more the coffeehouse and pizza-party type, filling places like the Cardinal Deli, Papaleno's, and the Berea Coffee & Tea Co. They'll head up the road to U.K. in Lexington if they want to go on a tear. There's usually live music and folk dancing on weekends at the Russel Acton Folk Center in town or at the Seabeary Center on campus. During the summer months, a series of bluegrass concerts and art fairs take place at the Indian Fort Theatre amphitheater.

Art Perspectives

Ceramicist Gwen Heffner, who sells her work through national craft shows and a local gallery, believes Berea is becoming a better place for contemporary crafts and painting. "People coming here tend to be aware of what really good crafts are, and they're the ones who are making an impact on the contemporary end of what's sold in Berea's galleries," she says. "Artists will come here because they've heard about the college's fine crafts traditions and will stay after they realize that this is a great place to live and make a living. The most popular art forms are still the traditional ones, but as Berea attracts more cultural tourists, we're seeing a wider acceptance of all kinds of art, not just the things people have come to expect from this town."

Details

Population: 10,000

Important Arts Events: The Mountain Folk Festival in April, May and October art fairs sponsored by Kentucky Guild of Artists & Craftsmen, Berea Crafts Festival in July, Traditional Music Festival in October

Must-See Art Galleries: Berea College Art Building Gallery, Contemporary Artifacts, Kentucky Guild of Artists & Craftsmen Gallery, Mitchell Tolle Gallery, Upstairs Gallery

Local Arts Agency: Kentucky Guild of Artists & Craftsmen

P.O. Box 291
Berea, KY 40403
606/986-3192

Natural Foods Store: Happy Meadows

Farmer's Market: Friday mornings at Berea Community School

National Public Radio: WEKU - 88.9 FM

Bookstores: College Bookstore, Appalachian Fireside Gallery

Chamber of Commerce: 105 Boone Street
Berea, KY 40403
606/986-9760

Belfast, Maine

Location

Maine's midcoast is a tremendously scenic area of bays, seaside cliffs, river mouths, islands, coves, and beaches. The idyllic region's northernmost seashore is dominated by Penobscot Bay, a 30-mile-long national treasure dotted with lighthouses, fishing villages, lobster sheds, and marinas. The closest Wal-Mart and airport are 50 miles away in Bangor.

Great Outdoors

During the glorious months of summer, all you'll need are a pair of deck shoes, a T-shirt, cutoff jeans, and a 40-foot sailboat. Some Belfast folks call themselves "Downeasters," even though the true "downeast" region doesn't start until your sailboat reaches the other side of Penobscot Bay. State parks, wildlife refuges, uninhabited islands, and quiet meadows (ideal for sleeping away a warm afternoon) line both sides of the bay, while the region's forested inland is filled with lakes, marshes, streams, ponds, and blueberry patches. The cost of this summer splendor is a bitterly cold, damp winter, so inhospitable that many local artists flee south to Florida, Mexico, and Costa Rica right after Halloween, working on their tropical tans until returning around April Fool's Day, the art world's next major holiday.

Lifestyle

The many artists, actors, musicians, poets, and craftspeople living in Belfast are so enthusiastic about their little seaside community that they bristle at the mere suggestion that their hilly haven of sea captain's homes and two-story brick buildings might some day be priced beyond the reach of the next wave of mid-career New York and Boston artists—the sort of folks who, several years ago, kicked off the town's first renaissance. The arts people here are hip, well-traveled, into having fun, and range in age from mid-30s to retirees. Belfast brims with clapboard churches, tree-lined streets, ocean views, and lobster sheds, where you can buy the day's catch straight off a fisherman's boat. Homes (well, carpenter's specials) start in the $70,000 range. People here realize that Belfast's prospects for a prosperous future are now brighter than ever, thanks in large part to the art scene's powerful economic impact.

Arts Scene

Cultural tourists from East Coast cities come to Belfast to check out local performing and visual arts events, which is why summertime opening receptions at the town's galleries are packed-house affairs and frequently result in sales of paintings in the $5,000 range. There's a cooperative visual arts gallery exhibiting work by ten or so artists, a couple of strong contemporary art galleries exhibiting mainly regional art, as well as a couple of galleries mixing more traditional paintings with the region's top-notch fine crafts work. Most local artists keep their studios open, by appointment, for direct sales.

The Belfast Arts Council schedules a year-round slate of performing arts that, during winter months, concentrates on art education projects in local schools and, in the summer, switches over to festivals and music performances in the 200-seat Abbott Room of the Belfast Free Library. At the Masker's Railroad Theatre, the Belfast Maskers theater company produces as many as ten plays annually. In nearby Northport, the Blue Goose dance hall is a local venue for blues bands, folk musicians, and rock bands. There's a year-round foreign film and art film series at the Belfast Free Library, and the new management at the Colonial Twin Cinemas offers innovative movie programming, changing the selection weekly.

Alternatives

Some of the alternative exhibition spaces for local visual artists include Bell the Cat, a coffee-house and venue for local jazz musicians, as well as Darby's restaurant and the 90 Main restaurant. The local arts council publishes a freebie artists resource directory. For nightlife, check out the three places exhibiting local art as well as Dos Amigos, the Mexican restaurant that made Harold Garde a household name among the cerveza set.

Art Perspectives

Landscape painter Linden Frederick is a local artist with a national reputation for his scenes of dusk and dawn moments. He feels these scenes strike responsive chords in most viewers. "I like working with artificial light against the ambient light of dusk, because that's when the 'magic hour' begins," says Frederick.

"I didn't realize this was going to become an artsy area when I moved here six years ago. I mean, the only reason you'd want to lock your car when you're in town is to prevent someone from putting a zucchini in your back seat. It's become a nice place to live, and I like the slow pace of life here. Belfast is a town that's got a total support system for the arts, from a co-op gallery to art fairs to studio tours to some fairly sophisticated galleries.

"It's a town that lives up to its reputation, and that's what's attracting so many creative individuals into the area. Belfast is a funky, do-what-you-want sort of place where a lot of educated people move to because they prefer living a life that involves working with their hands."

Details

Population: 6,300

Important Arts Events: Sankofa Ethnic Arts Festival in summer, Church Street Festival in early October

Must-See Art Galleries: ArtFellows and The Studio in nearby Northport, Frick Gallery

Local Arts Agency: Belfast Arts Council
P.O. Box 452
Belfast, ME 04915

Natural Food Store: The Belfast Co-op

Farmer's Market: Three mornings weekly at Reny's Plaza

National Public Radio: WMPR - 90.1 FM

Bookstores: Canterbury Books and The Fertile Mind

Chamber of Commerce: 19 Church Street
Belfast, ME 04915
207/338-5900

Deer Isle, Maine

Location

The two largest Deer Isles, at the tip of Maine's Penobscot Peninsula, are linked by Route 15, which runs through the small arts town of Deer Isle in the Acadia region of south-central Maine, an area of forested, rolling hillsides and breathtaking waterfront views. Commercial fishing forms the East Penobscot Bay region's economic foundation, with lobster, scallop, and sardine harvests employing local people nearly year-round. The closest city is Bangor, 75 miles north.

Great Outdoors

The Deer Isles hold quiet, small communities as beautiful as any you'll find along Maine's coast. During summer, pond lilies and blueberries weave a colorful tapestry across the landscape, and the isles' west-facing homes enjoy hours-long sunsets that local artists call magical. At Stonington, on the far tip of Deer Isle, is a ferry to Isle au Haut, part of Acadia National Park. A favorite way to pass languid summer afternoons involves a bottle of wine, a picnic basket, a grassy meadow, and the sight of yachts traversing Eggemoggin Reach and passing under the suspension bridge that links Little Deer Isle to North Deer Isle. Winter is typical Maine, which is why L.L. Bean earned millions from selling flannel shirts.

Lifestyle

Besides directing traffic on tourist-clogged roads, Deer Isle cops are about as busy as the Maytag repairman. Children are courteous, neighbors are friendly, and the biggest threat to public safety is the prospect of colliding with deer on winding country roads. Deer Isle's live-and-let-live attitude is one the local folk find both supportive and respectful of everyone's needs for privacy. People do socialize, especially during summer, but the general lack of commercial or population centers prevent the slightly frantic air that turns other Maine communities topsy-turvy from June through August. Other seaside towns offer whale-watching, schooner excursions, beaches, and waterfront quays packed with gift shops, but none of that exists on Deer Isle—nor do locals encourage it. Here, residents concentrate on maintaining the rural life that drew them to the Deer Isles in the first place; that's why modest family homes are still affordable at $75,000 and why people feel no need for security services to guard their homes.

Arts Scene

One of America's premier art institutions, the Haystack Mountain School of Crafts, is just a 10-minute drive from Deer Isle town. Though its reputation was built on the broad range of two- and three-week instructional seminars Haystack offers from May through early October, in recent years the school has expanded its community reach through a public performance series tied into its artist-in-residence programs in music, literature, dance, and poetry. Many of the artists and craftspeople living among the Deer Isles and on the Penobscot Peninsula were initially drawn to the region through their participation in Haystack seminars, and chose to stay because of the area's arts-friendly environment. Having concentrated on their art for several years, many of these same people are now established, nationally prominent artists; along with a visiting faculty drawn from the top artists and craftspeople from New York to L.A., they form the core of Haystack's faculty.

Another focal point for Deer Isle artists is the Maine Crafts Association, a state-wide organization whose retail shop in Deer Isle is among Maine's best craft galleries, selling creations by 70 of the group's member artists. MCA also publishes a free artists' directory (Maine Cultural Guide) and a bimonthly newsletter. The Deer Isle Artists Association's great gallery, open during summer, is downstairs at 6 Dow Road; the Haystack faculty sells its fantastic art work through the Blue Heron Gallery and Studio, also in Deer Isle town.

Alternatives

Open studios and small community galleries exist throughout the Deer Isles; the best way to locate them is through the Maine Cultural Guide. Most Deer Isle restaurants exhibit and sell local artists' work. Evenings out are another matter altogether, but many artists feel quite attached to the folk music and jazz evenings presented by the Left Bank Café in nearby Blue Hill.

Art Perspectives

Metalsmith Ron Hayes Pearson, who creates jewelry and dimensional sculpture in his Deer Isle studio, says one of the region's most attractive qualities is "its feeling of being far away from things yet not isolated or out of contact with the art world.

"People come here from across the country for an opportunity to do meaningful work, and they're recognized for their contributions to Deer Isle's arts community. Haystack's influence is a positive one, whether that's in respect to their programs for young artists and schoolchildren from around the state or for their seminars geared to mid-career artists.

"Artists here have gardens, root cellars, small sailboats, and lots of good friends. The only drawback to living here is you can't find a parking space in town during the summer . . . but most of those people are here to buy art, so its easy to overlook any inconvenience."

Details

Population: 3,500

Important Arts Events: Fishermen's Day, an Island, Fishermen's Wives craft fair in August, and five scholarship program craft auctions held during summer months at Haystack School

Must-See Art Galleries: Blue Heron Gallery and Studio, Deer Isle Artists Association Gallery, Maine Crafts Association Gallery, Turtle Gallery, Wheeler Gallery at Hill House

Local Arts Agency: Maine Crafts Association P.O. Box 228

Deer Isle, ME 04627
207/348-9943

Farmer's Market: Friday mornings at the Deer Isle Congregational Church

National Public Radio: WERU - 89.9 FM

Bookstore: Clifford Skeans Books

Chamber of Commerce: P.O. Box 459 Stonington, ME 04681 207/348-6124 3,500 (summers only) web HTTP:\\www.acadia.net\Deerisle

Lewiston, Maine

Location

The inland setting of this resurgent south-central Maine town places it within easy reach of salmon-filled lakes, nationally rated ski areas, beautiful covered bridges, and the city of Portland, 40 miles south. Lewiston and neighboring Auburn are separated by the Androscoggin River, which connects hundreds of the region's lakes, streams, and tributaries.

Great Outdoors

If it's the sporting life you want, this is the perfect place. One of the primary gateways to Maine's western lakes and mountains region, Lewiston has built a number of parks and inter-linked bicycle trails along the banks of the Androscoggin, parts of which are connected by a converted railroad bridge. Golf courses frame both Lewiston and Auburn, and the state's best beaches are less than an hour's drive to the coast. Range Pond State Park is ten miles west in Poland, Maine. For leisure of a more reflective sort, there's a Shaker museum 15 miles south, in New Gloucester.

Lifestyle

An ongoing historical preservation project has resuscitated this former manufacturing center's architectural vigor; several turn-of-the-century buildings have been successfully converted into mixed-use studio spaces. Lewiston and Auburn are loaded with many small neighborhoods, some of which have a distinct ethnic flavor imparted by the region's Franco-American residents.

A couple of decades ago, national urban renewal projects and the collapse of the region's textiles and manufacturing industries turned Lewiston into a depressed no-man's land. A subsequent community-wide political and social turnover ushered in enlightened leadership and a commitment to improve the region's quality of life, making Lewiston an attractive place for artists, telecommuting entrepreneurs, and small business owners. Well-built homes in safe neighborhoods start in the $80,000 range. There's some art instruction in local schools, as well as an artist-in-residence program coordinated by the local arts agency.

Arts Scene

Lewiston is creating an arts conscience primarily through the presentation of performing arts. Local government recently has thrown its weight behind a plan to create a downtown arts district incorporating exhibition space for both the visual and performing arts as well as artists' studios and living quarters in renovated former industrial buildings. Bates College is adjacent to the downtown arts district and provides Lewiston with year-round access to visual and performing arts presentations through its Olin Arts Center and other theaters. L/A Arts, the local arts agency, brings touring performance artists into town. Performances are also presented by The Public Theatre (an equity company performing at the Ritz Theatre), the Maine Music Society and the Community Little Theatre.

Visual and craft artists have one commercial and three nonprofit venues where they can exhibit. But outside of a few community festivals and fundraisers, the thing to do here is take advantage of the affordable studio spaces and concentrate on selling your work elsewhere.

The downtown's renovated Bates Mill Complex has attracted the Creative Photographic Center of Maine, an institution offering year-round seminars in fine photography and electronic imaging. One of the most exciting prospects for the community is the planned arts center. If funding can be nailed down, the city wants to create a downtown arts facility that could link the performing and visual arts scenes by offering exhibition space, a performance hall, classrooms, and studio/rehearsal rooms.

Alternatives

The Pleasant Note Coffeehouse in Auburn attracts the region's better artists, and more alternative venues are opening all the time. Some of the favorite local hangouts are the Great Falls Brewery, T.J.'s, and Austin's in Auburn, while over the bridge the artsy crowd hangs out at Nothin' but the Blues and The Seasons.

Art Perspectives

Mixed-media paper artist Martha Blowen is a founding member of the Artists of the Androscoggin, a group of several dozen visual artists. Her collaged pieces are represented in galleries and museums throughout the state.

"What we've got here is studio space like you wouldn't believe," she says. "Second-story, high ceilings, brick walls, incredible views across the river, great natural light—they're huge and cheap and ready to be used. What we don't have is a cultural tourism economy, yet there are enough cultural events taking place around the area to keep most anyone quite busy and involved, if they want to be.

"Artists living here, whether they're of a national reputation or local, tend to join the Artists of the Androscoggin and like working together to promote services that are important to artists. A new wave of creative people has begun moving in here 'from away,' and, for the most part, they're enthusiastic about this city, its heritage, and its future. We're becoming a multicultural community, with African Americans, Hispanics, and Asians moving in to join our already strong Franco-American population."

Details

Population: 39,757

Important Arts Events: Bates Dance Festival in July, Festival de Joie in July/August, Balloon Festival in August

Must-See Art Galleries: Atrium Gallery at Lewiston-Auburn Community College, Bates Museum of Art at Bates College, Gilbert Gallery on Lisbon Street, Pleasant Note Coffeehouse

Local Arts Agency: L/A Arts
49 Lisbon Street

Lewiston, ME 04240
207/782-7228

Natural Food Store: Axis Natural Foods

Farmer's Market: Fruit stands and farmers' stands on country roads outside of town

National Public Radio: WMEA - 90.1 FM

Bookstore: Waldenbooks

Chamber of Commerce: 179 Lisbon Street
Lewiston, ME 04243-0059
207/783-2249

Easton, Maryland

Location

The western coastline of Maryland's Eastern Shore isn't much of a beachfront, but it's a great place to live if you work in the nearby cities of Annapolis, Washington, D.C., or Baltimore. Easton's proximity to these regional population centers has created a paradoxical situation: people are moving into town from these cities and sharing in the community's strong arts scene, but they're also driving up the cost of living. Easton's expensive status not withstanding, its 11,000 residents are guaranteed plenty of company in the next few years.

Great Outdoors

Like other parts of the Eastern Shore, Easton is close to wildlife refuges, tidal marshes, and spectacular stretches of the Chesapeake Bay, giving rise to the community's most popular arts celebration, its annual Waterfowl Festival. Everything revolves around the bay and its outdoor opportunities, from duck hunting to oystering to sailboarding. For the less active, a favorite winter sport is building a fire in the living room hearth, boiling a kettle of water, and fixing a hot toddy to sip beside the fire.

Lifestyle

An average-sized home in Easton costs $125,000, but real estate becomes less expensive farther away from the Bay Bridge. This is a small, friendly, and accessible community, one in which newcomers can easily join local organizations and become involved in town life. The Academy of the Arts, an incredible facility with far-reaching programs for every sector of Easton's populace, is one of the main catalysts for the town. Much of the community's social life revolves around events at the academy, making it not only a gathering place for the region's creative community, but also a vehicle for integrating the arts, business, and government sectors. With limited funding, local schools rely on the academy's exhaustive programs to help educate Easton's children in the arts.

Arts Scene

With exemplary visual and performing arts programs and facilities, Easton stands out as an especially worthy small arts town. On the performing arts scene, there's the Avalon Theatre, a restored 400-seat art-deco masterpiece complete with computerized lighting and surround sound. The theater, owned by local arts supporters Ellen and John General, hosts local singers, bands, theater groups, and nonprofit groups, and attracts everything from Charlie Byrd to gospel choirs, chamber music, and community theater. It also holds regular coffeehouse presentations and several series of lectures, performances, and cinema arts.

The Academy of the Arts has an amazing 24,000 square feet of space used for more than 200 visual and performing arts programs annually. While the academy presents primarily classical music programs through a brown bag lunch series, its Artreach program brings in schoolkids from across Talbot County to attend exhibits and performances, while its Kaleidoscope program is a multidisciplinary summer arts camp for students. The academy also collects regional art, with a permanent collection of hundreds of works, names such as Grant Wood, James Rosenquist, Leonard Baskin, and Bernard Buffet. The academy offers a wonderful gift to community members: free or low-cost access to every activity it sponsors. Easton also hosts a commercial art exhibition space at the Weems Gallery, and the Tidewater Performing Arts Society stages jazz, classical, and pop music at the high school auditorium.

Alternatives

Easton's attitude toward the arts has had a positive impact on the town's local businesses, as well. Places such as Peach Blossom's, Mason's Café, and the Washington Street Pub exhibit the work of local artists on their walls, and most of the town's bed-and-breakfast inns and retail stores do too. The Tidewater Inn exhibits and sells the local art on its walls to a year-round flow of weekend visitors from the surrounding cities.

Art Perspectives

Sarah Kagan, a landscape and portrait painter, teaches landscape painting at the arts academy. "Here, there's great material to paint just five minutes from my back door . . . I'm not relying on the local arts market, but there are many people who do, and who seem to be making a living from it. The business community here realizes that their businesses do so well mainly because of the impact of the arts community, so we receive lots of support from them. The academy gives artists a place to gather, so the town has lots of camaraderie and, because of the Avalon, it has a lot of sophistication as well."

Painter Kay Holden, who was a commercial artist prior to moving into the Easton area, says the reasons local artists can make a living here are simple. "We've got a lot of people with big bucks moving in here, and they're the ones buying most of the local art. The tourists come in to buy decoys, like they always have. Lots of artists who want to be fairly close to a city are moving here, and even though they don't participate in the Academy's exhibitions, just having some limited access to them has helped to give us a sense of Easton as a place with a bright future for the arts."

Details

Population: 11,000

Important Arts Events: Summer Arts Festival in June, Waterfowl Festival in November, First Night in December

Must-See Art Galleries: Academy of the Arts, Weems Gallery

Local Arts Agency: Academy of the Arts
106 South Street
Easton, MD 21601
410/822-0455

Natural Food Store: Railway Market

Farmer's Market: Saturday mornings in the Town Hall parking lot

National Public Radio: WSCO - 89.3 FM

Bookstores: News Center, Rowen's Stationery

Chamber of Commerce: P.O. Box 1366
Easton, MD 21601
410/822-4606

Salisbury, Maryland

Location

This Maryland Eastern Shore town is two hours from both Washington, D.C. and Norfolk. Because it's not an oceanfront community, Salisbury is more a place the beach crowd drives through rather than stops in. So Salisbury's 25,000 residents have their historic community—complete with zoo, arts center, museum, and college—practically to themselves.

Great Outdoors

Surrounding the town is one of America's premier migratory-bird nesting grounds, and beside Schumaker Pond is the Ward Museum of Wildfowl Art. For decades the region's craftspeople were known as master decoy carvers, but today that reputation also covers a diverse range of wildlife artists. Their inspiration comes directly from the environment—from the Assateague Island National Seashore wild horse refuge (a 30-minute drive to the coast), and from Blackwater National Wildlife Refuge (a 30-minute drive to Chesapeake Bay). Water sports are accessible, from sailboarding on Tangier Sound to surf-casting from the Ocean City boardwalk.

Lifestyle

The regional dialect blends colonial British, Southern, and fishermen's patter, and easily identifies Eastern Shore residents. An historic community, Salisbury is filled with centuries-old estates and private homes. The town's 12-acre zoo, known for its waterfowl exhibitions, also holds exotics such as buffalo and jaguar. Salisbury is one of the few small art towns with its own African American cultural center, the Charles H. Chipman Center. Salisbury State University is an influential cultural and economic force, and its campus radio station, WSCO, provides important publicity for the community's arts organizations. The campus also houses an outstanding public-art collection, including contemporary sculpture and murals. Life here is extremely affordable—a fixer-upper in a nice neighborhood runs under $50,000; for a few thousand more you can find an average-sized home with a garage, garden, and shade trees.

Arts Scene

Salisbury is grateful to the SSU arts department, primarily for the fine-arts department's innovative and worldly exhibitions in its gallery. It's not unusual for Haitian art to be followed by contemporary Latin American and then a solo exhibition by an inner-city Baltimore artist. SSU's Holloway Hall Theatre presents classical music by touring chamber orchestras and soloists, as well as the Salisbury Symphony's winter performing arts series. The local Community Players theater group stages plays at the high school auditorium, a town church group offers religious-theme dramas, and SSU's minority affairs department sponsors occasional outstanding performances of ethnic dance companies, jazz, or off-the-wall theater.

    The town's visual arts center around the Art Institute and Gallery, a membership organization that promotes the region's many painters and craft artists through exhibitions at its downtown gallery space and through an ambitious program of adults', kids', and mid-career artists' education programs. AIG moved into new quarters last year, acquiring three classrooms as well as a 1,300-square-foot exhibition space for monthly solo shows, invitationals, and group exhibitions. The organization also sponsors City Arts week, an important means of raising Salisbury's awareness of its many professional-artist residents, of encouraging communication among the community's arts organizations, and of bringing artists together for a great show. The town's other high-profile arts organization is the Salisbury-Wicomico Arts Council, which re-grants state arts-agency funds to the community's many arts groups; it also stages an extremely popular First Night celebration downtown with 40 performing arts groups. Finally, the council presents the city-wide Salisbury Festival, which combines the visual and performing arts communities for a weekend in May.

Alternatives

Other than a few events at the college, Salisbury hasn't much of a nightlife. Popular places for the local creative crowd are La Roma, Market Street Inn, the Royal Exchange, and Goin' Nuts Cafe. Local restaurants and cafés have yet to learn that exhibiting locally created art not only draws a certain crowd, but generates more income.

Art Perspectives

Keith Whitelock, a realist painter of wildlife images and maritime scenes, says he's noticed a change in the way artists survive in the region. "When I first moved here, making a living as an artist was impossible. Wildlife and waterfowl painting and decoy carving got things started here several years ago, but now you're starting to see a lot of diversity in the local art market, especially in the wildlife art market.

"Some artists moving in here are not showing their work locally; they establish themselves somewhere else and move here for the affordable and peaceful lifestyle. What has the greatest sales impact on our arts scene is tourism from the D.C. and Baltimore areas. They're a pass-through crowd, but they do stop and buy art, especially when they come to the Ward Museum. For our arts scene to grow we need to do two things better: advertise the great artists and artwork that are already here, and improve the cooperation between the town's arts organizations and between those organizations and the college."

Details

Population: 42,000

Important Arts Events: City Arts Week in March, Salisbury Festival in May, First Night Eastern Shore

Must-See Art Galleries: Art Institute and Gallery, Finer Side Galleries, Objets d'Art, Salisbury State College Gallery of Art

Local Arts Agency: The Art Institute and Gallery
212 West Main Street

Salisbury, MD 21801
410/546-4748

Farmer's Market: Wednesday and Saturday mornings at Civic Center parking lot

National Public Radio: WSCO - 89.3 FM

Bookstores: Browseabout Books, Grassroots Two

Chamber of Commerce: 300 East Main Street
Salisbury, MD 21803
410/749-0144

Nantucket, Massachusetts

Location

It takes five hours by ferry to get to Nantucket Island, once the home port to the Atlantic whaling fleet. If ever an artist wanted a place to gaze off the end of the earth, this is the place. Interestingly, the warm ocean currents near the southeast flank of Nantucket produce a unique climate that brings an early spring and a late autumn.

Great Outdoors

To live here, you should love to sail or—at the very least—to canoe or kayak. Nantucket's pristine beaches are a national treasure, and tourists have flocked here since the turn of the century. Walks on the beach are de rigeur, whether on a breezy, summer night or a clear, crisp winter afternoon. Digging clams in tidal flats and casting a line from the shores of an isolated cove are other favorite means of communing with mother nature. About 7,000 beachcombers call Nantucket home year-round, but during summer months that number swells to 40,000.

Lifestyle

All this natural beauty comes with a price, and that price is the high cost of housing. Even your basic fixer-upper will set you back $200,000 or so. Although artists have fanned out across most of the island's 47 square miles, galleries concentrate in Nantucket's mile-long downtown, built in the 1850s and today peppered with realtors' offices. The town has been careful to preserve much of its maritime legacy, and there are a number of museums exhibiting artifacts from the whaling era. A wildlife center, an observatory, an aquarium, and a marine laboratory offer public programs and tours. Art programs in the local schools are still in the development stage, and generally art education is something that happens outside the school setting.

Arts Scene

The arts community here is full of genuine, earthy people. In many ways, the summer tourist scene and second-home economy are enough to make Nantucket a self-sustaining arts market for the local painters, craftspeople, and musicians. One glaring need is for an arts center where performances, classes, lectures, and organization offices could take place all under one roof. Every once in a while a suitable structure (such as an old church) hits the market, but slips through art folks' fingers for lack of a community-wide effort to secure it.

During summer months, the island's theater community kicks into high gear. The Nantucket Theater Workshop's annual plays competition is staged in venues such as Greater Light, the Children's Beach pavilion, and the garden of the Nantucket Athenaeum. Other local theater companies perform in the community's church halls, and the Musical Arts Society presents chamber music programs in the Congregational Church. Harbor Square Bandstand shakes and shimmies with free concerts on summer weekends.

The Nantucket visual arts scene has strengthened in the past two years. The (x) Gallery remains a key cooperative exhibition space selling truckloads of local art during the summer months. A new art exhibition space that has gained local attention is The Art Cabinet, exhibiting abstract work by top regional artists and serving as a sort of de facto visual arts center for the island's contemporary artists. Many of Nantucket's more traditional street painters are members of the Nantucket Artists Association, which has its own downtown gallery space. Another sign of continued health in the island's arts scene is the establishment of the Photographer's Alliance of Nantucket, a group that includes several renowned photographers. All of the island's arts organizations take part in Arts Alive, an October celebration featuring the Organ Crawl, a series of pipe organ performances in the churches, and the Wet Paint Auction, a fundraiser for the arts association.

Alternatives

Cambridge Street, a restaurant, hangs the work of local artists on its walls and employs some of those artists as bartenders, cooks, waiters and waitresses. The Cross Rip Coffeehouse, a volunteer-run café in the basement of the Methodist church, is another venue for exhibiting local art outside of the gallery scene.

Art Perspectives

Melissa McCloud, a painter whose contemporary images are exhibited at the (x) Gallery, says that living on the island has both its good and bad points. "It's great to be living somewhere where people can afford to buy the art that local artists are creating, and we all can sell to the market—from painters to weavers to potters and basket makers. But you've got that nagging thought in your head that maybe this place is too isolated from the art world's mainstream; maybe our access to contemporary thought is too much of an obstacle.

"Everyone can find somewhere to show their work. If you want to paint seascapes, there's the gallery run by the Nantucket Artists Association. If you create modern art that has an edge to it, then there's the (x) Gallery. If you want to show and sell in a commercial gallery, we've got plenty of those as well. Artists here are cooperative and supportive. Most of them have a fairly open studio policy and will sell art from their studios."

Details

Population: 7,000 year-round, 40,000 during summers

Important Arts Events: Printmakers' exhibition in August, Arts Alive in October, Christmas Craft Fair in December

Must-See Art Galleries: The Art Cabinet, Main Street Gallery, Nantucket Artists Association Gallery, Sailor's Valentine Gallery, (x) Gallery

Local Arts Agency: Nantucket Cultural Council
Town & County Building
16 Broad Street

Nantucket, MA 02554
508/228-4352

Natural Foods Store: Nantucket Natural Foods

Farmer's Market: Farm stands scattered on local roads

National Public Radio: WGBH 89.9 FM

Bookstores: Bookworks and Mitchell's Books

Chamber of Commerce: 48 Main Street
Nantucket, MA 02554
508/228-1700

Location

Nestled along the banks of the Merrimack River an hour's drive north of Boston, Newburyport is surrounded by natural splendor, from Plum Island's pristine seacoast to the Parker River National Wildlife Refuge. The lobster sheds in coastal Maine are only a 30-minute drive away.

Great Outdoors

Everyone here agrees that winters are long, windy, and cold, but they hasten to add that summers are incredibly glorious. Newburyport offers its residents easy access to one of the state's best-maintained outdoor recreation sites at Maudslay State Park, with nearly 500 acres of riding trails, hiking trails, and fishing holes. An hour's drive north will land winter sports lovers at some of New Hampshire's mid-size downhill ski areas; cross-country ski trails are even closer. But the real action in Newburyport takes place during summer, when locals flock to some of the best beaches on the East Coast. Nearby Plum Island's three miles of public beaches offer first-rate surf fishing and sailing, and occasional surfing.

Lifestyle

For the terminally employed, Newburyport is close enough to Boston to make commuting to work possible. But for those who have retreated from corporate America, Newburyport is a great place to set up shop and make a living selling advice, services, and of course, art. The town nearly shuts down when migrating humpbacks, finbacks, and minkes come within whale-watching distance. The local folks definitely have their priorities in order.

When its economy was booming in the early 1980s, Newburyport invested millions in renovating its historic downtown and gorgeous waterfront district. Now that the money has dried up, this enduring legacy is evidence that local government can occasionally do the right thing and sometimes even exceed expectations.

Newburyport's a beautiful town, with tree-lined neighborhood streets, architectural treasures dating from the community's past as a lucrative fishing port, a bustling tourist industry that creates low-impact jobs, and a model school system with a fully integrated K–12 arts curriculum. The drawback is that to pay for it all, local taxes are sky high, but at least the town has taken destiny into its own hands.

Arts Scene

Local artists know better than to expect to make their living selling art to Newburyport's home owners or tourists—people here on a day trip usually aren't in the right frame of mind to buy a painting. The local arts association maintains a sales gallery in the historic downtown, and some crafts artists are able to make a living selling to the tourist trade; the direct sales opportunities during Yankee Homecoming Days are lucrative. Still, most local artists use Newburyport as a base from which to tap into the Boston, Provincetown, coastal Maine, and ski-country galleries.

Newburyport's strong reputation as an arts community comes from the innovative and energetic programming of the performing arts sector. Maudslay State Park operates a seasonal Children's Theatre arts center and performance facility that runs a full schedule of outdoor music programs. The Custom House Maritime Museum is a gem, and there's also an extremely active community theater company.

Newburyport is home to one of the nation's premier small-town community arts centers, the Firehouse Center for Performing and Visual Arts. With 300-plus arts events offered during the year, the Firehouse's Arakelian Theatre programs everything from touring national jazz to historical society lectures to contemporary dance, classical music, piano recitals, comedy, drama, and ethnic music. Its proximity to Boston allows the Firehouse to tap into an incredible wealth of artistic talent. The Firehouse also has a visual arts gallery exhibiting 13 shows annually, with an emphasis on national and top regionalist painters and sculptors.

Alternatives

Most of the historic district's restaurants exhibit works by local artists—as long as they're traditional seascapes. For the contemporary artists in town, Caffe di Siena not only has a great name, it's also friendly to artists who want to take their chances on its walls. Fortunately, art sells here. Everyone meets at the Grog, as the saying goes. Ciro's, an Italian restaurant, is another favorite haunt.

Art Perspectives

Anna Smulowitz, a playwright and theater director, says that when it comes to the arts life in Newburyport, there's support from all directions. "It's in the beautiful landscape, the quiet and serenity of being surrounded by a river and the ocean. The seasons change dramatically, and in winter you intuitively know that it's time to stay indoors and create. People come into Newburyport from the surrounding towns for the specific reason of taking part in the arts. Selling out a show at the theater isn't at all unusual.

"We've attracted a huge community of classical and jazz musicians who make their livings performing in Boston but who choose to live here. Of course, they perform in Newburyport as well, which gives us access to some wonderful talent. We're a community that's culturally diverse, even if we're not one that's racially diverse."

Details

Population: 17,000

Important Arts Events: June Arts Festival, Yankee Homecoming Days in July and August, summer concerts at Maudslay Arts Center

Must-See Art Galleries: Firehouse Center, Lepore Gallery, Newburyport Art Association

Local Arts Agency: Firehouse Center for the Performing and Visual Arts
One Market Square
Newburyport, MA 01950
508/462-7336

Natural Foods Store: Greta's Grains

Farmer's Market: Many farm stands on local roads

National Public Radio: WGBX - 90.9 FM

Bookstore: Jabberwocky Books

Chamber of Commerce: 29 State Street
Newburyport, MA 01950
508/462-6680

Northampton, Massachusetts

Location

The Connecticut River cuts a fairly straight path through the central part of Massachusetts, once serving as the area's main transportation route and power source. Northampton, a small art town of 31,000 residents less than two hours west of Boston, used to rely on the river for the power that fueled its mills and factories. But with these industries gone and a new economic foundation in place, Northampton today is powered by a fantastic combination of cultural tourism and community access to a breathtaking range of performing and visual arts.

Great Outdoors

During the peak of autumn leaf season in mid-October, locals spend many hours biking, hiking, canoeing, fishing, and avoiding rural roads clogged with leaf-hunting tourists. For the rest of the year things are back to normal in rural Pioneer Valley, which for years has attracted artists, actors, musicians, and writers seeking an alternative to metropolitan living. From Northampton's centralized location, access to outdoor recreation is easy with the Mt. Tom ski area just a short trip south and the steeper slopes of the Berkshires about an hour's drive west. A few miles northwest of Northampton, you'll find two of the state's best cross-country ski areas at Hickory Hill and Swift River Inn. But if the snow's right, many locals hit the 8½-mile Norwottuck Trail, a converted railbed stretching between Northampton and Amherst. Others simply use the hiking trails leading up to Mt. Holyoke in Skinner State Park, just across the Connecticut River in Hadley. During the temperate months, the most popular backwoods hikes are in Holyoke Range State Park, just a short drive northeast of Northampton. Hikers walk along sections of the Metacomet-Monadnock Trail, which ends just shy of the small art town of Peterboro. Several central Massachusetts state parks are loaded with campgrounds, lakes, and hiking trails, including the DAR State Forest, Erving State Forest, and Mohawk Trail State Park. The state Audubon Society has its 500-acre Arcadia Nature Center and Wildlife Sanctuary in nearby Easthampton, and the Larch Hill Conservation Area is in neighboring Amherst. Canoeing along the Connecticut is another very popular summer getaway, and several times a year, white-water outfitters run sections of the Connecticut and Deerfield Rivers near the small art town of Shelburne Falls. Upper stretches of both the Deerfield and Westfield Rivers are known for their trout fishing.

Lifestyle

With five colleges in or near Northampton, (Amherst, Hampshire, Smith, Mt. Holyoke, and the University of Massachusetts) this town has many talented faculty members pursuing careers of their own in dance, visual arts, music, and theater. From one college town to another, there are great record stores, coffeebars, clothing shops, restaurants, and nightclubs. The town's blues, folk, rock, and jazz musicians make their living from these clubs which supplement their out-of-town gigs in larger cities. The region is full of arts organizations addressing every facet of the community's creative needs. These organizations are in large part run by graduates of the college arts departments who decide to remain in the area for its wealth of opportunities. Many Northampton performing arts groups are on the national touring circuit, spending part of each year performing locally, then taking their acts to venues across the U.S. and Europe. Northampton is similar to the small art towns of Santa Fe, Eureka, Asheville, and Oxford, in that its gay and lesbian communities are well-organized and integrated into the local arts scene.

The town's history museum is a collection of three restored historic homes dating back to the early 1700s. These antique furnished structures are used as both exhibition spaces and as models to show how early New England craftspeople used certain building techniques and hand tools. In nearby Amherst are the Emily Dickinson Homestead and the Pratt Museum of Natural History, while Hadley hosts the Porter Phelps Huntington House Museum (an historic home filled with antiques) and the Hadley Farm Museum. Just a short walk from the center of Northampton, Smith College Museum of Art maintains a fantastic permanent collection of work by major names in Impressionism, cubism, and European and American realism. Twentieth-century work is shown at the energetic Mount Holyoke College Art Museum, with its outstanding public lectures, films, gallery talks, and rotating contemporary art exhibits, and also by rotating shows at the Mead Art Museum in Amherst.

While other towns may offer college art museums, no other can claim the Words & Pictures Museum, an ultra-modern exhibition and education facility dedicated to "Fine Sequential Art," or comic book art. Founded by a local illustrator who made his fortune in Hollywood and turned philanthropist, the museum rotates monthly shows of fine sequential art created by international artists and illustrators of both comic books and Hollywood action-hero shows. It's educational outreach program introduces Northampton kids to this creative and sometimes lucrative field.

Ten years ago, when New England's economy was the nation's strongest, a large amount of state revenue was available for promoting the visual and performing arts. Real estate prices jumped so high that an average-sized home in Northampton currently runs in the $150,000 range. But today, Massachusetts' flat economy has resulted in huge cutbacks in state funding for the arts, and Northampton has had to dig deep within its own pockets for the money to fund an active, broad-based community arts scene. Fortunately, it has had success. The nonprofit Northampton Community Music Center is dedicated to the musical education of kids from the age of two through high school (adult programs are offered, too). The center teaches Suzuki flute, piano, and violin, and stages programs ranging from chamber music to jazz piano, using a faculty drawn mostly from the five Northampton area colleges. Though state cutbacks have crippled the Northampton public schools' once-exemplary arts education programs, there's still some instruction in visual art, music, and drama at the high school level, supplemented by the Northampton Arts Council's in-school artist residency projects. The Guild Art Centre offers some after-school kids art programs, as does the Northampton Center for the Arts.

Arts Scene

Northampton's most active nonprofit visual arts exhibition space is the Northampton Center for the Arts. Its two galleries exhibit the work of local artists through monthly one-artist shows and regional invitationals. The center organizes two annual juried exhibitions in different creative media, awarding prizes to approximately 75 artists. The local colleges all have galleries exhibiting student and faculty work. There are a number of commercial galleries in town, with work ranging from fine crafts and jewelry, to contemporary art, to more traditional landscapes and figurative pieces. The summer walk-in gallery crowd includes many New York collectors drawn to western Massachusetts for its Tanglewood musical performances and the Jacob's Pillow dance center near Becket.

Northampton's performing arts scene is in great shape, even though there are dozens of competing organizations under the stage lights throughout the year. The town's main performance venue is the Academy of Music, an old 800-seat opera hall. In addition, there are the Northampton Center for the Arts' 300-seat recital/performance hall, local churches and community centers, and the John M. Green Hall at Smith College for large events. The Northampton Center for the Arts presents nearly 100 yearly performances to raise its annual operating budget, bringing jazz, contemporary and ethnic dance, Shakespeare, film, and different styles of music into the center. Look Park's Pines Theater stages a summer Shakespeare festival in July, plus a summer music series, and the Northampton Arts Council's Transperformance Series, a series of satirical performances that raise funds for local school art programs.

Northampton's musical organizations include Commonwealth Opera, which tours central Massachusetts during its November to April season, and the Young-at-Heart Chorus, a campy group of seniors performing at the Academy of Music. The town also sponsors several choral groups including the De Camera Singers, the Northampton Chamber Players, and the Arcadia Players. Arcadia is a Baroque orchestra and chamber ensemble which plays at several venues, including the Academy of Music and the Sweeney Concert Hall at Smith College. All of the area colleges present their own performing arts series in their respective campus arts centers. The programs are always quite strong. The Massachusetts International Festival of the Arts is a spring festival of opera, modern music, classical, and jazz running from mid-April to mid-May. Also in town is the Northampton Film Festival, which screened more than two dozen films in six venues during its initial year in 1995. Pioneer Valley Ballet is Northampton's nonprofit dance education and presenter organization, using guest artists along with its young dancers for performances during winter and spring.

Northampton has a number of theater companies, some of which perform more regularly than others. The No Theater Company, focused on presenting new plays and experimental work, tours nationally and throughout Europe. Sleeveless Theatre tours shows with feminist themes regionally and performs locally at the Academy of Music and the arts center. Its actors also teach drama to Northampton kids at a local community center.

Northampton's two major public art events occur during the winter months. First Night, which draws 10,000 downtown revelers on New Year's Eve, is a well-organized, family-fun performing arts showcase that runs at many downtown venues from late afternoon to midnight. The Northampton Arts Council raises much of its locally awarded grant money through its Four Sundays in February series, four performing arts events staged at the Academy of Music. Funds from this series help the council acquire arts lottery funding from the state. It holds the distinction of being the only Massachusetts arts council to be offered two rounds of arts lottery funding. Each year's Four Sundays series offers performances by young artists, as well as a collegiate a cappella competition and a locally produced variety show. The main event is usually a new contemporary work in dance, music, or opera. In 1994, the Four Sundays series premiered The Passion of Joan of Arc, a performance that went on to win acclaim at the BAM Next Wave Festival.

Alternatives

Many great restaurants have sprung up around town, bringing some very creative interpretations of French, American, and Mexican food with them. Locally created visual art is so much a part of the Northampton restaurant and coffeebar scene that a recommended list of spots would run into the dozens. It's best just to walk into the first place you come to and look at the walls. Because this is a college town, Northampton has a serious local music scene. Touring national acts play at the Pearl Street Nightclub and the Iron Horse, while places like the Bay Street Cabaret showcase alternative bands. The Fire & Water Café is Northampton's jazz and folk club.

Art Perspectives

Sheron Rupp, photographer: "Northampton has an enlightening lifestyle, with great movie theaters, bookstores, galleries, and restaurants. The city has some of the most innovative arts programming I've ever seen, and you get a lot of exposure to performances coming from metropolitan areas. Northampton's become a commercial mecca, and prices in the downtown are starting to become too expensive for the kinds of stores we used to see starting here. But it's still a lovely community. There's still a rootedness to the lifestyle, and it's still a place where people genuinely care about each other."

Steve Calcagnino, director of the Northampton Center for the Arts: "The town has recognized that the arts are Northampton's largest industry, and that they're a draw for cultural tourism dollars, so the town's using the arts as the entre that promotes the community nationally and internationally. Businesses realize there's a direct correlation between the dollars that are invested in Northampton's arts and the amount of money they make."

Details

Population: 31,000

Important Arts Events: Four Sundays in February, Massachusetts International Festival of the Arts in April and May, Northampton Film Festival in November

Must-See Art Galleries: Don Muller Gallery, Ferrin Gallery, Hart Gallery, Michaelson Gallery, Northampton Center for the Arts, Peacework Gallery, Skera Contemporary Crafts Gallery, Smith College Museum of Art, The Artisan Gallery

Local Arts Agency: Northampton Center for the Arts
17 New South Street
Northampton, MA 01060
413/584-7327

Natural Foods Stores: Bread & Circus Whole Foods Market, Cornucopia Foods

Farmer's Market: Saturday mornings on Gothic Street

National Public Radio: WFCR - 88.5 FM, WAMC - 90.3 FM

Bookstores: Beyond Words Bookshop, Bookends, Broadside Bookshop, The Globe Bookshop, Space-Crime Continuum

Chamber of Commerce: 62 State Street Northampton, MA 01060
413/584-1900

Shelburne Falls, Massachusetts

Location

This quiet, back-country community of 2,000 doesn't receive much cultural tourism attention because it's in the middle of a lot of other places that are high spots on the tourism path. Shelburne Falls is far enough north that there's maple sugar harvesting in the spring, far enough west that there's land for family farms, and far enough south that winters are not as trying as in other parts of New England. Boston is a two-hour drive east.

Great Outdoors

This part of northwest Massachusetts has loads of outdoor recreation opportunities, and everything is accessible and affordable. Several of southern Vermont's mid-size ski areas are less than an hour's drive away (with a small area near town); and spring runoff is a perfect time for white-water rafting on stretches of the Deerfield River, which runs through town. Mohawk Trail State Forest is a magnet for the area's hikers and back-country campers.

Lifestyle

Shelburne Falls' industries went into a decline several decades ago, leaving behind an economically depressed area filled with inexpensive homes and vacant commercial structures perfect for conversion into studio and gallery spaces. Divided by the Deerfield River, which once powered the mills that built this town, Shelburne Falls is still quiet enough and affordable enough to attract a steady stream of Boston and other regional artists searching for a small, safe community with good schools and a lot of potential. One of the school system's problems has been its inattention to arts education, a situation local artists are trying to remedy by establishing a community arts center with classroom and studio space and programs aimed squarely at the town's children. Called the Art Bank—referring to the building's former life as a commercial bank—the center's planned future includes space for visual arts exhibitions and performances.

Art, in the form of cultural tourism, local arts programming, and the entrepreneurial efforts of newcomer artists setting up galleries and studios, is widely acknowledged as the economic power behind Shelburne Falls' mid-1990s revival. The town has developed a reputation as having a favorable climate for the arts, and even though local government doesn't have an adequate tax base to raise money that could fund more arts-related development, it does have an admirable commitment to doing whatever is within reasonable reach. Decent homes with yards and garages are in the $75,000 range, another reason why artists who can handle a little sheetrocking and carpentry find the town attractive.

Arts Scene

Many resident artists have moved from urban areas, once affordable and fun, that became sterile, lifeless yuppie havens. So the emphasis here is on keeping things low-key and avoiding the pitfalls of the past. Visual artists have a few local marketing opportunities through fine craft galleries and one visual-arts gallery, but many prefer to sell directly from their home studios or in the Salmon Falls Marketplace, a three-story converted granary that's packed with artists' studios and a couple of galleries. The Memorial Hall Theatre, upstairs in the community's town hall, presents classical and foreign films. This 420-seat theater is also home to the Mohawk Trail Concert Series of classical music programs and is where the community theater company stages its winter productions.

The public rooms at Arms Library are used for many of the town's children's arts events, and McCusker's Ballroom is another performing venue for local musicians and touring dance companies. There is not yet a community-wide celebration of Shelburne Falls' performing and visual arts, but a summer event called Riverfest celebrates the town's connection to the beautiful Deerfield River.

Alternatives

McCusker's Market & Deli has a solid reputation as a place where locally created art sells straight off the walls, and the Franklin Land Trust maintains a sculpture garden at its facility outside of town. Evenings find the local creative types crowding into the Buckland Bar & Grill and McCusker's, and the Shelburne Falls Coffee Roasters is a popular place to gather and gossip about the arts.

Art Perspectives

Christen Couture, who planted her roots here 17 years ago, is a contemporary artist who finds making a living in Shelburne Falls to be a matter of finding sales opportunities elsewhere.

"Things here seem to be developing quite nicely. We've been able to get the Art Bank open and there's a place to see movies at night; those are the sorts of community-wide efforts that make this little town so stupendous. In the past few years we've attracted a lot of self-employed professionals and a lot of artists—two kinds of individuals who are exactly the right people to bring new energy and vision to a small town, and I think we'll all benefit from it.

"We need to continue working toward building the town's acceptance of the arts as a central part of Shelburne Falls' new identity. We need more local people coming to gallery openings and other events, and not just have the same artists showing up."

Details

Population: 2,000

Important Arts Events: Movies at the Memorial Hall Theatre, Riverfest in summer, Bridge of Flowers 10-K road race in August

Must-See Galleries: Bald Mountain Pottery, McCusker's Deli, North River Glass, Salmon Falls Artisans Showroom

Local Arts Agency: Art Bank
22 Bridge Street
Shelburne Falls, MA 01370
413/625-6235

Natural Foods Store: McCusker's Market

Farmer's Market: Saturday mornings in front of Town Hall

National Public Radio: WFCR - 88.5 FM

Bookstores: Boswell's Books, The Wandering Moon

Chamber of Commerce: 75 Bridge Street
Shelburne Falls, MA 01370
413/625-2526

Hancock, Michigan

Location

Northern Michigan's Keweenaw Peninsula is so far north that some of Santa's elves live here and commute by snowmobile to their workshop jobs at the North Pole. Hancock, an art town of 4,547, sits on a strip of land surrounded on three sides by Lake Superior. The closest large city is Duluth, a three-hour drive west, weather permitting.

Great Outdoors

Hancock winters are long, cold, and dark, but the sweeping views of Lake Superior and the proximity of Isle Royale National Park (a pristine wilderness island 50 miles offshore, with hundreds of remote campsites) are ample compensation. The warmer months of the year turn this remote corner of the nation into an outdoor recreation haven. A national historic park strings 11 sites along the peninsula's 70 miles. Porcupine Wilderness State Park is Michigan's largest, with 60,000 acres and nearly 100 campsites. McLain State Park is a ten-minute drive from Hancock and has over 100 campsites. There are plenty of downhill and cross-country ski areas, as well as snowmobile trails up to 150 miles in length. The fishing in this part of the Great Lakes region is spectacular, with yearly runs of coho salmon, pike, rainbow trout, and lake trout. During the winter months, there's always ice fishing.

Lifestyle

Once old mining towns, Hancock and the neighboring village of Houghton have an abundance of structures that, in the good old days, were home to small businesses but, today, are not much more than empty spaces waiting for artists to move in. Housing is very affordable here: an average-sized home goes for about $40,000. There are two colleges in this two-town community—Michigan Tech University and Suomi College (part of a Finnish-American center).

The region's economy is rapidly shifting toward tourism, and cultural tourism has carved out a small niche for itself. The local arts agency, the Copper Country Community Arts Council, oversees the Community Arts Center, an education and exhibition facility in Hancock that houses a ceramics and photography studio; a performing arts hall is planned as well. School art instruction is still in the dark ages, so children's programs at the local art center are tremendously popular.

Arts Scene

In the past few years, the region's visual artists have surprised themselves with ever-increasing sales to the Houghton-Hancock area's cultural tourists. Buyers nobody really expected to show up have been making their way into town and liking what they see. The Kerredge Gallery at the arts center represents 160 or so regional artists in all media, exhibiting work in a large sales gallery and a children's gallery. Suomi College stages regular exhibits by Finnish artists and American artists of Finnish heritage, ranging from traditional crafts to contemporary painting.

Houghton tends to have more business activity, and that's where the TOSH Gallery,

Motherlode, and Marie's Gallery & Deli reach their buyers. Calumet, 15 miles from Houghton-Hancock, is the home of Omphale Gallery, and one of the community's banks has monthly rotating lobby exhibitions. The art exhibited in the region's galleries tends to be quite strong, partly because of the community's art-for-art's-sake attitude, and partly due to the local college art department's influence.

Michigan Tech is the community's performing arts lifeblood, using its 200-seat Walker Theatre as a venue for university theater productions, touring classical music groups, jazz bands, comedy acts, and pop music concerts. Third World music, rock, jazz, and other acts are presented in Fisher Hall. The other main venue for performing arts on the peninsula is the Calumet Theatre, a restored 1,200-seat opera house in Calumet. The Calumet is home to the Calumet Players community theater, the Keweenaw Symphony, a very active family and children's performing arts series, and a year-long Club Indigo film series that combines foreign food nights with its foreign film series.

Alternatives

Several bars and cafés make their livings from the Michigan Tech student population, and places like the Motherlode and Sub Urban Exchange draw the better-mannered crowds. Many local restaurants have regional art on their walls; the best of these is Marie's Gallery & Deli. Gemignani's Restaurant, the Library Bar, and Shutes Bar in Calumet are art-friendly, too.

Art Perspectives

Fiber artist and art teacher Phyllis McIntyre says the region's exhibition and sales opportunities are growing. "The peninsula's turning into a great place to sell art during the summer, but you've got to do everything you can do in those few months, and get your work into every gallery you can. The art fairs around here are also very good sales opportunities, so you can't miss those either. The way I see it, we're going to keep getting a broader tourist audience coming in here, which means the arts in this area are going to keep growing. It's an exciting time for the artists who live here."

Details

Population: 4,547 (Hancock), 7,500 (Houghton)

Important Arts Events: Pine Mountain Music Festival in June, Under the Arts Tent in June

Must-See Art Galleries: Kerredge Gallery, Marie's Gallery & Deli, Motherlode Gallery, Suomi College Gallery, TOSH Gallery, Walker Art Studio

Local Arts Agency: Copper Country Community Arts Council
126 Quincy Street

Hancock, MI 49930
906/482-2333

Natural Foods Store: Keweenaw Food Co-op

Farmer's Market: Saturday mornings in downtown Hancock

National Public Radio: WGGL - 91.9 FM

Bookstores: North Wind Books, Paynes Books

Chamber of Commerce: 326 Shelden Avenue Houghton, MI 49931
906/482-5240

Lanesboro, Minnesota

Location

In Bluff Country, the southeastern part of flat-as-a-pancake Minnesota, the terrain looks a lot more like hilly Arkansas than you'd expect. Steep escarpments and forested hillsides create a microclimate that shelters Lanesboro from some of the state's typically large snowfalls.

Great Outdoors

Lanesboro turned around 180 degrees the day the state's Department of Natural Resources converted a 41.5-mile stretch of retired railway to the paved Root River State Trail. Following the Root River Valley right into downtown Lanesboro, the trail economically revived this community by transforming it into an outdoor sports mecca for tens of thousands of bicyclists and cross-country skiers. Bike shops and trailside campgrounds now represent a growth industry in this part of the state, as do canoe rental businesses catering to the many visitors who boat and camp along the tremendously scenic Root River. A private foundation operates Lanesboro's Forest Resource Center, comprised of several hundred acres of hiking trails and campsites. It also oversees a commercial shitake mushroom cultivation project and an environmental education center offering classes for Lanesboro kids. State forest lands are abundant, as are groomed snowmobile trails, trout streams, spring-fed creeks, and breathtaking views from the tops of sheer bluffs. Beaver Creek Valley State Park is about 30 miles east, just across the Mississippi River.

Lifestyle

Much of Lanesboro's tourist traffic comes from the medical city of Rochester, less than an hour's drive north. They come to this once-prosperous forestry town for its historic beauty: all of Lanesboro's downtown and residential architectural masterpieces are listed on the National Register of Historic Places, and many of the turn-of-the-century mansions have been transformed into bed & breakfasts. Lanesboro is a very mellow place, one that prides itself on its "quiet sports," not the roar of snowmobiles and ski boats. The three neighborhoods in the town's residential area are refuges of treelined streets, parks, and porch swings. An average-sized home here sells for $45,000. Arts education programs in local schools are reasonably well-regarded, though not known for their farsightedness. Fortunately, two arts organizations partially meet the arts needs of Lanesboro's kids: the Cornucopia Arts Center, housed in one of the historic downtown's two-story brick structures, has a year-round schedule of multidisciplinary art classes for kids and adults; and the Commonweal Theatre Company stages its plays in the 126-seat St. Mane Theatre, uses local kids in an annual production, and runs a two-week summer conservatory program for high school students.

Arts Scene

In their wildest dreams, none of the artists living in this town ever thought they would see the day when $1,000 paintings would be sold in Lanesboro. But with the development of the Root

River Trail came just the right kind of outdoorsy cultural tourist who could not only spot good art but could also afford to buy it. Of course most of the work sold in this town costs a lot less than four figures, but the point is that a surprising amount of art does get sold, and artists are moving here to tap into that market. The Cornucopia Art Center rotates one-artist and group exhibitions through its gallery space every two months, and serves as the region's creative nerve center by tying together artists and the arts community. Cornucopia shows all kinds of art work, from traditional craft to contemporary painting. Many local artists are contemporary craftspeople who make their living on the Midwest craft fair circuit.

Performing arts are the province of the Commonweal Theatre Company, staging drama and musicals from late May through Christmas. The company produces one new experimental play each season, as well as productions like 1995's The Mousetrap, Medea, and The Nerd.

Alternatives

The town's restaurants are big supporters of Lanesboro's artists, and both the Parkway Pub & Restaurant and the Old Village Hall Restaurant & Pub have a track record for selling the local art that hangs on their walls. One of Lanesboro's favorite artists' hangouts is Das Wurst Haus, a schnitzel-and-beer kind of place, where the owner makes his own root beer and serenades diners with his accordion.

Art Perspectives

Frank Wright, a woodworker and sculptor, says that one of the best aspects of living in Lanesboro is the town's sense of community. "Artists here aren't estranged from what's going on elsewhere in town. Here you can sell work that's affordable, because the people coming into Lanesboro are here to have a good time, and they're knowledgeable about what's going on in the arts. For artists, this is a place where you can do some of your sales in the local market, but where you've got to have other outlets in order to survive."

Details

Population: 858

Important Arts Events: Art in the Park in June, Buffalo Bill Days in August, Holiday Market in December

Must-See Art Gallery: Cornucopia Art Center Gallery
507/467-2446

Local Arts Agency: Lanesboro Arts Council
P.O. Box 15
Lanesboro, MN 55949
507/467-2525

Natural Food Store: Preston Co-op

Farmer's Market: Saturday mornings in Sylvan Park

National Public Radio: KLSE - 91.7 FM

Bookstore: Avian Acres

Chamber of Commerce: P.O. Box 20
Lanesboro, MN 55949
800/944-2670

New York Mills, Minnesota

Location

Residents of New York Mills would like to boast that their village has a population of 1,000, but so far the most heads anyone has counted is 972. Tucked into the northwest corner of Minnesota, New York Mills is a long way from everything. It's as flat as a slice of cinnamon toast and so cold in winter that half the local people are driven into isolation within the confines of their ice-fishing shacks. The region is so sparsely populated that it seems the majority of people must have packed their bags several years ago and returned to Finland.

Great Outdoors

As might be expected from a community whose largest employer is the Lund Boat Company, fishing is almost a form of religious worship around this town. In the months when Ottertail County's thousand-plus lakes aren't frozen over, locals endure a rash of natural indignities such as thunder storms, mosquitoes, and chilling, Levis-soaking rain showers just for the pleasure of being able to catch their own dinners. New York Mills even has a town Fishing League, filled with teams with names like the Happy Hookers, Dominators, and Goodfellas. During the winter months, a favorite pastime is to sit on ice that's several feet thick, stoke kerosene heaters inside ice fishing shacks, and beg for something weighing about seven pounds and wearing fins to come banging on the basement ice door. Another favorite winter activity for the fishermen is cursing the hordes of snowmobiling teenagers who whip around the countryside on snowcats so overpowered that they have more in common with a Corvette than a jet ski. For half the school year, these kids have the choice of riding a yellow bus, driving a parent's second car, or flying across snowdrifts at 60 m.p.h. with terrified buddies clawing for survival on the snowmobiles' rear seats.

Itasca State Park, one of Minnesota's outdoor recreation treasures, is just an hour's drive north of New York Mills. Loaded with pristine beaches, a rustic lodge, more than a hundred campsites, and dozens of miles of hiking trails, Itasca's a favorite for residents who need to get away for a while. It's the home of the Mississippi River headwaters, and from one side of the park, the ground water flows into the Mississippi and on into the Gulf of Mexico. From the other side, the ground water flows into the Great Lakes and eventually into the Atlantic. State forests, parks, lakes, rivers, campground resorts, and Indian reservations are everywhere you turn, giving the residents of New York Mills incredible access to unspoiled natural wonders.

Residents also have a passion for baseball diamonds, and they seem determined that the next Rod Carew will be a New York Mills kid who will donate a few million dollars to build the town its own domed stadium. Until then, the semi-pro New York Mills Millers will make their annual quest for glory under the lights at Miller Park. Additionally, there are several great parks around town, as well as a public pool, tennis courts, a playground, and an RV park.

Lifestyle

In the 1870s a lumber mill owner from upstate New York sent his lackeys out to this part of the wilderness to buy up and cut down the region's virgin stands of white pine. After a few decades, with the forests stripped and the New Yorkers run out of town on a morals charge, the only people brash enough to move into the region were dirt-poor Finnish farmers, who immediately set about the hard work of clearing stumps and turning the barren landscape into productive farms. (Today, second-growth white pines continue to survive in the area alongside fifth-generation descendants of those hardy Finns.)

In the late 1960s, New York Mills fell on rough economic times as the Nixon administration's policies caused the bottom to drop out of the agricultural industry. This set off a chain of events that continues to batter and bruise many small midwestern communities whose local economies are hot-wired into the Beltway's agricultural policies. Fortunately, the financial impact of the town's Lund Boat Company helped keep the economy stable while the farmers adjusted to their industry's shifting terrain. Today the notion of prosperity in New York Mills remains a speck on the horizon, but the town is surviving and maintains a "we're-doing-okay" mentality that has prevented the local spirit from falling into despair. A house in this small town runs about $30,000, which is part of the reason New York Mills is attracting artists from not only from the Twin Cities, but from places further east and west.

Basic art education is provided by the local school district, but it is not very extensive. The community's local arts agency, the New York Mills Regional Cultural Center, offers a broad calendar of inventive, multidisciplinary art classes throughout the summer. The center also organizes an arts education travel program that buses kids and grandparents to such places as the North Country Museum of Arts, the Red River Museum, and the interpretive nature lodge of Itasca State Park. It also sponsors an international visiting artist's residency program which has, as part of its community involvement component, an artist demonstration and discussion series. Finally, the center holds two annual student art exhibitions in its gallery space: one for elementary levels and the other for students in middle school and high school.

Arts Scene

The arts scene that turned New York Mills into one of the nation's most unexpected cultural tourism success stories was started by one man, John Davis. A native New Yorker whose art career in Minneapolis was interrupted by long stretches behind the wheel of a pizza delivery truck, Davis moved to New York Mills in the mid-1980s under the mistaken impression that the town had a fantastic kosher deli selling the best latkes this side of the Bowery. His dreams dashed, he nonetheless stayed on in New York Mills, patching together a life as a full-time house painter and part-time artist until he raised enough money to convert his farmhouse residence into an Artists' Retreat Center. He hoped the center would attract visiting artists to New York Mills for short periods of time, during which they would teach a thing or two about art to the local school kids.

In 1990 the first visiting artist arrived. From the Alsatian community of Montpellier in eastern France, he rolled his gear into town and the entire program was kicked off to a fine start. (Today that same retreat has completed nearly 40 artist's residencies with a pool of creativity drawn from across the U.S., Europe, and Latin America.) Later that same year, a local couple retiring from their furniture business donated their two-story brick building in central New York Mills to the town, along with a $7,500 endowment tagged to "start a cultural center." Davis took action and began securing pledges from enthusiastic townsfolk, eventually raising $35,000.

At the same time Davis was fundraising, the city, which had estimated the cost of refurbishing the old furniture store at $275,000, was actually considering tearing the building down and starting a cultural center elsewhere in town. Davis maneuvered himself into a showdown with the City Council over the question of whether the old building could be saved. A do-or-die meeting was scheduled, but fortunately for Davis, on the afternoon of the crucial session, the entire council spent the better part of the afternoon getting hammered on the local bathtub version of chokecherry wine. Davis stood before the council, asked nicely for matching funds for his $35,000, and was promptly handed the keys to the council's piggy bank. His only instructions : "Get us a case of cold beer and keep the change, bucko." (Strange, but true!) The renovations were completed for $120,000, and the New York Mills Regional Cultural Center was born.

The center opened its doors in 1992 to reveal a gallery space and lecture hall, classrooms and studios, and the administrative offices of the community arts scene. It also serves as a regional contact point and distribution center for the highly regarded Minneapolis-based Walker Art Center. Through the Cultural Center's exhibition space and gift shop, regional artists sell their jewelry, ceramics, pottery, textile art, greeting cards, and toys for children. The center hosts visual artists' monthly meetings (important for keeping artists in contact with one another), as well as a regular literary roundtable meeting with visiting authors, playwrights, and poets. The center's visual arts exhibition space rotates shows monthly and features both local and visiting artists as they build their national reputations through the Minneapolis arts scene. The center also runs a monthly film series, an espresso bar, its own Web site, and an active performance series of music of all varieties, from chamber baroque to blues to contemporary folk to rock and jazz, much of which is performed by touring national artists. Finally, it coordinates three large annual arts and culture celebrations: the Laskainen Festival of Finnish Sami culture in February, The Continental Divide Music & Film Festival in July, and The Great American Think-Off in June.

It's The Great American Think-Off that has brought New York Mills its greatest national attention, and only a mind as open as Davis' could have come up with a scheme so grand. The Think-Off is an armchair philosopher's battle of intellects that attracts 700 philosophers from across the nation, each of whom submit a 750-word essay dealing with an esoteric topic such as the 1995 theme, "What Does Society Value More—Money or Morality?" A panel of local wise men and women weed through the entries, sorting for the most cogent philosophical arguments, then invites the top four entrants to New York Mills for an all-expenses paid weekend and the opportunity to publicly battle it out for a $2,000 prize. This final battle has become so popular that the event has had to be moved from the Cultural Center to the town Sports Center, where hundreds of people pay $8 to sit and listen to philosophical arguments. And that's not the only entertainment—that same weekend New York Mills marches two Philosophy Parades right down the middle of Main Street: one for the kids and one for adults.

Davis, who continues to roam New York Mills' streets, is working on his next blockbuster project for the town. His sights are set on converting a closed school building into a center for science, imagination, technology, and education (to be called S.I.T.E.). The new institution will attract scientists-in-residence to New York Mills to collaborate with both the Cultural Center's artists-in-residence and the townspeople in developing high-tech projects to fuse arts, science, technology, and local culture.

Alternatives

Eagle's Café is everyone's favorite, with a close second place going to the Cultural Center's espresso bar. There are a number of art galleries that have opened lately, most of which are operated by artists drawn into town by the Cultural Center.

Art Perspectives

Linda Strand Koutsky, a contemporary painter and multimedia artist, says she moved to New York Mills after reading about the Cultural Center. "Artists move here from Minneapolis to work on their art, to open their own studios or galleries, and to take part in a town's revival. There's a lot going on around here, and that's surprising to all of us who once thought of there being nothing in this part of the state. The people who live here and the artists moving here all feel they have an investment in what's taking place at the Cultural Center."

Details

Population: 972

Important Arts Events: Laskiainen Midwinter Festival in February, The Great American Think-Off in June, The Continental Divide Music & Film Festival in August

Must-See Art Galleries: Batikworks, New York Mills Regional Cultural Center Gallery, Ottertail Oaks Pottery

Local Arts Agency: New York Mills Regional Cultural Center
24 North Main Avenue

New York Mills, MN 56567
218/385-3339

Natural Foods Store: Down Home Foods

Farmer's Market: Farm trucks park on town streets

National Public Radio: KBPR - 90.7 FM

Bookstore: Books & Things

Economic Development Director: City Hall
New York Mills, MN 56567
218/385-2213

Clarksdale, Mississippi

Location

Mississippi's northwest corner is delta country, the area that blues and country-western performers love to sing about. Elvis Presley's from around here, and so are Robert Johnson, B.B. King, and Muddy Waters, to name just a few. About an hour's drive south of Memphis, Clarksdale is light-years from mainstream U.S.A.

Great Outdoors

So what do 22,000 blues-loving local residents do in the great outdoors? Fish, for one thing. The Little and Big Sunflower Rivers teem with catfish, as does the Big Muddy, 20 miles west of town and the site of popular Great River Road State Park campground. Ten-mile-long Enid Lake recreation area is less than an hour's drive east. The beach is just five hours south.

Lifestyle

Clarksdale's motto is "We Got the Blues," and a huge public party is thrown each year for Muddy Waters' birthday. Visit Clarksdale around this local son's anniversary, and you'll see strolling blues musicians, blues bands gettin' their mojo workin' in public parks and on street corners, and half the town's businesses closed for part of the day. The many great bluesmen (and blueswomen) who lived here—including W.C. Handy, Son House, Robert Johnson, Sam Cooke, Ike Turner, Howlin' Wolf, and John Lee Hooker—are why the Delta Blues Museum draws thousands of tourists from all over the world to Clarksdale each year. They prowl Clarksdale's sleepy streets, visit Muddy Waters' log cabin home north of town, shake his wax-museum-exhibit hand at the Delta Blues Museum, and check out Clarksdale's wild and woolly juke joints. This is, after all, the place where a millionaire Brit blew into town one day, bought a local juke joint, loaded it onto flatbed trailers, and trucked the whole thing to Hollywood, where it became the House of Blues. The area also has a powerful gospel music scene; every summer the Sunflower River Blues Festival includes a Sunday gospel music festival with performers from Memphis, Jackson, and Arkansas.

Besides Clarksdale's musical gods, there's also the town's native literary lion, Thomas Lanier "Tennessee" Williams. Tom Williams (who went on to raise all types of hell during his stormy life) receives the spotlight each October during the annual Tennessee Williams Festival, a literary bash including an academic component, a new-plays festival, Williams readings, and community-wide performances of Williams plays at every possible venue in town.

Clarksdale's home prices are vintage 1960s—nice places with lawns and porch swings sell for just over $40,000. Local schools' art instruction includes the incredibly successful Delta Blues Education Program run by bluesman "Mr. Johnnie" Billington and the Delta Blues Museum.

Arts Scene

The heart of Clarksdale's music scene is the juke joints, where regional bluesfolk play, and the Delta Blues Museum, dedicated to preserving and presenting this most American of music forms. Housed since 1979 in Clarksdale's Carnegie Public Library, the museum hosts monthly blues concerts, book-signings, visual art exhibitions, and summer artist-in-residence programs for Clarksdale kids. ZZ Top is a major supporter of the museum, donating not just cash but also blues-musician artifacts and occasional public appearances in Clarksdale. The museum is renovating Clarksdale's 14,000-square-foot railroad depot, converting it into Clarksdale Station and Bluesland, a combined performance venue and new home for the museum. WROX, the local blues radio station, ties the blues scene together through its on-air DJ legend, Early Wright. Juke joints include J.J.'s Social Club, Red's, Margaret's Blue Diamond Lounge, and the Rivermont Lounge.

The Delta Blues Education Program is run by bluesman Johnnie Billington, a Mississippi legend who works with the region's school system to find and teach children who want to play the blues. Started in the early 1980s, this program also helps the kids form bands, which then play paid gigs in Mississippi juke joints around the state. Forget "Dance of the Sugar Plum Fairy"—by the time these Clarksdale kids hit high school they can boogie with the best! Who needs a paper route when Mr. Johnnie's around to book gigs and transport you to the show?

Alternatives

Everything in Clarksdale is an alternative.

Art Perspectives

Mr. Johnnie says the future of blues music is the Delta children. "I organize them, I teach them to play, I find places where they can perform, I buy them their instruments, and I drive them to and from the shows. It's a good program. It keeps kids off the streets and gives them a way to make some money—and teaches them the importance of working.

"People are surprised when these boys and girls get on stage and warm up, but once they start playing they're really surprised. NBC came down here and was blown away! The blues is history, with songs made up from things that really happened around here. When you teach these kids the blues you're teaching them their own history. They learn fast that the lessons in the songs are lessons for their own lives."

Details

Population: 22,000

Important Arts Events: Delta Jubilee in June, Sunflower River Blues and Gospel Festival in August, Tennessee Williams Festival in October

Must-See Art Galleries: Bobo Store, Delta Blues Museum, Do Drop Inn, J.J.'s, Red's, The Rivermont

Local Arts Agency: Delta Blues Museum 114 Delta Avenue

Clarksdale, MS 38614
601/627-6820

Natural Food Store: Boss Hog's Bar-B-Q

Farmer's Market: Throughout surrounding area

National Public Radio: WKNA - 88.9 FM

Bookstore: Delta Blues Museum

Chamber of Commerce: P.O. Box 160 Clarksdale, MS 38614 601/627-7337

Oxford, Mississippi

Location

For the nine months that Ol' Miss is in session, this northern Mississippi art town of 10,000 doubles its population. An hour's drive south of Memphis, Oxford has a sultry climate: long, humid, Southern summers with only occasional fleeting glimpses of winter.

Great Outdoors

Ten minutes from town, Sardis Lake boasts some of the South's best duck-hunting terrain, with state parks, boat ramps, campgrounds, and bass fishing within its 15-mile stretch. The same can be said for Enid Lake, half the size of Sardis and a 30-minute drive south. The favorite sport in Oxford seems to be watching college football games, even if Ol' Miss has a reputation for disappointing local fans. There are also several city parks around town.

Lifestyle

Up until a few years ago, Oxford was strictly a college town. Sure, William Faulkner had lived here, but this place was best known as a bastion of the Old South. Things started shaking loose when a trickle of the state's better artists returned to the town in which they had received their art degrees after finding that life in Oxford was a safer, more affordable alternative to their bohemian ways in New Orleans, Memphis, and Atlanta. Today Oxford is chock-full of artists, writers, musicians, and actors who have successfully diverted the community's attention from college student antics to the cultural opportunities right on its doorstep. The town has developed a reputation as a mandatory stop for touring acts of all types, from the up-and-coming to the established. These enhance its already respectable nightlife scene of blues and alternative music. Oxford also attracts its share of serious authors and playwrights, most of whom find each other at Square Books, a place where agents' names are traded, projects shared, and dinner parties brainstormed.

As is often the case in small towns with universities, Oxford's public schools deliver on the high expectations education pros place on their teachers. Curriculum-integrated art programs are available, if a little behind the national curve. Some of the town's arts education slack is addressed by the local arts agency through its visiting artists and matinee performance series, and by artist-in-residence programs using local visual and craft artists. Within walking distance of the action at the historic town square, average-sized homes in quiet, safe neighborhoods are easy to find in the $60,000 range.

Arts Scene

Oxford lacks a suitable exhibition forum to help the region's visual artists attract cultural tourists. Unfortunately, unless a visual arts center is established or more galleries open, most of the town's artists will continue to be better known in places like New Orleans than they are at home. For now, smart collectors have to scope out the walls of the town's many cafés, restaurants, and the Southside Gallery—Oxford's one great visual arts space—looking for new buys.

Local performing arts are already in great shape, and things are set to go straight through the roof when the University of Mississippi opens its $24 million performing arts center in 1997. An interesting sidelight to Oxford's thriving blues and alternative music scene is the University of Mississippi International Conference on Elvis Presley each August, when hundreds of Elvises do their thing in the town's many nightclubs. The university's Blues Archive houses one of the country's foremost collections of sheet music and recordings of America's homegrown music. The Ol' Miss campus scatters its performances to Fulton Chapel, where classical music, dance, and some theater take place; to Meek Hall Auditorium for chamber performances and recitals; or to its large auditorium for touring drama and ethnic music programs. Oxford's community theater group uses the Hoka Theatre, a 100-seat venue that also hosts a foreign film series, lectures, children's theater, and musical acts.

Oxford's literary scene steps into the spotlight at the annual Faulkner & Yoknapatawpha Conference, staged by the university's Center for Southern Culture. This mid-summer blowout of academics, authors, and book dealers follows the Oxford Conference for the Book, a literary conference held in April.

Alternatives

Until the local gallery scene develops more strength, Oxford artists will continue to use the Harvest Café and City Grocery as key sales venues. After nightfall, bump into the creative crowd at Proud Larry's, Lafayette's Bar and Grill, or the Square Books Café.

Art Perspectives

Sculptor Gregg Shelnutt notes that one of Oxford's main attractions is its cost of living. "You can get a studio space here for next to nothing, and a lot of the best art shows are the ones where several artists move their work in one studio for a couple of weeks. Galleries here do better then you would think, which goes to show you that at least some football fans buy art. Our art scene is a homegrown but good one, because the artists here have traveled and lived in other places. There's a café society, a music scene, and a respect for people's talents—all of which is very new for Oxford."

Details

Population: 10,000

Important Arts Events: Oxford Arts Festival in April, Festival of Southern Theatre in June, Faulkner & Yoknapatawpha Conference in July/August, International Elvis Conference in August

Must-See Art Galleries: Basement Gallery, Bryant Hall Gallery, Creative Sources, Huckleberry Hill Collection, Southside Gallery

Local Arts Agency: Yoknapatawpha Arts Council
P.O. Box 544

Oxford, MS 38655
601/234-9243

Natural Food Store: Harvest Café

Farmer's Market: Hollowell's Market

National Public Radio: WKNA - 88.9 FM

Chamber of Commerce: 299 West Jackson Oxford, MS 38655
601/234-4651

$\bigwedge$rrow Rock, Missouri

Location

The central Missouri art town of Arrow Rock has a glorious Wild West past dating back to Lewis and Clark, who spied a bluff overlooking the Missouri River and described it a perfect place to build a town. Within a few decades, 1,000 people named the site Arrow Rock and made it their home. Today, there are only 70 full-time residents in Arrow Rock, which is two hours west of Kansas City.

Great Outdoors

Once a stopping point near the head of the Santa Fe Trail, Arrow Rock owes its continued existence to the Missouri River, which flows past the town's outskirts, providing excellent fishing, boating, and bird watching. There are several wildlife refuges in the region, the nearest being Grand Pass, 30 miles west of Arrow Rock. Lake of the Ozarks, an enormous freshwater lake sprawling across the central part of the state, is the region's most popular summer recreation area. An hour's drive past the lake brings you to the Ozark Mountains and the Arkansas border, an area replete with state parks, hiking trails, and wilderness.

Lifestyle

Arrow Rock is both a National Historic Landmark and a State Historic Site, which means that the state owns much of the local real estate, even operating its own campground and interpretive center. The community prospers from its active summer tourism industry, allowing a number of traditional craftspeople as well as a summer repertory theater (the state's oldest) to make a living.

Because of its size, there aren't many places to live or operate a crafts shop in Arrow Rock. The state has a lid on things, so there's a high demand from folks who want in on the action. From the look of things, business is strong enough in Arrow Rock to allow the town's craftspeople to make the bulk of their annual income sitting in their shops, creating and selling. Some of the local residents dress in period costumes, working in their bed and breakfasts, antique stores, craft shops, and cafés looking as if they just stepped off a covered wagon.

Arts Scene

For the town's craftspeople who work in Arrow Rock during the daytime, the local approach to making a living is folksy. Artists and craftspeople work in public settings where a visitor can wander up and ask them about their work. If they generate enough curiosity and enthusiasm in the tourist, he or she will buy the craft and take it home with them. It's a simple formula, and in this small town it works like a charm. The town has shops that sell a variety of traditional crafts: a craftsman who resilvers mirrors and frames, a textile arts gallery and loom shop, a potter who makes functional stoneware, a broom-maker, and more.

The big surprise in Arrow Rock is the Lyceum Theatre, an 1872 church converted into a

400-seat theater that recruits a repertory company each year for its summer season of musicals, drama, and comedies.

"We cut down our production budget a few years ago," says Michael Bollinger, the theater's artistic director. "We decided instead to put our focus on acting. Our job is to work hard to bring a wider audience into Arrow Rock. Last summer we sold 27,000 tickets to people from all over the state. In season, we employ 30 people, keep most of the town's room rentals filled up, and get tremendous support from the business community. When you walk into Arrow Rock, it's like stepping back in time. That's what I love about living here."

The town's Community Center is also used as a performance space, staging everything from children's plays to meetings of the local arts community to an occasional classical music performance.

Alternatives

Craft artists who don't own one of the few shops in Arrow Rock can participate in the town's Boardwalk artists program, which allows visiting artists to set up their working equipment in the city's historic downtown, selling their crafts as they create them. Many of the community's B & Bs have craft work as well as locally created paintings for sale in their lobby areas. The historic Arrow Rock Tavern hangs the work of regional visual artists on its walls.

Art Perspectives

Tom Beamer, Arrow Rock's broom maker, says the town draws a specific type of tourist: "There aren't any amusement parks in town, so people who come here like to attend the theater or they're interested in history. We do a lot of sales here, but I still have my electrician's license to help out in the off-season. Some of us are concerned about shops which might want to sell ice cream or T-shirts, but so far nobody has tried to do things that don't fit into Arrow Rock's character. I'd like to see more good craftspeople move in. The town's the kind of place that has to be just right for you. But if it is, it's great to live here."

Details

Population: 70

Important Arts Events: Spring Festival of the Arts in May, Lyceum Theatre season from June to September, Heritage Craft Festival in October

Must-See Art Galleries: Arrow Rock Pottery, keelor Handweaving, The House of Mary B, The Old Library Shop

Local Arts Agency: Historic Arrow Rock Council
P.O. Box 15
Arrow Rock, MO 65320
816/837-3443

Bookstore: The Old Library Shop

Hannibal, Missouri

Location

Hannibal's setting along the Mississippi River has molded America's perception about what takes place in this art town of 18,200. Sure enough, Tom, Huck, and Becky were all important to the community's past, as was American treasure Mark Twain. But Hannibal's riverfront location, its two-hour drive into St. Louis, and its wealth of historic homes and commercial buildings are attracting a new group of residents who expect this small town to meet high artistic standards.

Great Outdoors

The mighty Mississippi dominates Hannibal's relationship to the environment, providing outdoor recreation at the town's doorstep. Mark Twain State Park, with its 18,000-acre lake, is the area's most popular place for bass fishing. You can hike on its 2,500 forested acres and camp at one of 450 campsites. Hannibal is also close to the Ted Shanks Wildlife Area, a wildlife and migratory waterfowl refuge that stretches along ten miles of the Mississippi riverbank. Hannibal's climate is hot and humid during the summer, and in this part of the state you're far enough north to get blasted by the same winter storms that batter Iowa.

Lifestyle

This historic community went through an era of prosperity in the mid- to late-1800s, a period that endowed Hannibal with dozens of massive homes set on bluffs overlooking the Mississippi, as well as with hundreds of smaller residences referred to by locals as "river shacks." Of course, they aren't shacks at all unless you compare them to the mansions on the hills above. This architectural legacy has largely been preserved by Hannibal's residents and business community, which is one of the main reasons why the town has for decades attracted a steady stream of tourists lured by its Tom Sawyer-ish charm. There are plenty of places in Hannibal to get in touch with the Twain legacy—the author's boyhood home, Becky Thatcher's house, and a few dozen shops that use Twain as a retail theme. Housing is not especially expensive here; the average cost of a home on one of the town's tree-lined streets is $55,000. Relocated Californians, New Yorkers, and retirees from large Midwestern cities have settled into Hannibal, buying many of the town's larger historic homes and renovating them from top to bottom.

Arts Scene

Hannibal is attempting to reinvent its tourist appeal from the kitschy (the Haunted House Wax Museum comes to mind) to the cultural. For years this town has lived off its old image, and change comes slowly. Half the town's businesses seem happy to continue hawking ice cream and T-shirts, while the other half are trying to redirect Hannibal's growth. For now, there's a great deal of optimism over the community's first serious attempt at a gallery that exhibits locally created fine art. Even though the Hannibal Art Council's Gallery 1221 is a small space, it's starting to sell surprisingly large amounts of original art, and there's hope that the surge portends Hannibal's new identity. The community is experienced at staging summer festivals, the most important one for local artists being the River Art Fair over Memorial Day Weekend. The Historic Folklife Festival brings nearly 100 fine craft artists, children's theater companies, storytellers, and bluegrass musicians to town in October.

The Hannibal Concert Association uses the downtown historic Orpheum Theatre, a 1,100-seat, turn-of-the-century vaudeville house, as a venue for its winter series of classical, jazz, and ethnic music performances by touring companies. Other local organizations use the Orpheum as well, bringing in ballet performances, piano recitals, and even the occasional flamenco guitarist. There are a couple of dinner theaters in Hannibal whose evening shows are cheesy, Music Man–meets–Huck Finn affairs, as well as a summer outdoor theater production that covers roughly the same territory.

Alternatives

Hannibal's restaurants and cafés don't quite grasp that local artists would like to have their work exhibited in places other than Gallery 1221, so artists have to find places in nearby Quincy or even St. Louis that will hang their work. The Café is a favorite meeting places of local artists

Art Perspectives

Hettie Marie Andrews, a painter, says the artists of Hannibal need to assume a higher profile locally. "The downtown businesses are worried about why their business has been falling off, and so they're more open now to the idea of seeing the local artists as somehow important in the way Hannibal's able to bring in tourists," she says. "We could use some more galleries, especially places that are run professionally and know how to display art without making their interiors look like a gift shop. A lot of us local artists look to Quincy as a place that's more progressive in its attitude toward the arts . . . though it's a slow process. Each year, I'm seeing more and more original things coming into the Hannibal stores, and that's a good sign."

Details

Population: 18,200

Important Arts Events: Bluegrass Music Festival in February, River Arts Festival in May, Historic Folklife Festival in October

Must-See Art Galleries: Gallery 1221

Local Arts Agency: Hannibal Arts Council
P.O. Box 1202
Hannibal, MO 63401
314/221-6545

Farmer's Market: Farm stands on area roads

National Public Radio: WQUB - 90.3

Bookstores: Copperfield's in Quincy

Chamber of Commerce: 623 Broadway
Hannibal, MO 63401
314/221-1101

Bigfork, Montana

Location

Bigfork calls itself the Village by the Bay, a title that may sound absurd to anyone who hasn't seen the spectacularly beautiful Flathead Valley, Flathead Lake, and the mountain ranges that drop off dramatically into the lake's edges. Bigfork's 4,500 residents live at the lake's northeast corner, right where the Flathead River enters the lake. The small art town of Kalispell is just 20 miles away, and the largest nearby city is Spokane, a four-hour drive west.

Great Outdoors

In this corner of Montana, the landscape and economy are dominated by Flathead Lake and Glacier National Park, a jewel in the National Park system and a tremendous draw for this region's fast-growing tourism economy. A million-plus acres of jagged mountains, turquoise lakes, glaciers, and thick forests make up Glacier, a park so massive its boundaries spill northward across the border into Alberta. Glacier Park is full of hiking trails, back-country lodges, campgrounds, and swimming holes. In late autumn, hundreds of eagles migrate to the park's western lakes to feed off the annual run of migrating salmon. Lake McDonald, inside the park, and Hungry Horse Reservoir are favorite summer recreation areas, but if you live in Bigfork, Flathead Lake is right at your doorstep—25 miles of the West's best freshwater sailing, lake fishing, and water skiing. At the south end of the lake is the National Bison Range; to the northeast is Flathead National Forest, with trout streams, campgrounds, snowmobile trails, and millions of wilderness acres. Big Mountain ski area, in nearby Whitefish, is less than an hour's drive from Bigfork.

Lifestyle

The tourism economy has always been important to Bigfork's well-being, but recently the community has grown tremendously from a less-than-welcome influx of urban refugees. As Kalispell and Glacier Park have grown in popularity, so has Bigfork, with shopping centers, office buildings, and newcomers' sprawling homes appearing much too quickly. The benefit of this growth is that it has allowed many local folks to prosper from the improved business climate. Local schools are improving their arts education programs, recently implementing a revised arts curriculum at the elementary levels. Older kids benefit from an artist-in-residence program that involves volunteer local artists.

Arts Scene

The dominant visual art is Western, especially cowboy art from the Charles Russell/Frederick Remington schools of creative thought. Sculpture here is better, artistically and financially, than the painting, largely because of the region's two fine bronze foundries, Kalispell Art Casting and Arrowhead Bronze. Western artists I've met tend to fall into one of two categories: commercial illustrators from Brooklyn who, tired of working at an ad agency, packed their bags, bought a Stetson, and moved west or Western-states natives who have worked on ranches and are largely self-taught artists. Bigfork's eight commercial western art galleries show a little of both. The town's nonprofit exhibition site is the Village Square Arts & Crafts Center. Village Square originally concentrated on touring exhibitions, which received mixed local approval; currently it focuses on local and regional art. Demonstrating the wide range of local art appreciation, Bigfork's two contemporary commercial galleries have also found substantial audiences for their work.

The performing arts have helped make Bigfork one of America's best small arts towns. The Bigfork Summer Playhouse has been packing in audiences for decades. Its 400-seat theater, Bigfork Center for the Performing Arts, is a gem of a facility used year-round by regional arts organizations. The Playhouse's five-play season runs from late May to late August. Then the Bigfork Community Players opens a three-play season that stretches through the long, cold Montana winter. The center also presents a year-round concert series of touring kids' theater and popular and contemporary folk music. A great summer event is the Riverbend Concert Association's series at Bigfork's Sliter Memorial Park. The family-entertainment flavor of these open-air concerts provides a nice counterpart to the sophisticated professionalism of the Flathead Music Festival's two-week July run, which brings national names in pop, classical, jazz, and ethnic music primarily to Kalispell, but also to a performance in Sliter Park.

Alternatives

The Bridge Street Gallery and Restaurant is one of Bigfork's premier exhibition locations, with changing monthly shows by regional artists; it has a legendary reputation for selling lots of art. The Bigfork Inn also exhibits work by local artists.

Art Perspectives

Pamme Reed, owner of Art Fusion (a contemporary gallery), says, "Selling contemporary art here is a struggle, but I've made it through eight years by developing some local clients and lots of out-of-state clients who collect contemporary art. I think it's important to support the work that's created by contemporary artists . . . to help them make their livings. I've noticed a lot more local people coming through my doors in the past year. I think they're finally starting to develop an appreciation for the kind of work I exhibit."

Details

Population: 4,500

Important Arts Events: Bigfork Festival of the Arts in August, PEO Art Show in October

Must-See Art Galleries: (Bigfork Art) Center Gallery, Bridge Street Gallery, Art Fusion, Yellowhorse Gallery, Kootenai Gallery, Riecke's Bayside Gallery, Corbertt Gallery

Local Arts Agency: Bigfork Art & Cultural Center
525 Electric Avenue
Bigfork, MT 59911
406/837-6927

Natural Foods Store: Withey's Health Foods (in Kalispell)

Farmer's Market: Thursday afternoons in Flathead Bank parking lot

National Public Radio: KUFM - 89.1 FM

Bookstores: Electric Avenue Books, Bay Books & Prints

Chamber of Commerce: P.O. Box 237
Bigfork, MT 59911
406/837-5888

Dillon, Montana

Location

Dillon's picture-perfect setting in the Beaverhead Valley of southwest Montana places it smack in the middle of a near-wilderness filled with trout streams, mountains, wildlife refuges, and peaceful farming valleys. Five thousand full-time residents and 1,000 or so students at Western Montana College call this town home. The closest population center is Butte, an hour's drive north.

Great Outdoors

Everything you would expect to find in a Rocky Mountain community is practically on Dillon's doorstep. Foremost is fishing, with hundreds of streams and lakes producing trophy-sized grayling and trout. The fishing is so legendary here that it's one of the big summer tourism draws, employing dozens of guides and outfitters. Beaverhead National Forest surrounds Dillon, as do 70 miles of designated National Recreation Trails, dozens of campgrounds, five lakes, and hundreds of miles of snowmobile trails. Two hours south, canoers and campers find paradise at Red Rock Lakes National Wildlife Refuge, a 43,000-acre habitat for trumpeter swans and all the usual sportfishing species. Clark Canyon Reservoir, 20 miles south of town, is Dillon's summer watersports magnet, complete with marinas, campgrounds, and summer homes. Maverick Mountain Ski Area is just a short drive from town, and Jackson Hole is just a few hours east.

Lifestyle

The tourist industry and Western Montana College are Dillon's top employers. Because WMC is the state's main teacher-training college, Dillon's schools are especially strong. The college runs an extensive children's summer arts camp that covers crafts, dance, nature photography, and visual arts. Adults use the college's Elderhostel program as a summer arts educational supplement. The region's arts agency, Southwest Montana Arts Council, sponsors an artist-in-residence program. The program brings performing artists into local schools for daylong events and to the college for extended residencies and master's classes.

The Beaverhead Valley's other main employer is the ranching industry. Settled by gold-miners in the mid-1800s, the landscape is littered today with remnants of those boom times. Bannack State Park, 25 miles west of Dillon, is an especially notorious ghost town, where the local sheriff teamed up with a gang of outlaws to loot, kill, and terrorize hundreds of the town's citizens (they eventually hired some gunfighters to do the job). Bannack's July Festival commemorates this wild-west past, as do the summer theaters operating in nearby Virginia City's nineteenth-century Opera House Theatre. A bit west of town is the Big Hole Battlefield National Memorial, an historical site and interpretive center commemorating one of the last battlegrounds of Chief Joseph's band of Nez Percé Indians.

Arts Scene

Western Montana College has one of the oddest museums in the West. The Seidensticker Wildlife Museum fills its walls with trophy heads of elk, bear, cougar, and other animals hunted in the region. (Just the place for visiting taxidermy students.) On the brighter side, the school's Main Hall gallery space exhibits contemporary work by the college's art faculty and students, and displays shows on loan from other Montana museums. Southwest Montana Artists Gallery is the community's other arts center, a nonprofit, artist-run cooperative exhibiting the work of Dillon's many fine painters, craftspeople, and sculptors. Of the several commercial galleries in the region, foremost are the Lonesome Dove Gallery and the Cathy Weber Gallery.

Dillon has two community theater groups as well as a very ambitious performance series presented by the local arts council. The council's Celebrate Montana series uses the college's 500-seat main auditorium for its touring shows of classical music, contemporary dance, children's theater, and folk music. One of the truly outstanding children's art programs in any of the nation's small towns is the annual two-week residency conducted in Dillon by the Missoula Children's Theatre, the country's premier performing arts organization for children.

May through September, you can catch the Shortline Players' Wapiti Dinner Theatre at the Dillon Elk's Lodge, while the Montana Vaudeville Players, whose repertory covers gold-rush days slapstick and a Roaring Twenties theme show, play at the Old Depot Theatre. The theater is a renovated Union-Pacific railroad depot filled with log homes and other historic structures on the grounds of the Beaverhead County Museum.

Alternatives

Sweetwater Coffee hangs the work of local artists, as do the Centennial Inn and a student-run coffeehouse and live music club on the Western Montana College campus.

Art Perspectives

Victoria Fridley, director of the Southwest Montana Arts Council, notes, "We've started a summer program called Lunch in the Park that brings free musical performances into the downtown area. That's helped the local business owners realize that the arts community can draw more business into their stores. Our town's a lot like other Montana towns in that it's growing with a new group of professionals—the type of people who support the arts and want to help things improve. We're a conservative area, but we're live-and-let-live, and I think that's why artists like living here."

Details

Population: 5,000

Important Arts Events: Boardwalk Arts & Crafts Show in July, Summer season of the Montana Vaudeville Players and the Shortline Players

Must-See Art Galleries: Cathy Weber Gallery, Lonesome Dove Gallery, Southwest Montana Artists Gallery, Western Montana College Gallery

Local Arts Agency: Southwest Montana Arts Council

P.O. Box 1416
Dillon, MT 59725
406/683-9476

Natural Food Store: Mountain Valley Grocery

National Public Radio: KUFM - 99.3 FM

Bookstore: The Bookstore

Chamber of Commerce: P.O. Box 425
Dillon, MT 59725
406/683-5511

Helena, Montana

Location

Montana's capital, Helena is a small-town community of 27,000 residents in the west-central part of the state. The drive north to Great Falls is less than an hour now that national speed limits have been returned to their Evel Knievel standard of "safe and sane."

Great Outdoors

The town is surrounded by Helena National Forest's million-plus acres, bringing wilderness areas, the Continental Divide, back-country campsites, hundreds of miles of hiking, biking, and cross-country skiing trails, and fantastic fly-fishing all within an easy drive of the Greek Renaissance-style capitol. In Helena, the great outdoors is right in your backyard. Canyon Ferry Lake, with nearly 20 miles for water-skiing, sailing, camping (two dozen recreation areas and campgrounds), and houseboating, is just a few minutes from downtown. Throwing a line into the lake (for rainbows and brown trout) and sunning on its shores are sacred Helena rituals. Sleeping Giant Recreation Area and Mt. Helena City Park, on the outskirts of town, are easily accessible hiking spots; Gates of the Mountains Wilderness is a short drive north. Helena's closest ski area is Great Divide, just a 30-minute drive from town.

Lifestyle

As the state capital and a regional center for federal government, Helena is loaded with bureaucrats, lawyers, legislators, and lobbyists. Home values in Helena's quiet neighborhoods have bucked the national trend in recent years as a flood of coastal urban refugees has poured into town, hoping to find the legendary hospitality and friendliness of the American West. You can still find decent homes for $90,000 or so, but the hardest thing to come by in Helena is a job; well-paid state and federal positions are not often voluntarily vacated. Highly qualified newcomers are a dime a dozen in Helena, which is why many of each year's crop of job-hunters become discouraged and move on to their next community of choice . . . wherever that might be. Local school art education programs are on the upswing as a result of their Art Plus program, a fairly recent development aimed at improving theater and dance education programs in the schools. Art Plus consists of teacher training, a local artist-in-residence program, and a Classroom Series that brings touring performers into schools for art workshops.

Arts Scene

Helena's most prominent visual arts site is the 10,000-square-foot contemporary art exhibition space in the Holter Museum of Art. The Holter exhibits as much regional work as it does national, and on occasion will mount a show of historical or traditional-style paintings. Its gift shop does double duty as one of Helena's two fine crafts galleries, and every spring the Holter hosts an exhibition of local student art. The Myrna Loy Center, housed in an ornate building that once was Helena's jail, mounts monthly exhibitions of work by Helena's contemporary artists, and its basement gallery is occasionally used for installations. There are many other exhibition venues around Helena at restaurants, bank lobbies, and government offices, but the town's commercial gallery scene is minimal, forcing Helena's visual artists to exhibit and sell their work outside the community. The town's unique Archie Bray Foundation Center, one of the nation's foremost artist residency and education programs for ceramicists, is located in an old brickyard on the edge of town. The Archie Bray attracts top international talent for its ten residency spots, and participating artists do everything while they're here: teach children's and master classes, create work in their own studios to mount exhibitions at the Archie Bray and the Holter, and even help tap beer kegs at the Archie Bray's annual summer Brickyard Bash.

The performing art scene is a different story altogether. Helena Presents uses the Myrna Loy Theater for its highly successful performing arts programs and its year-long film series, which includes foreign, independent, and first-run releases. Helena Presents provides the town with everything from classical music and touring theater to contemporary dance, ethnic music, and jazz during its nine-month performing arts series. Two theater organizations, Helena Theatre Company and Toadstone Theatre Company, use the Myrna Loy for their plays. Helena's most prominent theater group, Grandstreet Theater, stages its six-production, September-to-May season in a converted Unitarian church. The 60-musician Helena Symphony Orchestra performs at the 2,000-seat Civic Center, a converted Shriner's auditorium, occasionally along with the Helena Chorus. Also at the Civic Center, Helena Community Concert Association presents touring classical musicians, chamber orchestras, and soloists from the Helena Symphony.

Alternatives

Helena's musicians make a portion of their income performing at places like the Morning Light, Bert & Ernie's, The Wall Street Café, and J.D.'s Nightclub.

Art Perspectives

Arnie Malina of the Myrna Loy Center notes, "One of our strongest commitments is to progressive jazz, and we're known for bringing in good, national name acts. Almost anything that's presented here does well, as long as it's contemporary and shows people something they didn't already know."

Details

Population: 27,000

Important Arts Events: Dixieland Jazz Festival in June, Brickyard Bash in August

Must-See Art Galleries: Ghost Art Gallery, Holter Museum of Art, Montana Historical Society Museum, Myrna Loy Center

Local Arts Agency: Myrna Loy Center
15 North Ewing
Helena, MT 59601
406/443-0287

Natural Foods Store: The Real Food Store

Farmer's Market: Saturday mornings at Memorial Park

National Public Radio: KEMC - 91.7 FM

Bookstore: Montana Book Company

Chamber of Commerce: 225 Cruse Avenue
Helena, MT 59601
406/442-4120

Scottsbluff, Nebraska

Location

In western Nebraska, the Midwestern landscape begins to give way to the dramatic contours of the Rocky Mountains. If it weren't for this region's frequent winter blizzards, visitors to Scottsbluff would swear they were in southern New Mexico. Spring comes early to this edge of the Midwest, and summers are clear and hot. The closest city is Denver, a four-hour drive south.

Great Outdoors

When late-1800s pioneer families traversed their way toward the Pacific Northwest, they marked their progress along the Oregon Trail by landscape monoliths such as Scotts Bluff, now a national monument a few miles west of Gering, and Chimney Rock, now a national historic site 20 miles east of town. The region is laced with rivers, and the North Platte cuts right through town. Abundant wildlife can be found in the North Platte National Wildlife Refuge and around Lake Minatare. The lake is Scottsbluff's most popular summer recreation site, and during certain times of the year, its 2,000 surface acres attract flocks of migratory waterfowl. Wildcat Hills State Recreation Area, ten miles south of town, is a buffalo and elk refuge as well as a popular place for day hikes. It's also the site of a nature center presenting year-round adult and children's education programs. Colorado's ski areas are nearby, with the great art town of Steamboat Springs about a five-hour's drive.

Lifestyle

Agriculture is the area's largest employer, and though Scottsbluff's economy is diversified, there's no denying the important role that sugar beets and cattle play in local paychecks. Over the past 20 years, the area has attracted hundreds of Mexican farmworker families, many of whom have become American citizens and now own small businesses in Scottsbluff and Gering. Spanish-speaking families pack restaurants like El Charrito, Taco Town, and Rosita's on weekends for their fix of menudo, fajitas, and cerveza. But the all-out party takes place during the September 16th Fiesta and Cinco de Mayo, complete with dancing in the streets.

Historical museums in the region include the visitors center at Scotts Bluff National Monument, which owns a collection of paintings by artist William Jackson. There's a reconstructed fur-trading post at Carter Canyon, the Wyo-Braska Museum of Natural History, a railroad museum, and the North Platte Valley Museum. All are either right in town or within a few miles. Real estate prices are still very low, with homes selling in the $40,000 range. Artists from Denver and even the small art town of Loveland have started moving into the area. Scottsbluff's schools teach the standard visual art, music, and theater classes, but the major arts education here comes courtesy of the West Nebraska Arts Center. Located in a former Carnegie Library building, it's equipped with classroom and performance spaces used year-round for adult and children's art education programs, including a summer teacher's program.

Arts Scene

The center's visual arts exhibition space serves a wide swath of this region's many painters, sculptors, and craftspeople. Artists from 100 miles away consider this to be their home turf, reflecting a very high level of community interest. Arts center exhibitions change monthly and emphasize work created by western Nebraska's wonderfully diverse group of artists. As a result, residents are exposed to a photography invitational one month, a Native-American art show the next (the state borders on the Sioux Reservation), followed by anything from fine crafts to Chicano art. A nearby bronze foundry in Mitchell casts work for many of Loveland's top sculptors, several of whom have moved here to be close to the foundry. An hour's drive northeast takes you to Carhenge, a roadside attraction dreamed up by artist Jim Reinders. Carhenge uses junker cars sticking straight out of the ground to simulate the pillars of Stonehenge. (A similar attraction stands outside of Kerrville, Texas.) If you're going to be in Nebraska on the night of summer solstice, this is the place.

The art center also serves as Scottsbluff's performance headquarters, presenting theatrical productions by the Foothills Theatre, a semiprofessional community group, plus touring contemporary dance, jazz, and blues groups, children's programs, and holiday shows. Western Nebraska College's 600-seat auditorium stages performances by the Panhandle Symphony, touring classical musicians, and the Valley Voices chorale.

Alternatives

The Java Hut is a multifaceted venue that meets a variety of local arts needs. It includes a visual arts exhibition space with rotating shows and a music stage for blues, folk, Christian, rock, and Latino acts. It's also the place to relax and grab a cheesecake and a cup of espresso.

Art Perspectives

Painter Pat Hall reports, "Artists here teach, do the summer art fairs, take part in the art center's shows, find galleries in Colorado—whatever it takes to survive. One of the nicest things about Scottsbluff is our Mexican-American community. They've brought us great restaurants, wonderful fiestas, and strong families. It helps you to feel connected to the rest of the world."

Details

Population: 14,000

Important Arts Events: Sugar Valley Arts and Crafts Fair in June, Art in the Park (North Platte) and Western Art Fair in July, Native American Pow-wow in September

Must-See Art Galleries: Artworks, Image Makers Gallery, Java Hut, West Nebraska Arts Center Gallery

Local Arts Agency: West Nebraska Arts Center
106 East 18th Street

Scottsbluff, NB 69363
308/632-2226

National Public Radio: KTNE - 91.9 FM

Natural Food Store: Tamarack's Foods of the Earth

Farmer's Market: Wednesdays and Saturdays in downtown park

Bookstore: Copperfield Books

Chamber of Commerce: 1517 Broadway
Scottsbluff, NB 69361
308/632-2133

Carson City, Nevada

Ranked #44

Location

This legendary Wild-West town is one of the nation's smaller state capitals, but the 45,000 residents of Carson City don't seem to lack much. Lying just outside the beautiful Lake Tahoe region, this artistic community is 30 miles from Reno and just a five-hour drive from San Francisco.

Great Outdoors

Some of the nation's foremost downhill resorts are right at Carson City residents' fingertips, including Heavenly, Squaw Valley, Alpine Meadows, and Mount Rose. In November the town's high elevation brings snow, and every hiking trail and city park becomes a cross-country skier's haven. Heading out on the Tahoe Rim Trail, which hugs Lake Tahoe's shores for 75 miles, is a must-do at least once each winter (and a must-bike in summer). The nearby lake means that sailing, water skiing, and canoeing are naturally part of everyone's summer fun. Loaded with hiking trails and campgrounds, Lake Tahoe State Park backs up against Carson City's west side, while Toiyabe National Forest stand to the north. The rest of Nevada's desert landscape is an easy drive in any of three directions, and Yosemite National Park is just a few hours southwest.

Lifestyle

Carson City is decidedly a government town, filled with educated, socially aware individuals who own many of the mid-1800s historic district homes. The town has developed into a retirement magnet of sorts, and flanking eastern Carson City are more than a few strip malls and condo towns. But this is also very much a Western town, a place where cowboy clothing stores proliferate and country-music bars are one of the few alternatives to the casino scene. Carson City has casinos in all varieties, from the bankrupt and boarded-up to the glitzy palaces spawned by their Las Vegas parents. Surrounded by mountains and just a few minutes from Lake Tahoe, much of Carson City's young population takes outdoor recreation seriously. Being in shape is almost as much of a civic duty here as in the sports-crazed art town of Durango. Homes in Carson City's historic neighborhoods aren't easy to come by, but when they do show up, $150,000 and up is about the norm. As an alternative, an average-sized residence in one of the look-alike newer developments runs in the $100,000 range.

Arts Scene

Carson City's visual arts scene is centered around the two nonprofit exhibition spaces inside the Brewery Arts Center, a two-story brick structure downtown known as the home of Tahoe Beer for nearly 100 years. The building became Carson City's arts center in 1976 and now houses the community's largest artists' group, the Nevada Artists Association, and its exhibition space. The Brewery Art Center's facilities include a pottery studio and two studio/classrooms, as well as a contemporary art gallery that seats 140 for dance, theater, and musical performances. Adjacent to the art center's gallery is Artists' Association space used for member artists' shows, a monthly lecture series, and regular art classes. The Brewery Art Center has a strong education focus, programming year-round adult and children's classes in visual arts, drama, dance, and music.

Carson City's commercial gallery scene is still in its developing stages, expanding slowly as the town's reputation for affordable art reaches more of the Californian collectors. Some of the better-known commercial spaces are Abell House Gallery, Great Basin Gallery, Java Joe's Gourmet Coffee Gallery, and Austin Arts. Carson City is one of the few small art towns with a Native American arts facility—the Stewart Indian Cultural Center presently exhibits historical work but plans an expansion into commercial space.

The town's performing arts are well-addressed, with big-name country music, classical, jazz, reggae, and rock at the city community center; and dance, folk, and some jazz at the Brewery. For community theater, Western Nevada Musical Theatre is a zany group presenting musicals from one end of the year to the other. During summer, Mills Park presents an outdoor music series at its 2,500-seat Pony Express Pavillion. Western Nevada Community College operates a small children's theater, and there's a children's museum in Carson City's historic district. Several historical museums maintain Carson City's ties to its Wild-West past, including the Nevada State Museum, the Nevada State Railroad Museum, and the J.D. Roberts House Museum.

Alternatives

Local artists exhibit in the lobby of the *Nevada Appeal*, Carson City's daily newspaper, and in the City Café Bakery.

Art Perspectives

Painter John Hunt notes, "Artists here have to do everything they can to make a buck, and that includes Victorian-style portraits of famous prostitutes. Our business community hasn't caught on to the fact that artists are starting to bring their own kinds of tourists into town, because all they can see is the glare of the casinos. The exhibitions in Carson City get better each year, we sell more art each year, and the artists are unified."

Details

Population: 45,000

Important Arts Events: Stewart Indian Museum Pow-Wow in June, Folk Arts Festival in August, High Desert Jazz Fest in August, Bower's Mansion Bluegrass Festival in September, Cowboy Art Exhibit in October

Must-See Art Galleries: Abell House Gallery, Brewery Arts Center Gallery, Great Basin Art Gallery, Nevada Artists Association Gallery, Kristan Lane Gallery

Local Arts Agency: Nevada Artists Association, Brewery Art Center 449 West King Street

Carson City, NV 89703
702/882-6411 or 702/883-1976

Natural Food Store: Life Dream

Farmer's Market: Wednesdays in front of the St. Charles Hotel in summer

National Public Radio: KUNR - 88.7 FM

Bookstores: Kennedy Books, New World Books

Chamber of Commerce: 1900 South Carson Street
Carson City, NV 89701
702/687-7410

Virginia City, Nevada

Location

More than a century has passed since the era of Virginia City's glory, but the architectural legacy of its former residents who mined more than $400 million worth of gold and silver remains. This small art town (population 850) is 30 minutes from Reno and 25 miles from Lake Tahoe.

Great Outdoors

The views in Virginia City are spectacular, stretching nearly 100 miles in several directions. The vista down Six Mile Canyon to the Forty Mile Desert and on to distant, snow-covered peaks is one of the local favorites. It snows here in winter, sometimes a lot—which is just fine with Virginia City skiers. They travel to Lake Tahoe for downhill skiing or glide on the cross-country trails around town. Virginia City's landscape is typical high desert, and the summers here can be hot. Several state parks with hiking and fishing are within an easy drive of town, and Yosemite is a few hours' drive south.

Lifestyle

Virginia City and its neighbors Gold Hill and Silver City are part of the Comstock Historic District. Visitors here are treated to a look at what life was like in the boomtown era of the mid-1800s. If you've got $100,000 to spend on a home, there are more than a few elegant Victorians in Virginia City that need some time and attention.

Old West-style casinos, complete with honky-tonk pianos, have in large part kept this town's economy alive. A nearby real estate development has finally started to blow some wind into the local economy's sails, and it's bringing a new group of residents to town who want and expect to find lots of arts-related activity.

Unfortunately, the town's art center, housed in an elegant old building that once served as a hospital, is limited in its focus, offering art classes to mostly out-of-towners.

Arts Scene

You'll find Western art in Virginia City's casino restaurants and gift shops, but in recent years, as artists and entrepreneurs have moved into town, a promise of change has appeared on the horizon. The Comstock Arts Council has become the most active voice on Virginia City's arts scene and has staged exhibits at both the Fourth Ward School, a historical museum with a visual arts exhibition space, and the Sun Mountain Artworks Gallery. The council has made progress with the county's schools, taking over the regional artist-in-residence programs and placing local artists within the system.

The town's performing arts series is Comstock Art Council's most visible project. Each year the council presents a wide range of touring and local performing arts groups and individual artists. Some of its classical music concerts and contemporary dance programs are presented at the high school's 250-seat auditorium. Theater, poetry readings, and visual art exhibitions are staged at the middle school's 350-seat gym and at the Sun Mountain Artworks. Other music programs take place at the town's Knights of Pythias Hall and occasionally outdoors in Miner's Park. Every so often one of the casinos will bring a well-known musical act into town.

Alternatives

Virginia City's casinos give this small art town all the alternative action it needs.

Art Perspectives

Rick Magistrali, Comstock Arts Council, says, "The idea behind our performance series is to put money back into the community, and that's why we mix our touring artists with our local performers. We need a place where kids and adults from town can have art classes, and we need a performance space that isn't part of another entity. Piper's Opera House would be perfect, if it was priced more reasonably."

Says Karen Kreyeski, Virginia City painter, "Our performing arts events are always filled, which is why artists like coming here to perform. The town's business community could do a lot more to support the arts."

Details

Population: 850

Important Arts Events: Beer and Bard in February, Camel Races in September, Boar's Head Feast in December

Must-See Art Galleries: Buckskin and Lace Gallery, Fourth Ward School, Sun Mountain Artworks

Local Arts Agency: Comstock Arts Council P.O. Box 81 Virginia City, NV 89440 702/847-9278

Natural Foods Store: Life Dream in Carson City

National Public Radio: KUNR - 88.7 FM

Bookstores: Kennedy Books, New World Books in Carson City

Chamber of Commerce: P.O. Box 464 Virginia City, NV 89440 702/847-0311

Peterborough, New Hampshire

Location

Southwest New Hampshire is an outdoor paradise of covered bridges, trout streams, forested hillsides, and cross-country ski trails. In the recent past, the region's economy was driven by water-powered mills, and many of the large brick structures that once turned out clothing and manufactured goods still stand. Boston is a 90-minute drive when the roads are clear.

Great Outdoors

Summers in the Monadnock region are a time when hundreds of lakes are turned into swimming holes and thousands of tourists flood the area. Winters are moderate by New England standards, but are productive months for the visual, craft, performance, and music pros. The hiking and snowshoeing haven of Monadnock Mountain (elev. 3,165 feet) dominates the eastern horizon, and the seacoast's lobster sheds are less than a two-hour drive. Cross-country ski trails are everywhere, but the more challenging slopes are an hour's drive north.

Lifestyle

Newcomers who fit into the area's laid-back lifestyle are welcome additions to Peterborough's talented group of local residents. Lacking the madness of a year-round tourist season, Peterborough takes its community life seriously. There's a strong emphasis on family, and affordable rural homes in the $75,000 range are plentiful. In recent years an influx of home-based computer-industry pros have bought rural acreage, and the area has recovered nicely from the region-wide economic downturn of a few years ago.

Arts Scene

The arts scene is impressively varied for a small community, with lots occurring locally and even more within easy reach of town. The MacDowell Colony is one of the nation's most sought-after writers' retreats, bringing national figures into town for occasional public readings. Peterborough is home to the New England Marionette Theater, a prominent children's performance group active throughout the summer and autumn. Kids will also enjoy the Monadnock Children's Museum in nearby Keene. The town takes its history quite seriously, and the local historical society, which operates a museum, is one of the most influential groups in town.

The Peterborough Players is an Actor's Equity company producing five plays each summer in a renovated 1940s barn. The company is professionally run and attracts experienced actors and directors from across the nation, because it has built a formidable reputation within theater circles over the years. Another outstanding local arts organization is Monadnock Music, presenting orchestra, opera, and chamber performances from mid-July to late August. The group attracts a stellar series of guest artists to its bucolic setting, the 400-seat Pine Hill Waldorf Auditorium in nearby Wilton. During winter months Keene's restored Colonial Theater schedules an admirable range of performances, from metropolitan-area ballet companies, to locally produced plays, to top names in pop and jazz. Peterborough also has a movie theater occasionally showing classic films, and there are regular slates of foreign flicks at both the Wilton theater and at the Colonial. The Peterborough Unitarian Church presents a July and August lyceum series focused on national and international social issues.

The one component of the Peterborough arts scene that could benefit from more exposure is its visual arts. Peter Pelletier's gallery does a great job of showing nineteenth- and twentieth-century American and regional master artists, but there are few places dedicated to the commercial presentation of Monadnock's impressive contemporary artists. The Thorne-Sagendorph Gallery at Keene State College brings in strong touring exhibitions and occasionally hangs local art, while four miles south of town, the Sharon Arts Center's main gallery intersperses touring exhibitions with member artists' work. Though there's an absence of a strong fine crafts gallery, many area shops sell local craft artists' creations.

Alternatives

Grand Monadnock Arts Council's spring Art Walk places regional art in Keene storefronts. Many local artists successfully mine these month-long demonstrations and exhibitions for sales opportunities, along with the large August crafts fair in nearby Newbury. Restaurants exhibiting the work of Monadnock artists are 176 Main, the Bagelworks, Brew Bakers, Latacarta, and the Boilerhouse. The Peterborough Folk Music Society (at the Unitarian Church) shows local art on its walls, hosts local musicians on weekends, and runs a craft shop next to its busy dining area.

Art Perspectives

"Our population's growing, but it's growing with the right kind of people," says James Bolle, founder and artistic director of Monadnock Music. "Organizations are finding it possible to survive because the people living here want these programs to survive. All of us have to appeal to the tourist market to some degree or another, but for a place without a large university, the community has an attitude and a level of sophistication that's rare in a small town."

Says Molly B. Wiese, executive director of the Grand Monadnock Arts Council: "The arts are mainstreamed into the area's daily life, and you can really see that reflected in the audiences turning out for everything that goes on around here—and people do turn out."

Details

Population: 5,200

Important Arts Events: Downtown Keene's Art Walk and Arts in the Park in May, opening night party for Monadnock Music in July, Pumpkin Festival in October, First Night in downtown Keene

Must-See Art Galleries: Keene Art Association Gallery in Colony Mill Marketplace, Killian Gallery and Law's House Gallery at the Sharon Arts Center, Peter Pelletier Fine Art, Thorne-Sagendorph Art Gallery

Local Arts Agency: Grand Monadnock Arts Council

P.O. Box 835
Keene, NH 03431
603/357-3906

Natural Food Store: Maggie's Marketplace

Farmer's Market: Many farm stands on country roads

National Public Radio: WNHQ - 92.1 FM

Bookstore: The Toadstool Bookshop

Chamber of Commerce: Greater Peterborough Chamber of Commerce
P.O. Box 401
Peterborough, NH 03458
603/924-7234

Cape May, New Jersey

Location

This art town is as much a national architectural treasure as it is the end of the rainbow for hundreds of painters, writers, actors, and dancers. Cape May, an elegantly preserved Victorian community of 5,500 residents at the southern tip of New Jersey, may be in a Northeastern state, but its southerly orientation and proximity to warm ocean currents gives it a climate more like that of the Carolina coast. Philadelphia is a 90-minute drive, and the great art town of Lewes, Delaware, is just a 70-minute ferry ride across the Delaware Bay.

Great Outdoors

Life's rules are simple in this idyllic setting: During the winter, take long walks on the beach and be grateful for those frequent February days when a sweater is enough to keep you warm. And in early April, when the town becomes a riot of brilliant blooms, start waxing your boogie board and prepare for six straight months of beach weather. Another way residents enjoy nature is by birding at the many nearby migratory nesting grounds, especially at the 200-acre Cape May Bird Observatory.

Lifestyle

If the $200,000 Victorian homes along the coast seem unreasonable, $100,000 could land you an average-sized home an easy drive from town. It's not uncommon for artists moving into the area to set up house in a place like Wildwood or West Cape May to gain access to Cape May's performing and visual arts scenes.

Arts education hasn't caught on with Cape May schools, forcing local arts organizations to step in and fill the gap. One of these groups is Access to the Arts, which brings a strong performing arts schedule to Cape May and some of the schools. The other major children's program is operated by the Cape May County Art League, offering classroom settings in painting, dance, music, and theater.

Arts Scene

What this town needs is a medium-sized performing arts facility. As things stand, potential options are the city's 600-seat convention center (a hulk of a building that's used for roller derby contests on winter weekends), and a few church halls, hotel ballrooms, and banquet rooms at restaurants. The Mid-Atlantic Center for the Arts hopes to move its operations into an old school building to create a 500-seat performance venue, but the city government has yet to back the idea.

Cape May Stage is the area's equity theater company, and the community theater group is the East Lynne Company. During summer the Cape May Playhouse offers a children's theater schedule.

The visual arts scene in Cape May is centered around programs and exhibitions at the Emlen Physick Estate, also the home of the Cape May County Art League. A huge Victorian mansion built in the late 1800s, its carriage-house galleries are used for touring regional exhibitions and solo shows by Cape May painters. There are several commercial galleries in Cape May, and traditional plein-air painters work on the town's waterfront streets hoping to sell their seascapes to tourists.

Alternatives

Many local artists join the art-fair circuit during the warmer months. The major events, such as Victorian Week, Wings 'n' Water Festival, and the Tulip Festival all have arts and crafts components. Two of the better alternative exhibition venues for local artists are the Chalfonte Hotel and the Mad Batter café.

Art Perspectives

Alice Steer Wilson, a painter specializing in Cape May landscapes, notes that growth has been a hot issue among Cape May's arts community. "Some of the artists moving into this area don't want to take part in what's going on in the community. And that's unfortunate. Some people get the feeling that Cape May's becoming overcrowded, and that's created problems between the retirees who are part of the Cape May County Art League and the young people who are moving in with new ideas and who want to see the Mid-Atlantic Center for the Arts grow. Our city government seems afraid to get behind any ideas that will promote Cape May as an arts community. Sure, they know what cultural tourism means to the area, but it seems like they would just as soon see all of us go away."

Neal McPheeters, a contemporary painter who has recently relocated to Cape May from New York City, finds the town attractive for its lifestyle. "Everything's laid-back. There's no rush, no hurry to get anywhere. Of course, the environment's a difficult one for artists who are trying to sell their work, so you've got to have things pretty well set up before you make that move into Cape May. But what you get in return is a place that's historic, natural, and friendly."

Details

Population: 5,500

Important Arts Events: Cape May Music Festival in May and June, Victorian Week in October, Cape May Jazz festival in November

Must-See Art Galleries: Carriagehouse Galleries of the Cape May County Art League

Local Arts Agency: Mid-Atlantic Center for the Arts
P.O. Box 340
Cape May, NJ 08204
609/884-5404

Natural Foods Store: Our Daily Bread

Farmer's Market: Roadside stands are everywhere

National Public Radio: WSCL - 89.5 FM

Bookstore: Foundation Books

Chamber of Commerce: 609 Lafayette Street
Cape May, NJ 08210
609/884-5508

Red Bank, New Jersey

Location

Though only an hour's drive from Philadelphia and New York City, Red Bank's 12,000 residents live in a setting that's neither rural nor a metropolitan sprawl. For the next few decades at least, New Jersey's central coast should remain more country than city. The lowland coastal setting means winters are mild, spring arrives in early April, and warm weather lingers until nearly Halloween.

Great Outdoors

Red Bank is just a few minutes' drive from Gateway National Recreation Area, a 1,600-acre treasure of Atlantic beachfront and sand dunes sheltering Sandy Hook. Everything you could ever want from a beach is here, from hiking trails and campsites to premier East Coast surf-fishing. Farther down the Jersey Shore are more great beaches, state parks, and places for a weekend tent and baking in the summer sun. The land is fairly flat, so if you need to ski, you need to drive, and it's at least a couple of hours to reach a decent downhill area. Of course, being this close to New York City, some locals would rather spend their outdoor recreation hours trekking the urban jungle.

Lifestyle

The past several years have been good to Red Bank; the community has recovered from a regional recession. One innovative approach Red Bank used in reviving its economic fortunes was to create the Red Bank River Center shopping district, which includes the Red Bank Galleria, a generic structure housing the community's children's theater and a commercial art gallery. The town draws day-trippers from across the region because of its attractive commercial shopping district and dozens of restaurants—which means that local people can easily find retail or restaurant jobs, and entrepreneurs who want to start their own retail businesses have a ready-made market walking the streets on weekends. Red Bank's high school is a regional magnet school for children studying music, visual arts, and theater. Housing costs and living expenses are a problem in Red Bank, as in most communities within commuting distance of New York City. An average home here runs nearly $150,000.

Arts Scene

The 1,435-seat Count Basie Theatre, an old vaudeville house that today is one of the region's most popular venues for touring rock, jazz, blues, folk, and classical music acts, is the focal point for the community's cultural life. The theater stages hundreds of performances each year, bringing evening crowds into the downtown shopping and restaurant district, and providing the community with a true nightlife. According to Basie Theatre director Tom Tkach, profits from ticket sales on big-name acts allow the theater to help fund the Monmouth County Arts Council, housed at the Basie Theatre. The council's activities include a schoolchildren's theater performance program, exhibits in the theater's main lobby, and a subsidized ticket program for the community's low-income families. The Basie hosts other performing-arts groups as well, such as the Monmouth Symphony and the Monmouth Civic Chorus. Red Bank has two dance companies, and the Meadow Theatre at the galleria building focuses on children's theater productions and family shows.

Visual artists who participate in Red Bank's developing arts scene exhibit their work through nonprofit venues at the Art Alliance of Monmouth County's downtown gallery, the Basie Theatre, and several other commercial galleries. This isn't a town where an artist can survive on local sales alone, but neither is it overlooked by art collectors. The community's prime sales opportunities for craft artists are during the Red Bank Streetfair in September, and during the extremely popular First Night program that fills Red Bank's downtown on the last day of the year. For cinéastes, the Sony Theatre shows the latest in art and foreign releases.

Alternatives

Red Bank's four coffeehouses are known not only as great places to spot local art on the walls, but also for their evening music performances. House of Coffee, No Ordinary Joe, Laughing Bean, and Upstairs Coffee House are all worth checking out. Other popular hangouts for the creative crowd are Picasso's Palate, 2 Senza, and Murphy's Grill.

Art Perspectives

Charlotte T. Scherer, a painter whose work is influenced by the bold colors of Mexico's Yucatán, says the Red Bank area has attracted artists whose work is exhibited in galleries across the nation, but who keep a low local profile. "Some of the artists exhibiting here do quite well, and even people from New York City are coming here to buy art, if you can imagine that! The downtown business community is very supportive of local visual and performing artists . . . they know that what's good for us is good for their stores, eventually. Red Bank was a depressed area not too long ago, and that's what brought the artists in. Even now, the place isn't too expensive for being so close to the city, but we've got to make sure it doesn't get overpriced. What we are isn't kitschy, it isn't low end, but whatever it is, we've got to keep it that way."

Details

Population: 12,000

Important Arts Events: Riverfest Jazz & Blues Festival in June, Red Bank Streetfair in September

Must-See Art Galleries: Art Alliance of Monmouth County, Art Forms, Chetkin Gallery, Kingsley Gallery, Lloyd's Gallery

Local Arts Agency: Monmouth County Arts Council
99 Monmouth Street

Red Bank, NJ 07701
908/224-8778

Natural Foods Store: Red Bank Health Food

Farmer's Market: Roadside stands are everywhere

National Public Radio: WMCX - 88.9 FM

Chamber of Commerce: 170 Broad Street Red Bank, NJ 07701908/741-0055

Madrid, New Mexico

Location

The Turquoise Trail, a winding ribbon of two-lane blacktop connecting Albuquerque and Santa Fe, skirts the east side of the Sandia Mountains as well as the Ortiz and Cerrillos ranges. While the turquoise and coal mines that once lined the highway (officially known as NM 14) have long been closed, several of the towns that sprung up to house and service the mining families remain. One of them, the former coal mining community of Madrid, has become a small arts town. Its 350 residents live a half-hour's drive south of Santa Fe.

Great Outdoors

Two ski areas are within easy reach of Madrid: Santa Fe Ski Area is a one-hour drive north, and Sandia Peak is a 30-minute drive to the south. The Santa Fe National Forest, which covers the Sangre de Cristo mountains behind Santa Fe, is loaded with hiking trails, old logging roads, and access roads that in summer are perfect for day hikes and in winter are ideal for cross-country skiing. The Pecos Wilderness, about an hour's drive northeast of Madrid, is a back-country hiking and camping region that draws lots of summer visitors from Texas and southern New Mexico.

Lakes are hard to come by in this part of the country, which is why the strange moonscape surrounding Cochiti Lake is nonetheless appreciated by the people living in nearby Madrid. In summer months, swimming is possible at Cochiti Lake or the Abiquiu and El Vado reservoirs, which are several hours away.

Lifestyle

Madrid retains a rugged, miner's-town appeal. It was still very much a ghost town until the mid-1970s, when hardy pioneer types started moving back into the abandoned miner's homes and opened up a few of the town's dusty old storefronts. Today Madrid is a refreshing, Old-West alternative to the glamour and high prices of Santa Fe. The town's main street has several clothing stores, crafts shops, jewelry stores, leather shops, and art galleries, most of which are owned by Madrid residents.

The same miners' shacks that sold for a few thousand dollars two decades ago run upwards of $90,000 today, but there are still plenty that need major repairs and can be bought for considerably less.

Arts Scene

As it continues to grow, Madrid will need a community arts center. But for now the town's commercial galleries are doing a good job of representing the wide range of talented individuals who are moving into Madrid as an affordable alternative to nearby Santa Fe. A mix of contemporary and traditional works are exhibited here, most created by Madrid artists, but some by those from Albuquerque and Santa Fe. What holds this town's arts scene together is its affordability; people come to Madrid to find quality art that beats the high prices in Santa Fe galleries. The art here is less expensive because overhead gallery costs are much lower; Santa Fe monthly rents can easily top $1 per square foot.

Madrid's performing arts scene flourishes with both a summer melodrama theater and a summer outdoor music festival. The Engine House Theatre Melodrama Company performs a melodrama repertory of three productions running from late May through October at the Coal Mine Museum, which adjoins the historical Mine Shaft Tavern & Restaurant. The Mine Shaft is famous for its cold draft brews and huge burgers. Madrid's outdoor blues music festival is held at the Madrid Ballpark, a 1930s field of dreams that was built as part of New Mexico's WPA projects. The Madrid Blues Festival is held from late-May to mid-July, drawing New Mexico's best blues musicians and huge crowds from all over the northern half of the state.

Alternatives

Local art is exhibited at Maya Jones, a Latin American import shop on Madrid's historic boardwalk, and at Primitiva, an imported furniture shop adjoining Maya Jones.

Art Perspectives

Roger Blake, gallery owner: "I've found that the cultural tourists who come to Madrid are looking for local work—they certainly don't want inexpensive junk, and they want something different than what they can find in Santa Fe or Albuquerque. Our visitors are very astute about fine arts and fine crafts."

Details

Population: 350

Important Arts Events: Madrid Blues Festival from May through July, Madrid Melodrama from May through October, Madrid Christmas Open House in December

Must-See Art Galleries: Gold Hills Gallery, Hal Leedom Gallery, Jack of All Arts, Soulskin Gallery

Local Arts Agency:
Madrid Merchants Association
2851 State Road 14
Madrid, NM 87010

Natural Foods Stores: Alfalfa's, The Marketplace, Wild Oats (all in Santa Fe)

National Public Radio: KUNM - 89.9 FM

Bookstore: Maya Jones Imports

Raton, New Mexico

Location

The northeast corner of New Mexico is a fantastically scenic part of the state, where the rolling grasslands of the High Plains' westernmost edge meet the eastern flank of the Rocky Mountains' southern tier. Cold, windy winters keep Raton's 8,000 residents bundled up well into April, wondering when tourist season will arrive.

Great Outdoors

If you've wondered how the Great Plains looked in the centuries before sod-busting wheat farmers sliced and plowed them into agricultural productivity, visit Comanche National Grasslands, a two-hour drive east of Raton. With the slightest imagination you'll picture thundering herds of bison, galloping bands of Comanche and Apache raiders, and long lines of Buffalo Soldiers, all competing for dominance over this elegant landscape's waving terrain of four-foot grasses. Truly an incredible place and unlike any other corner of the West, for decades Comanche National Grasslands has inspired not only Raton's landscape painters but also the master artists of nearby Santa Fe and Taos.

Capulin Volcano National Monument, a short drive from Raton's historic downtown, is another must-see for breathtaking views from the edge of an inactive volcano's rim. Raton is home to the National Rifle Association's Whittington Center, a 35,000-acre camping, hunting, and shooting reserve loaded with some of the nation's best firing ranges for all kinds of weapons, from short-range pistols to elephant guns. New Mexico's law enforcement agencies use Whittington for training, and the facility is open to visitors who call ahead. The Santa Fe National Historic Trail cuts right across Raton, pointing the way into the Sangre de Cristo Mountains and toward Taos, which is a two-hour drive away. In winter this road leads skiers to the slopes; in summer, boaters take it to Eagle Nest Lake.

Lifestyle

Close to the Sangre de Cristos and located on the main rail route connecting the Southwest to the East Coast, Raton grew largely because of its mining and transportation industries. Amtrak trains stop here several times each day, bringing summer tourists to the community's compact downtown. The mining industry's cyclical nature has given Raton as many good times as bad, and recently many artists (from Santa Fe and points east and north) moved into town when mining-economy downturns caused Raton's real estate prices to plummet. A fair amount of boarded-up storefronts stretch along Raton's main drag, but you'll see many old neighborhoods with tree-lined streets and homes selling in the $50,000 range. The school system's art education programs are minimal, as in the rest of the state, which makes the efforts of the Raton Arts and Humanities Council that much more important to local children—such as in-school residencies by visiting artists brought in by the arts council, and a subsidized ticket program for schoolkids wanting to attend performances at the town's restored theater. The arts council's programming also addresses cultural needs of Raton's large Hispanic population, sponsoring performing artists such as the Maria Benitez flamenco dance company, folk musicians playing songs with a south-of-the-border flavor, and holiday shows that preserve the Hispanic religious pageantry rooted in more than four centuries of Hispanic presence in the state.

Arts Scene

For years, Raton's promise as an emerging arts center has been hobbled by New Mexico's chronic legislative indifference to funding arts programs. Nonetheless, the Raton Arts and Humanities Council has put together an energetic arts scene by using what was available: the renovated, historic Shuler Theater and a small visual arts space that doubles as the council's administrative offices. The council has recently obtained federal funding to restore Raton's old Wells Fargo Express building into a regional visual arts center, and if the project becomes real in late 1996, as planned, the town's arts scene could take a dramatic leap forward. For now, the community's nonprofit visual arts exhibition space is the Old Pass Gallery, with monthly shows by local artists. The shows range from exhibitions of children's art and traditional Hispanic santeros' works to paintings by Raton artists, all very much tied into the intriguing cultural mix that pulls Raton's arts community together. The real challenge for professional artists in this area is to have work exhibited in the nearby Taos and Santa Fe galleries, where they can mine the cultural tourism dollars that pour into these two arts markets from around the globe.

Raton's performing arts happen primarily at the 450-seat Shuler Theater, a restored vaudeville house, with some shows also at the high school auditorium. The local arts agency brings in Missoula Children's Theatre, touring drama, orchestral music, and children's shows.

Alternatives

Raton has yet to develop much of an arts conscience, but the nearby towns of Las Vegas and Taos are plastered with art, making up for its deficiency.

Art Perspectives

Barbara Carlini, director of the Raton Arts and Humanities Council, says, "The Wells Fargo arts center will enhance Raton's historic district. It's a smaller place, but a better financial deal for us. We're waiting for final approval on the construction. If it goes well, we'll be in by early 1997. The space will be used for visual arts, humanities lectures, and small performances."

Details

Population: 8,000

Important Arts Events: Raton Arts & Crafts Fair in August, International Art Show in September, Northern New Mexico Classic Exhibition in November

Must-See Art Galleries: A.R. Mitchell Museum of Western Art in Trinidad, Colorado, Old Pass Gallery

Local Arts Agency: Raton Arts and Humanities Council
140 W. First Street

Raton, NM 87740
505/445-2052

Farmer's Market: Tuesday and Saturday mornings at Second and Tiger Drive

National Public Radio: KENW - 101.9 FM

Bookstore: Eureka Books

Chamber of Commerce: P.O. Box 1211
Raton, NM 87740
505/445-3689

Taos, New Mexico

Location

Since the early 1900s, the dramatic beauty of the high desert surrounding Taos has drawn artists, art collectors, vagabonds, and black sheep. This quintessential small art town lies at the base of 13,161-foot Wheeler Peak, the tallest mountain in New Mexico and one of the jewels of the Sangre de Cristo range. Only 5,000 people live here, but of that number fully 25 percent of the population identifies as "an artist."

Great Outdoors

One of North America's greatest ski areas, Taos Ski Valley is just a half-hour's drive from the town's gorgeous Plaza. Many non-skiers are amazed when they hear that Taos is an alpine town and not a desert outpost of saguaro cacti and scampering iguanas. The Plaza's elevation is nearly 7,000 feet, and with the southern end of the Rocky Mountains flanking the east side of town, winters come in cold and early and leave late. Taos Ski Valley is intensely challenging, with a high percentage of expert-only terrain and an average annual snowfall of nearly 30 feet. Miles of cross-country ski trails on the town's outskirts wind through the enormous Carson National Forest that cradles Taos and the adjacent tribal lands belonging to Taos Pueblo.

The closest lake is at Eagle's Nest, about an hour's drive east through the ski town of Red River. But the main summer watersports action in Taos is the booming white-water rafting scene on the Rio Grande. Each year, after mountain snowmelt raises water levels, tourists and locals flock to the river. Until the Bureau of Land Management says differently, white-water trips will course through the spectacular Taos Box Canyon from spring to mid-summer.

Taos is well known in birding circles for its range of unusual desert species that fly here in the early summer when the lower deserts in the south get too hot for comfort. You might not see any roadrunners (the New Mexico state bird), but chances are good you'll spot orioles, cardinals, wrens, hawks, and eagles.

Because it's located in the heart of an outdoor recreation haven, Taos supports a number of back-country outfitters and guide services who put together everything from llama treks to fishing and snowmobile excursions. One of the more interesting of these is the Taos Indian Horse Ranch, a Pueblo-based enterprise that takes people on daylong horseback rides in the summer and sleigh rides in winter. Hiking around the rugged Taos landscape is little more than simply deciding which trail you want to take and heading toward the mountains from there. One of the most popular area hikes, however, is a daylong trek that descends into Taos Canyon, an enormous gash in the high desert, and follows the banks of the Rio Grande.

Lifestyle

Taos is very much an Hispanic community, populated by descendants of Spanish conquistadores and farmers who settled on the upper reaches of the Rio Grande nearly 500 years ago. But while the Hispanic presence here dates back to 1540, the Native American presence in Taos dates back to 3000 BC, and to this day exerts a vital influence on the region's tri-cultural population. Taos Pueblo, the most spectacular of the Southwestern Native American pueblos, looms above the landscape just north of the Taos Plaza. It is home to a large population of Taos Indians, people who have continually inhabited this land since long before Coronado ever set foot north of the Rio Grande. The intertwined histories of the Native American and Hispanic peoples have resulted in lots of shared bloodlines and family names, as well as a respect for each other's cultures.

It's the Anglo population that is Taos' newcomer group, along with Mexican laborers who move here for employment in the construction trade. Although the Hispanic and Native American people of Taos had developed sophisticated art forms of their own well before Anglos arrived, the artists who gravitated here in the 1920s popularized Taos as one of the nation's first destinations for cultural tourists. In many ways, the Taos Society of Artists, a sophisticated group of Eastern-educated landscape painters, was responsible for attracting people like D. H. Lawrence, Georgia O'Keeffe, and Mabel Dodge Luhan to the area. These artists are referred to today as the "Taos Founders." Their present-day descendants include a diverse and talented group of painters, sculptors, fiber artists, jewelers, fine craftspeople, ceramicists, writers, poets, musicians, designers, and actors.

Artists move to Taos for different reasons, but mainly to be around a dynamic community of like-minded individuals. Walk into any bar or store, pull into any gas station, chat up any waiter or waitress at any café, and chances are you'll be talking with someone who is an artist—maybe not a full-time artist, but certainly someone who understands and appreciates creative expression. Taos isn't a place where people come to find corporate jobs and the security of a steady paycheck. Rather, it's a place where risk-taking folks relocate to immerse themselves in a freethinking, creative, and nurturing environment.

Taos is peppered with small adobe homes, the norm in this part of New Mexico, but on the outskirts of town you'll find recent development that definitely breaks the mold, including "earthships" built from used car tires filled with dirt. Because it has long been a destination for cultural tourists, Taos has a disproportionate number of restaurants (80) and art galleries (90) relative to its population. There's some degree of coming and going, but a surprising number survive and prosper. Everyone connected to the arts scenes in both Taos and Santa Fe are thankful that tourists from all over North America come to the area not just for a vacation, but specifically to buy a piece of art.

Arts Scene

Taos is home to 90 commercial galleries, seven museums, a performing arts theater, a community arts center, huge arts festivals, two annual classical music festivals, an annual film festival, nationally prominent poetry bouts, and several famous authors. Some artists move here because they can make most, if not all, of their living selling to the cultural tourism market. The Taos version of an artist's hat trick is to have gallery representation not only in Taos but also in Santa Fe and Aspen. If you combine representation in those towns with galleries in Jackson and Scottsdale, you've got automatic entry to the "I-made-a-million-from-my-art" hall of fame. Yes, some artists are in it for the money, but the art-for-art's-sake attitude flourishes here, too. Taos is a fabulous place to build a career and develop a broad base of collectors who base their buying decisions on quality.

Many Taos artists get their start by exhibiting work at the visual arts exhibition space operated by the Taos Art Association, a nonprofit group that operates the Fine Art Gallery inside the Stables Art Center. The shows here are designed to include not only the usual opening night reception, but a follow-up "TalkBack" artist lecture/discussion, and an arts workshop conducted by the featured artist or artists. This is an exemplary way to increase artists' contact with others in the community and helps to develop the strength and integrity of Taos' arts scene.

Taos' seven museums, all foundation-supported, are the Blumenschein Home & Museum, Kit Carson Home & Museum, Hacienda Martinez, The Fechin Institute, The Harwood Foundation Museum, Millicent Rogers Museum, and the Van Vechten-Lineberry Taos Art Museum. All but the historical Kit Carson and Hacienda Martinez are fine arts museums.

Taos' commercial galleries are dedicated predominantly to traditional work. Landscape paintings executed in the representational style of Taos artists of decades past are very popular, and Western realism in all of its forms, from cowboys to cavalry to Sioux warriors, is given lots of attention. A few galleries exhibit contemporary paintings, and there are lots of fine crafts galleries exhibiting everything from Native American crafts to fiber art, contemporary weavings, art glass, and jewelry.

Taos has done a great job of promoting its two big yearly arts events, the Spring and Fall Arts Festivals. The two events coordinate gallery openings and many associated activities, but each year's arts calendar is loaded with special events at the museums and galleries; so, as popular as they are, the spring and fall art fairs are also seen as the brackets marking the beginning and end of the town's busy summer season.

The year-round focal point of Taos' performing arts scene is the Taos Community Auditorium, a 280-seat facility frequently configured into a 75-seat black box. Taos Art Association is by far the largest presenter organization at the auditorium, and its very active schedule covers it all: touring contemporary dance, children's and experimental theater, classical music soloists, chamber players, orchestras, and ethnic dance; and a year-round film series that presents the best of foreign and independent filmmakers, productions by its own Taos Readers' Theatre Company, and other theater productions. The auditorium is the venue of choice for the many performing arts organizations that call Taos home, including the Taos Children's Theatre; Taos Chamber Music Group; independent music promoters bringing in folk, jazz, and classical concerts; and the extremely popular Taos Talking Picture Festival which showcases Native American, Hispanic, and independent filmmakers.

Two major classical music events take place in Taos during the summer months—The Taos School of Music's Chamber Music Festival and the Music from Angel Fire festival. The chamber music festival brings in several top chamber quartets along with a number of nationally prominent soloists and nearly two dozen young musicians who have shown exceptional artistic promise. Music from Angel Fire—which performs its concerts in Taos, Raton, Las Vegas (New Mexico), and Angel Fire—takes place late August through early September. Taos also has a very active rock, blues, and folk music scene, which cranks up to full steam during the ski season when the clubs and hotels at Taos Ski Valley pull in thousands of skiers each night. Independent music promoters also book the Kachina Lodge for rock, reggae, and contemporary folk shows, and the Café Tazza is a popular small performance venue for folk musicians.

Alternatives

Most of the local restaurants and cafés exhibit local work, especially Café Tazza, Apple Tree, Bent Street Deli, Lambert's Restaurant, and the Taos Inn.

Art Perspectives

Cecelia Torres, owner of New Directions Gallery, thinks the arts scene in Taos has changed dramatically in recent years. "We're not seeing anywhere near as many of the walk-in buyers that used to come through our doors. Most of our sales now go to people who have been clients for some time, who we deal with over the phone, and who know the work they're buying. Then again, my largest single sale last year went to a man who just wandered in here and made a fast decision on a very, very expensive painting. So you can't just move your business off the street, because there are still those types of people coming through town. Sales here are frequently for large sums of money, and, nearly every day of the year, there are quite knowledgeable people walking through the door.

"The contemporary art I exhibit doesn't sell as well as the representational work most galleries exhibit, but I'm committed to Taos contemporary artists, because that's what I'm most comfortable with. Our market can be pretty soft at times, and this past year has been one of those times. But if artists are willing to wait, if they work hard and take their time to build a solid foundation for their careers, Taos can be a very generous place for them."

Details

Population: 5,000

Important Arts Events: Spring Arts Festival from late April to early May, Taos School of Music Chamber Music Festival from mid-June to early August, Music from Angel Fire from late August to early September, Fall Arts Festival from late September to early October

Must-See Art Galleries: Blumenschein Museum, Fechin Institute, Fenix Gallery, Harwood Foundation, Millicent Rogers Museum, New Directions Gallery, Taos Art Association Fine Art Gallery, Taos Artisans Co-op Gallery, The Parks Gallery, Van Vechten-Lineberry Museum, Weaving Southwest

Local Arts Agency: Taos Art Association
133 North Pueblo Road
Taos, NM 87571
505/758-2052

Farmer's Market: Weekends at parking lot on Paseo del Pueblo Sur

National Public Radio: KUNM - 91.9 FM

Bookstores: Moby Dickens Book Shop, Mystery Ink Bookstore, Taos Book Shop

Chamber of Commerce: P.O. Drawer 1
Taos, NM 87571
505/758-3873

Alfred, New York

Location

Alfred, set in the rolling hills of western New York's Allegany County, is rural, affordable, and full of creative talent. A college town, it's the home of the state-supported College of Ceramics at Alfred University, a draw for some of the world's top creative talents. It's a two-hour drive to either Buffalo or Rochester, and Toronto is only three hours away.

Great Outdoors

Nature has provided Alfred with plenty of forests and water. Fishing is a popular pursuit, and the area has dozens of stocked trout streams and bass lakes. Deer hunting brings in lots of tourist dollars each autumn, while summer action concentrates on the area's lakes and rivers, where canoes are as popular as sailboats. During winter it's a mixed bag of cross-country skiing and snowmobiling on the wide-open land of Allegany, Stoneybrook, and Letchworth State Parks.

Lifestyle

Alfred is one of the best bargains in the nation for artists. $30,000 will buy a fixer-upper wood-frame home, $50,000 will secure a colonial residence with a yard and garage, and $100,000 will procure not only several acres of land, but a large house, studio, front porch, and full basement. Artists move here because they want a safe place to live and raise their families—a place where they have easy access to high quality arts programs and excellent educational opportunities for both themselves and their children.

An historic, vibrant community, Alfred is as much a college town as it is an arts town. Though technically an outpost of the vast State University of New York system, Alfred University feels more like a private liberal arts college. This is a cultured, highly educated town. Its natural attributes and easy lifestyle are the primary drawing cards for the teaching talent lured here from across the nation. Communities are characterized by tree-lined neighborhoods, kids riding bicycles, and folks who know one another and stop to chat in public places. Main Street is only a block long, yet it has both a city green and a bandstand for free summer concerts.

Arts Scene

The hundreds of artists in Allegany County pursue all branches of the arts, from playwriting, to sculpting, to contemporary painting. But in Alfred, there's an incredibly talented group of instructors, students, and visiting artists attracted by the ceramics school. On campus is the Scholes Library of Ceramics, a small sales gallery for instructors' creations, and the Fosdick-Nelson Gallery of contemporary visual arts and fine crafts.

In the past year Alfred University has opened a new multimillion-dollar performing arts center with a 250-seat theater, a black-box rehearsal space, and a maple-sprung dance floor. The college presents a challenging touring artists calendar to inspire and promote its own performing arts programs and students. And people expect things to get even better.

The driving force of the Allegany County arts is the Allegany Arts Association, a minimally funded umbrella organization that coordinates important get-togethers for the county's creative talent, contributing to the widespread feeling of support from one artist to another. Local theater companies present their dramas and musicals in Wellsville's Howe Library and at the Fillmore Fire Hall. Chamber music and classical concerts take place at the Cuba Presbyterian and Belvedere First Congregational churches, as well as in Alfred University's Harder Hall. At the opposite end of the county, Houghton College hosts a Spring Strings Festival that brings local schoolkids and professional conductors together to rehearse and perform an afternoon concert.

Though the area is developing more sales and exhibition opportunities for visual artists, for now their challenge is to market their work elsewhere. In addition to the exhibition spaces at Houghton College, the Technical College, and Alfred University, the arts association maintains an exhibition space in Wellsville. The foreign film series at the university is one of the most popular events during winter months.

Alternatives

The Summer Arts festivals are prime sales opportunities for local craft artists. Hot Dog Day in April is a spring-fever celebration with an arts component. Visual art is exhibited at Manhattan West Bar and Coffeehouse in Alfred, and Hangups is a Wellsville frame shop exhibiting local work. At night, two of the favorites are Classic Espresso and Alex's Bar.

Art Perspectives

Hope Zaccagni, a graphic designer with a talent for goldsmithing and puppetry, observes, "What the artists of this region need is their own visual arts center. That would give us a better place to show our work and it would give the arts community a place to hold classes and lectures. One of the best places to do that would be in the town hall theater, which is in desperate need of renovation. We get some very good shows at the university's gallery, and one of the most popular events of the year is the graduating seniors' exhibition. Our arts association is getting stronger, but making a living here is still very difficult."

Details

Population: 5,000

Important Arts Events: Spring Strings Festival in April, Hot Dog Day in June (try a not-dog for lunch), Summer Arts Festival in July and August, Renaissance Fair in September

Must-See Art Galleries: Allegany Arts Association Gallery, Fosdick-Nelson Gallery, Scholes Library of Ceramics

Local Arts Agency: Allegany Arts Association 84 Schuyler Street

Belmont, NY 14813
716/268-5078

Natural Food Store: Kinfolk

Farmer's Market: Saturday mornings in Wellsville

National Public Radio: WOLN - 91.3 FM

Bookstore: Box of Books

Chamber of Commerce: 43 North Main Street Alfred, NY 14802
607/587-8222

Corning, New York

Location

Corning, a sophisticated community with a thriving arts scene and a healthy economy, is located in Steuben County, part of New York's Finger Lake Region. More than 12,000 people call Corning home. The cultural activities of the community are tied to nearby Elmira.

Great Outdoors

Like the rest of upstate New York, Corning is close to a range of natural resources, from the pristine shores of the Finger Lakes to the Catskills' ski areas. The rolling terrain of this region's countryside isn't just a great place for hiking and camping, it has also served as inspiration for many of the fine artists who have lived here. The lakefront state parks—Bluffpoint's Keuka State Park and the enormous Watkins Glen State Park—both have plenty of campsites, hiking trails, and boat launches. Spencer Crest Nature Center, a 250-acre park right in Corning, is a favorite place for hiking, fishing, and cross-country skiing.

Lifestyle

Corning has always been a prosperous place because the Corning corporation, the nation's leading glass manufacturer and glass technology company, is a smart, civic-minded employer that can ride out economic cycles and still contribute financially to regional arts. Commercial and fine art glassblowers have lived here for as long as anyone can remember. In their honor, their corporate employer recently built the high-tech Corning Museum of Glass, which contains historic, scientific, and Steuben glass-blowing exhibits.

Corning is also home to the Rockwell Museum, a facility housing a large collection of Western paintings and sculpture, as well as an enormous collection of antique toys and Steuben glass. Nearby Patterson Inn Museum is dedicated to exhibiting historical artifacts from the region's frontier days.

Corning's business district is in a classic, turn-of-the-century style, renovated and restored to reflect its charming historical heritage. The rows of brick, terra-cotta, and wood commercial structures are ideal places for artists seeking second- and third-story studio spaces with north light. Homes in Corning include both fixer-uppers and mansions built by corporate executives. Average house prices start at $65,000.

The town's schools are an enormous source of community pride. Corning is exemplary in integrating arts-based education into each grade level's curriculum. There are also weekend and weeknight art education classes offered through ARTS of the Southern Finger Lakes, which funds regional in-school projects and pays for teacher-training.

Arts Scene

Corning's visual arts scene is centered around the exhibition action at 171 Cedar Arts Center, which focuses on contemporary work by regional artists. The Rockwell Museum rotates historical exhibitions in its gallery space, as does the Corning Museum, which also mounts technological exhibitions. The most prominent commercial gallery in Corning is West

End Gallery. Artists Studio Gallery and the Hands on Glass Studio are also very popular. In nearby Elmira, the Arnot Art Museum exhibits work by European and American masters as well as works by regional artists, and operates a comprehensive arts education program. Elmira's Allen Smith Gallery is another of the region's best commercial spaces.

The performing arts scene in Corning is diverse and committed to presenting challenging material. 171 Cedar throws open its doors year-round, bringing in a range of classical music, modern dance, jazz, and folk music culled from New York, Boston, Washington, D.C., and regional artists. These activities are supplemented by a series of lectures, opening receptions, book signings, and classes. In nearby Elmira, the Clemens Center (Mark Twain is buried in Elmira's Woodlawn Cemetery—much to Hannibal's chagrin) is the region's premier performing arts venue. Every weekend, the Center presents rock concerts (Elmira College students fill the seats), touring theater productions, community and college theater, comedy, opera, and orchestra. Elmira and Corning share a ballet company and a symphony orchestra. During the summer months, the region supports three summer stock repertory companies entertaining Finger Lakes tourists.

Alternatives

Corning has attracted a large population of resettled city types who seem to drive this town's happening night scene. The west end of Market Street is where you'll find Medley's Cafe, the town's most popular live music venue. Pizza? Corning has Rico's, a favorite local hangout.

Art Perspectives

Thomas Buechner, a Corning painter who creates different types of work but is known nationally for his portraitures, says he likes the feeling of arts ownership in Corning. "Here, people from all parts of town are involved in planning what happens in the arts in addition to attending events. Corning is a model of democracy in action. Artists here know one another, enjoy one another's company, and help one another. All we need is a good arts school, the kind of place that would bring artists into Corning to teach. If we could sustain something like that, this place would take off."

Details

Population: 12,000

Important Arts Events: Market Street Festival of the Arts in August, World Folk Music Festival in August, Corning Crafts Fair in November, Annual Regional Art Exhibition at Arnot Art Museum in Elmira

Must-See Art Galleries: Allen Smith Gallery, Arnot Art Museum, Artists Studio Gallery, 171 Cedar Arts Center, West End Gallery

Local Arts Agency: ARTS of the Finger Lakes 1 Baron Steuben Place, Suite 8

Corning, N.Y. 14830
607/962-5871

Natural Food Store: Naturally Nice

Farmer's Market: Farm stands in countryside

National Public Radio: WSKG - 91.1 FM

Bookstore: Bookmarks

Chamber of Commerce: 42 East Market Street Corning, N.Y. 14830
607/936-4686

Jamestown, New York

Location

Forested and sparsely populated, this lakeside town in the southwest corner of New York is within a three-hour drive of Toronto, Pittsburgh, Cleveland, and Rochester. The largest city in Chautauqua County, Jamestown is a blue-collar community that has managed to roll with the nation's economic punches by redefining itself as competent, creative, and resourceful.

Great Outdoors

Jamestown sits at the southern tip of Chautauqua Lake, a scenic summer recreation magnet stretching nearly 18 miles (stopping just short of Lake Erie). Nearby Allegheny State Park provides year-round outdoor recreation; the area offers mountain trails, a 30-mile reservoir, and back-country campsites. This remote corner of the state is a prime breeding ground and migratory area for waterfowl, songbirds, and butterflies. The National Audubon Society's premier environmental education facility, the Roger Tory Peterson Institute, is located on a 600-acre nature sanctuary just ten minutes from Jamestown.

Western New York is famous for its brutal winters, which play havoc with road conditions but make for great winter sports opportunities. Cross-country ski trails are plentiful near Jamestown, and the downhill skiing is moderately challenging 30-minutes away at Cockaigne.

Lifestyle

Jamestown's story is a model for how the arts can be integrated into a community's business and social life. Like many other old manufacturing cities in the East, Jamestown's economy hit a wall in the 1980s. When things got rough and people started looking for new solutions, local government teamed up with the business community and the area's fledgling arts organizations to develop a plan for the town's future.

The groups driving Jamestown's revival as an arts community were more than adept at finding money. They received millions from state and federal government, and philanthropic sources, and they put those dollars into the right projects. The key downtown project was the purchase, restoration, and rebirth of the community's 1,260-seat vaudeville theater. The Reg Lenna project was an enormous, city-wide undertaking that drew volunteer help and contributions from all of Jamestown's ethnic, economic, and social sectors. When the theater reopened in late 1990, the entire community shared in the pride of its success. The new Reg Lenna Civic Center, an award-winning, art-deco masterpiece, now serves as headquarters for the Arts Council of Chautauqua County. Jamestown's spirit was reborn the night the civic center reopened.

The Arts Council of Chautauqua County has been involved in renovating several old commercial buildings into office, retail, and artists' studio spaces, in hopes of drawing talented artists to Jamestown. The council wants to turn these spaces into rental properties and is willing to rent them for a pittance compared to what similar property would bring in other parts of the state.

Jamestown is still the home of thousands of well-paying jobs in the manufacturing industry. Cummins Engine Company, one of the main funding sources for the region's arts group, builds diesel engines, and other community-involved corporations manufacture things like ball bearings and furniture. Homes in Jamestown's neighborhoods are very affordable; $30,000 is the average cost of a starter home and $50,000 will buy a place with a few bedrooms, a garage, a vegetable garden, and fruit trees in a large back yard. The outlying communities in Chautauqua County have a New England charm and are virtually crime-free.

Art education is highly valued in Jamestown's public schools, and instruction is provided at all grade levels. The Cummins Corporation recently awarded the arts council a large grant to formThe Creative Learning Partnership, a program aimed at employing local artists for residencies in Chautauqua County's schools. The program's aim is to develop specific curriculum goals that are fully integrated into the educational experience.

The Reg Lenna Civic Center's mainstage series includes an ambitious children's outreach and performance component that books music and dance professionals for nearly two dozen performances throughout the school year. During February and March, a professional dance company and a classical music organization are in residence at the Lenna, working with gifted dance and music students from county schools to produce a mainstage performance. During the year the Lenna also presents a children's film series, and the Roger Tory Peterson Institute offers everything from children's nature photography classes to field research instruction.

Arts Scene

Jamestown is part of an arts and cultural scene that includes nearby Dunkirk, Chautauqua, and Fredonia. Fredonia, a 30-minute drive from Jamestown, is home of the Rockefeller Arts Center, a 1,200-seat performing arts facility on the campus of Fredonia State College. The Fredonia Opera House, a restored, turn-of-the-century, 400-seat performance hall, presents its own mainstage series. The Chautauqua Institution, a 20-minute drive from Jamestown, is a summer getaway for families from East Coast metropolitan areas. Chautauqua's arts calendar is full from late June to late August, with performances by resident symphony, dance, theater, and opera companies, as well as visual art exhibitions and lecture series, and a national issues lecture series.

The rest of the year is another matter entirely. The county arts council stages a comprehensive, September through May film series in the Lenna Theater with an emphasis on foreign and independent releases. Most of these same films are cycled through two other venues, the Fredonia Opera House and the Warren Library Theater. The arts council's live performance programming concentrates on children's education, but it also produces several events (ethnic music and touring dance companies, for example) as well as a low-cost year end subscription series. The Fredonia Chamber players stage classical music performances at both the Lenna Civic Center and the Rockefeller Arts Center in Fredonia. The Rockefeller's season includes the college's theater productions and some touring musical presentations, while the Jamestown Concert Association and the Community Music Project present classical and chorale music programs at church venues around Jamestown.

Another important performing arts facility is the Lucille Ball Little Theater, a 426-seat repertory playhouse named for Jamestown's most famous home-grown celebrity. The theater serves as the headquarters of Jamestown's annual Lucille Ball Festival of New Comedy, a three-day spring fiesta celebrating the career achievements and comedic art of Ms. Ball. Now in its sixth year, "Lucy Fest" brings some of the nation's top comedy pros into town. The event also features a national film and video competition, plays by local playwrights, and an auction of

Lucille Ball memorabilia. The auction is a fund-raiser for the Lucille Ball/Desi Arnaz Center for Comedy, another Jamestown success story that houses nearly 1,000 objects donated from the estate of Lucille Ball in a gallery setting. The resident company at the Lucille Ball Little Theater stages four productions during its season.

Dozens of community arts fairs scattered across the county are used by craft and visual artists as important direct sales opportunities. The Roger Tory Peterson Institute mounts touring national exhibitions of wildlife painting and photography, and the Prendergast Library Gallery in Jamestown is an important nonprofit exhibition space for the area's visual artists. Westfield's Patterson Library Octagon Gallery fills a similar role at the far end of the county.

Touring shows and the work of regional artists are shown at the Forum Gallery at Jamestown Community College and at the Rockefeller Center art gallery in Fredonia. The Chautauqua Art Association and Logan art galleries are located on the grounds of the Chautauqua Institution, and Gloria Plevin's gallery is located nearby. Two of the best places in the region to find fine crafts are the Crary Gallery in Warren, Pennsylvania, and the Portage Hill Gallery in Westfield. Scattered among the communities lining Chautauqua Lake are a number of summer-operated galleries doing gangbuster-business for three months of the year, while the Trails End Gallery in Ashville manages to stay open year-round. Griffis Sculpture Park is a 400-acre nature preserve with ten miles of hiking trails, 200 pieces of three-dimensional installation work, and a national reputation for innovation in its collection and exhibitions. In Jamestown, next to the Lenna theater, the Chautauqua Originals gallery mixes fine craft, traditional craft, and visual art in a retail setting, and Framemasters has an exhibition space for rotating shows by local painters.

Adams Art Gallery in Dunkirk is the region's premier art exhibition space for contemporary work. It stays open year-round, mounts an aggressive series of touring national and regional invitational shows, has a far-reaching children's art education program, hosts master classes by visiting artists-in-residence, and hosts events such as an art film series, ethnic music celebrations, and meetings of the region's artists' association. The summer Blue Heron Music Festival in Sherman features regional rock, folk, and ethnic bands, and the Busti Apple Festival in Busti includes one of the county's best outdoor fine crafts exhibitions.

Alternatives

Since the direct sales opportunities for artists in Jamestown are primarily defined by the summer tourism season, it's important for artists to take part in the better arts and craft fairs such as the Busti Apple Festival, and to exhibit their work in the many cafés and restaurants. Nellie's Deli in Jamestown is one of the best, as is the Ironstone restaurant. In Fredonia, the Upper Crust Bakery is a prime alternative exhibition space, as is the White Inn.

Art Perspectives

Roy Nedreberg, a painter with a studio in one of the renovated industrial buildings, says Jamestown's climate for local visual artists is a welcoming one. "We all communicate well, and we have a lot of fun together. Realism, especially those front porch-and-shaded-street scenes you find at Chautauqua Institution, are the big sellers with the summer arts crowd. If you're not doing that sort of realism the opportunities for exposure in this area can be pretty frustrating.

"For contemporary artists, the challenges are getting accepted into the group shows at the Adams Gallery, and finding commercial galleries in Buffalo, Pittsburgh, and Cleveland to carry your work. I like living in Jamestown. I've got a couple thousand square feet of studio space in an industrial loft setting, lots of musician friends who make their livings playing in the clubs and bars around the area, and a feeling of support from the art center's involvement in the community. If more artists don't want to move in to this town, I feel they're missing out on a great opportunity."

Sarah Baker Michalak, a papermaker in Fredonia, says that the region's summer sales opportunities are strong for artists who know how to reach their markets. "The tourists coming through here are from large cities and they know good art when they see it. Artists like living here because of the cost of living and the quiet, rural communities they can choose to live in. I've noticed a number of mature, older artists who have established themselves in other places starting to move into this area—especially fine craft artists who like to do a few big shows each year, then stay home and work the rest of the time. I'm optimistic about the way things are shaping up."

Kay Collins, the director of the Adams Gallery, says her facility addresses numerous aspects of the arts community's needs. "This town is a place that's ready to grow into being an arts center, and the support is here for that to happen. Dunkirk and Fredonia still have their turn-of-the-century manufacturing infrastructures standing, and to drive through these towns is to realize that the potential is right there. Our focus in one gallery is on contemporary shows, and we have a second gallery for more traditional works. Each summer we work with the Chautauqua Institution to exhibit an international fiber arts show. Our Saturdays are largely given over to kids art classes."

Details

Population: 34,500

Important Arts Events: Lucy Fest in May, Chautauqua Institution's programming in visual and performing arts in summer, Blue Heron Music Festival in June, Keeper of the Western Door Pow-Wow in Salamanca in July, Bisti Apple Festival in September

Must-See Art Galleries: Adams Gallery, Gloria Plevin Gallery, Portage Hill Gallery, Prendergast Library Gallery, Rockefeller Art Center Gallery, Roger Tory Peterson Institute Gallery

Local Arts Agency: Arts Council for Chautauqua County

116 East Third Street
Jamestown, NY 14701
716/664-2465

Natural Food Store: The Nutt Tree

Farmer's Market: Thursday and Friday mornings on Brooklyn Square

National Public Radio: WNED - 89.7 FM

Bookstore: The Paperback Exchange

Chamber of Commerce:
101 West Fifth Street
Jamestown, NY 14701
716/484-1101

Peekskill, New York

Location

A Hudson River Valley town north of New York City, Peekskill was once a thriving manufacturing center. Today, its 20,000 residents (including hundreds of recently arrived artists) live an hour's drive from the Museum of Modern Art.

Great Outdoors

Peekskill is close to several state and regional parks. Challenging ski areas are within an hour's drive, while just across the Hudson River are Harriman and Bear Mt. State Parks, both laced with trails for winter cross-country skiing and summer hiking. The adjacent Blue Mountain Reservation is a large county park that's part of a 20-mile bike trail system. Ecological restoration has made the Hudson River a summer magnet for sailing, canoeing, and other sun sports.

Lifestyle

Peekskill has become an alternative community for hundreds of creative professionals who are looking for a way out of New York City, but want to retain access to big-city theaters, galleries, museums, and nightclubs. In the late 1980s, in a desperate attempt to bring economic activity to the town, the Peekskill government established the Downtown Artists District. Artists started moving in, a few articles appeared in New York City newspapers about the renovation program (headed by consultant Ralph DiBart), the Paramount Center for the Arts began serving as an exhibition venue for visual and performing arts, and Peekskill surprised even itself as it developed its reputation as an arts community.

   Peekskill schools offer art education, but most local artists feel there's plenty of room for improvement in this area. The Paramount presents Art Attack, a program that brings regional schoolkids into the theater for matinee performances by touring groups booked for its mainstage shows. The cost of living here is much less than in the nearby city, with fixer-upper homes priced slightly under $100,000 and lots of the apartment and industrial-loft spaces that make New York City transplants feel at home. In Peekskill they find larger studio spaces for less rent, as well as an environment loaded with artists and creative pros who make a living through gallery and performance gigs in the city, but who enjoy Peekskill's small-town life.

Arts Scene

Peekskill's performing arts are in great shape because of the Paramount Center's influence. Using the 1,000-seat restored vaudeville house for classical and pop music and adult and children's theater programs has given Peekskill an arts conscience. With so many seats to fill, the Paramount keeps ticket prices low, bringing higher revenues through increased sales. September through May, the Peekskill Rep stages four productions at the Paramount. A smaller performing arts space is next door at Paramount East, and in summer, Peekskill's Riverfront Green hosts music concerts under the stars. Local folk bands and solo acts are booked into One Station Plaza, while orchestral and dance performances appear in Eisenhower Hall at the U.S. Military Academy at West Point, just 20 minutes away.

The community's visual arts scene has become a popular alternative for the region's art collectors. In the eight-block area that forms the art district, a number of galleries have become successful, which in turn has attracted more artists eager to rent studio space. Five buildings are already packed with artists' living and studio spaces, and more are coming. Cooperative JJENTH Gallerie continues to be a focal point for the visual arts scene, recently joined by the Driftwood Gallery, the Paramount's exhibition spaces, and Creations Gallery. Some artists try to get their work into these venues, while others make direct sales through the district's self-guided open-studio tours on Saturdays. Still others only open their studios on the third Saturday of each month—a widely distributed studio map contains addresses and phone numbers. The Valley Artists Association coordinates local art displayed in some of the district's storefronts, and the recently established schedule of Peekskill art classes through the Westchester Arts Workshop has been an important catalyst for some of the community's artists.

Alternatives

Even the mayor's office exhibits local artists' work, and many restaurants and cafés sell paintings. Susan's Restaurant is right in the middle of it all, and Connolly's Bar & Grill mixes local blues, art, and artists. The Bruised Apple Café does the same, with a less-amplified music mix, and Zip City Brewing, a brew pub exhibiting local art, is Peekskill's pride and joy.

Art Perspectives

Sarah Haviland, who left New York City two years ago for Peekskill, is a sculptor who enjoys the town's friendliness and potential. "I've seen a lot of artists working together on projects like organizing shows, and that's a great way to meet the other active people in the community. Peekskill's met my expectations, but it took me a while to get adjusted, to get over the feeling that I had to be commuting in and out of the city every few days.

"I don't think that living here has changed my work, but it's definitely given me a focus by its nature of being a quiet, more productive place to work."

Details

Population: 20,000

Important Arts Events: Open Studio Tour Saturdays, Summer Street Fairs in July and August, Riverfront Green Wednesday concert series in July and August

Must-See Art Galleries: Driftwood Gallery, Hudson Valley Institute for Art and Photographic Resources, JJENTH Gallerie, Rotating Gallery of the Valley Artists Association, The Up Gallery

Local Arts Agency: Paramount Center for the Arts
1008 Brown Street
Peekskill, NY 10566
914/736-9585

Natural Foods Store: Member-run cooperative without a storefront

Farmers Market: Saturday mornings on Bank Street

National Public Radio: WNYC - 93.5 FM

Bookstore: Bruised Apple Bookstore and Café

Chamber of Commerce: One South Division Street
Peekskill, NY 10566
914/737-3600

Asheville, North Carolina

Location

Compact and beautiful, the art town of Asheville is really a small city, and with 63,000 residents it's among the largest communities included in this book. Perched in the glorious western end of North Carolina, at a point where the Smoky Mountains meet the Blue Ridge, Asheville is the cultural, economic, and educational center for not just this part of the state but also most of eastern Tennessee. The closest big city is Charlotte, a three-hour drive.

Great Outdoors

An outdoor recreation paradise, Asheville's at the doorstep of everything you could want, from the Great Smoky Mountains National Park wilderness area, to skiing in nearby Boone and fantastic white-water rafting throughout the region. The climate is on the "mountain" end of the scale, but moderately humid and warm summers are followed by spectacular autumns. If you have a need to roll around in salt water, the drive to the Carolina coast takes nearly six hours—so find the quickest way to Lake Lure and count your blessings.

Lifestyle

For several years Asheville has been one of the two favorite destinations for Carolinians from Charlotte, Raleigh, Winston-Salem, and elsewhere who want to move their businesses and lives to a bucolic, affordable community (the other is Carolina Beach). And who can blame them? Asheville's an eminently livable place. Everything here is within easy reach, from quiet neighborhood homes in the $100,000 range, to the community's wide range of arts programs and performances. One of the Southeast's most influential arts and economic development organizations, Handmade in America, is based in Asheville. Right now, Handmade's focus has narrowed to communities in western North Carolina; but its push to revive small towns by developing cultural tourism potential could soon be adapted throughout the five nearby states.

Arts Scene

Asheville's arts scene is well-balanced, with plenty to see and do and lots of opportunity for all kinds of visual and performing artists. Community planning a few years back resulted in the formation of an arts alliance that works to centralize Asheville's arts funding resources and keep the art town's many different groups from bumping into each other. Crafts are important, but not dominant, in Asheville's arts scene. The nearby Biltmore Village crafts fair and the two yearly Southern Highlands crafts fairs are major direct-sales events, but Asheville's craft artists tend to be "road warrior" types who make their livings at outdoor shows from Ann Arbor to Nova Scotia. The nationally famous community of Penland contemporary glass artists is here and in nearby Toe Valley, with hot shop masters who exhibit their work in major galleries across the U.S. and Europe.

For painters and sculptors, Asheville's an enormously attractive place to live, with its art museum, nonprofit galleries, and many commercial galleries in the Pack Square downtown district. Many of Asheville's visual artists supplement their incomes through the Mountain Arts

Program, which places artists in school residencies throughout the region. Pack Place is Asheville's cultural hub and home to the city's art museum, African American cultural center, kids' science museum, and 520-seat Wortham Theatre. The Wortham houses the community's classical concert series, kids' theater, contemporary dance performances, and summer Shakespeare festival. The Asheville Symphony and big-name music acts that tour through town could use a larger concert hall; currently they're forced into the Civic Center, a place better suited for roller derby and custom-car shows. The Asheville Community Theatre performs six months annually in its own 240-seat downtown space, and an interesting local arts scene takes place at the Broadway Arts center, home to several alternative theater groups, poetry bouts, musical performances, and ethnic dance shows. Cinematique is the town's full-time art and foreign film showcase.

Alternatives

Like other college towns, Asheville has a few great live-music places, from bars showcasing alternative music acts to contemporary folk musicians at coffeehouses and even a couple of jazz bars. Beanstreets, Barleys, and Café on the Square are a few more-favored artists' gathering places, as is Vincent's Ear, known for both its food and the great local art hanging on its walls.

Art Perspectives

Linda Wilkerson, an arts administrator, says Asheville's downtown business community has not yet caught on to the arts' powerful influence on the region's rising economic fortunes. "I'd like to see more resources going toward the professional organizations that are here. The people are in place, but we're being taken for granted and aren't widely recognized for the contributions we're making.

"In the past few years I've seen lots of artists coming in, from young artists starting their careers to some big national names who just buy a home somewhere in the area and don't really take part in local happenings. It's a beautiful town, a place where people get to know their neighbors, and a place where there's so much expertise that you can make some great contacts to help build your career."

Details

Population: 63,000

Important Arts Events: Southern Highlands Crafts Fairs in April and October, Anything that Floats Boat Parade in June, Biltmore Village Crafts Fair in August

Must-See Art Galleries: Blue Spiral One, New Morning Gallery, Village Galleries, Zone One Gallery, Vitrum Gallery

Local Arts Agency: Arts Alliance
P.O. Box 507
Asheville, NC 28802
704/258-0710

Natural Food Store: Earth Fare

Farmer's Market: Weekend mornings at the Grove Arcade

National Public Radio: WCQS - 88.1 FM

Bookstores: Malaprops, The Captain's Bookshelf, Once Upon a Time, Downtown Books & News

Chamber of Commerce: 151 Haywood Street Asheville, NC 28802
704/258-6101

Blowing Rock, North Carolina

Location

The northwest corner of North Carolina is a mountainous playground filled with ski areas, trout streams, hiking trails, and forested wilderness. Blowing Rock's 1,500 residents are closer to Johnson City, Tennessee than they are to Charlotte, but because this is the Tarheel State they'll make that three-hour drive at the drop of a hat.

Great Outdoors

The east coast's tallest peak is the Southern Appalachians' Mt. Mitchell (6,684 feet), just an hour's winding drive from Blowing Rock along the Blue Ridge Parkway. Blowing Rock is surrounded by the beautiful Pisgah National Forest, an outdoor recreation gold mine offering everything from back-country wilderness to some of the best Eastern skiing outside of Vermont (when conditions are right). This area gets a whole lot of winter; snowfalls in mid-October are not unknown. Summers are cooler and less humid than those in the Piedmont lowlands, which explains Blowing Rock's success in attracting cultural tourists, summer-home owners, and urban refugees.

Lifestyle

Because it's a popular place for vacation-home owners who want to ski or get away from the humid southern summers, Blowing Rock real estate values are much higher than in nearby towns. Average-size homes can still be found in the $60,000 range, but it helps if you're handy with drywall and a pipe wrench. The nearby college town of Boone is an important cultural asset to the residents of Blowing Rock, as Appalachian State University presents a performing arts series featuring classical, orchestra, pop, and occasional rock music. Artists move to this area largely because of the region's historic tradition of functional crafts, and because the area's year-round tourist trade brings in visitors who prowl the town's galleries and gift shops. While there's a strong local market for art, it's important to develop sales outside the region; many local artists show in galleries in Atlanta, Washington, D.C., Charleston, and Hilton Head.

Arts Scene

Blowing Rock's highly successful summer series of seven art festivals—Art in the Park—is one of the Southeast's premier art fairs. Painters, jewelers, ceramicists, and creative professionals from throughout the region compete to be juried into these shows, and once they get in they rarely leave. For local artists, Art in the Park and its tens of thousands of visitors is a huge sales opportunity, whether you're standing in one of the 120 artists' booths at Blowing Rock Memorial Park or having an opening at one of the community's several art galleries. A half-dozen galleries and studio galleries are in Blowing Rock's tiny downtown, sprinkled among the pricey clothing shops and import stores. Most local artists prefer to sell directly from their studio galleries, developing important sales contacts through the buyers breezing into Blowing Rock from Florida, South Carolina, Georgia, and North Carolina.

For performing arts, Blowing Rock is a lot like your typical small town. A popular community theater performs in the ancient auditorium of the Blowing Rock elementary school, and a symphony performs occasionally at one of the nearby condo resorts. Summer gazebo concerts in the town's Memorial Park feature some of the area's highly skilled bluegrass and mountain music pros, and sometimes a bagpipe act from the Grandfather Mountain area. During summer, the community theater brings in actors and technicians from Southeastern colleges, which helps improve the onstage presentations.

Alternatives

Years ago, due to a quirk in North Carolina's liquor laws, Blowing Rock was famous as the only community for miles around where you could buy a drink and sit in a bar like a normal person. Today, things have quieted down significantly, mostly because the college kids in Boone can now get rowdy much closer to home. There are still a few good bars in Blowing Rock, and a couple of the local hangouts such as Vance's Café and the Cosmic Coffee House exhibit work created by Blowing Rock artists.

Art Perspectives

Ronald Tharp, jeweler and gallery owner, says that recent years have brought noticeable changes to Blowing Rock. "When I first opened Fovea Gallery I was concerned because the work I show there is contemporary—but to my surprise it's gotten strong acceptance. I knew there was always a lot of creative talent here, but in the past few years artists from the Northeast and the Midwest have settled into Blowing Rock, and they've added a great deal to our image of this place as an arts community.

"The arts are an important part of this area's economy, and most of the businesses around here realize that. The town itself could do a better job of promoting Blowing Rock's arts, and not stay so focused on its same old attractions. But things are shifting around here, and shifting quickly. I can tell by the types of people coming into the gallery and visiting here for Art in the Park that we're developing more of a reputation for quality, more acceptance of contemporary work, and—thankfully—more buyers."

Details

Population: 1,500

Important Arts Events: Art in the Park from April to October, Old Time Mountain Music Festival in October

Must-See Art Galleries: Brookside Gallery, Expressions Gallery, Fovea Gallery, Ragged Garden Inn Gallery of Contemporary Italian Art

Local Arts Agency: High Country Gallery Association
P.O. Box 1210

c/o Fovea Gallery
Blowing Rock, NC 28605
704/295-4705

Natural Food Store: Raspberries in Boone

Farmer's Market: Saturday mornings in Boone at Horn in the West

National Public Radio: WDAV - 89.9 FM

Bookstore: Bookmasters

Chamber of Commerce: P.O. Box 406
Blowing Rock, NC 28605
704/295-7851

Salisbury, North Carolina

Location

Can you say "Paris of the Piedmont"? The 26,000 people living in Salisbury can, and they've got escalating real estate values to prove it. Halfway between sophisticated Charlotte and "are-we-sophisticated-yet?" Winston-Salem, Salisbury offers its artists access to rural life, pro sports, quaint neighborhoods, international airports, low taxes, and major league performing arts—an unbeatable combination.

Great Outdoors

One of the nicest things about Salisbury is that it backs up against High Rock Lake and the Yadkin River. The 15,000-acre lake and its Yadkin River tributaries stretch clear down to the South Carolina border, taking on several different names along the way and providing nearby water recreation opportunities for those not crazy about the four-hour drive to the Carolina coast. Locals find great hiking and back-country camping in the Pisgah National Forest, slightly more than an hour's drive west, and the ski areas outside Boone are just another hour past the forest turnoff. Salisbury itself has a half-dozen municipal parks ranging from the historic setting of Sloan Park to the family recreation focus of Dan Nicholas Park.

Lifestyle

Close enough to Winston-Salem and Charlotte to be within commuting distance, Salisbury's reputation as an arts center has made it a somewhat fashionable place to live. As a result, homes that just a few years ago sold for $60,000 are now listed in the $80,000 and higher range. But the community still retains much of its leafy-neighborhood, small-town charm. Salisbury has earned its reputation as a great place to raise a family and has kept its downtown area from going the way of Mallsville, U.S.A. The downtown's Meroney Theatre, a restored vaudeville house, draws evening foot traffic into local restaurants, while a half-dozen galleries and craft shops draw day-tripping visitors.

Arts Scene

The focal point for Salisbury's visual artists is the Waterworks Visual Arts Center, a renovated public building that today houses classrooms, studios, an exhibition space, and a sensory garden for the visually impaired. Waterworks is a big player in Salisbury's arts education, plugging hundreds of local schoolkids into its annual printmaking program, leading art tours for low-income children, and scheduling after-school and weekend art classes for the artistically gifted.

Salisbury's strength as an arts town lies in its diverse and readily accessible performing arts scene. The Meroney is home to the Piedmont Players, an accomplished community theater company staging seven annual productions. Catawba College's theater arts department pursues a more cutting-edge style of theater, using its 1,500-seat Keppel Auditorium for Shakespeare and contemporary dance, its 100-seat Experimental Theatre for plays by the likes of Vaclav Havel, and its 250-seat Little Theatre for an annual new plays competition.

Salisbury's community concert association presents a winter series of more than two dozen performances of big band, folk music, and classical concerts by touring national acts such as the Rio Trio and the Aspen Wind Quintet. Also at Keppel through the winter months are the many concerts of the Salisbury Symphony Orchestra, an organization offering Salisbury's kids an after-school strings program. There's also a choral society that performs in the St. John's Lutheran Church and runs a children's chorus program during the school year.

Alternatives
Sweet Meadow Café has jumped onto the local arts bandwagon in a big way by exhibiting and selling locally created visual arts. La Cava café, Las Palmas cantina, and DJ's Bar are favorite artists' hangouts after exhibitions and performances.

Art Perspectives
Ceramicist, potter, and Clayworks Gallery owner Denny Meecham says that one of the more noticeable trends in Salisbury's arts scene is growth. "Our local artists group has turned into an arts center, and there are a lot of artists working hard to build Salisbury's downtown into a place recognized for its visual arts. The main performing arts groups here, the symphony and the community theater, could do more bridge-building with the other Salisbury arts groups. We all could benefit from shared creative energies and administrative expertise.

"Artists here make a living by teaching and creating. Some work will sell to the tourists coming here, some has to be sold at the regional crafts fairs, and some has to be wholesaled, but you can do it if you work hard. I see buyers coming into my gallery from all over the state, people who like to come in and talk about art. They're interested in us, we're interested in them, and that's creating a nice dynamic here."

Details
Population: 26,000

Important Arts Events: Downtown Arts Celebration in April, Downtown Gallery Gallop in October

Must-See Art Galleries: Clayworks Gallery, Duck Blind Gallery, Waterworks Gallery

Local Arts Agency: United Arts Council P.O. Box 4234 Salisbury, NC 28145 704/638-9887

Natural Food Store: Simply Good Natural Foods

Farmer's Market: Wednesday and Saturday mornings in Town Pharmacy parking lot

National Public Radio: WDAV - 89.9 FM

Bookstores: Bookmasters, Rainy Day Books

Chamber of Commerce: P.O. Box 559 Salisbury, NC 28145 704/633-4221

Lancaster, Ohio

Location

The 36,400 residents of Lancaster live in the wooded, rolling hills of Fairfield County, about an hour's drive southeast of Columbus. All four seasons assert their presence in this part of the Midwest, with frigid winters and hot, humid summers repaid by a long, beautiful springs.

Great Outdoors

Lancaster's neighboring Hocking County is known as one of Ohio's prime spots for outdoor recreation. Campgrounds, state forests, lakes, and reservoirs are all within 60 minutes of Lancaster's historic downtown. Lake Erie's beaches are four hours north, and it takes at least that long to reach the ski areas in Pennsylvania and West Virginia.

Lifestyle

For most of the year, Lancaster is the kind of town that attracts a variety of tourists. Some of them come for the town's art galleries and traditional craft shops, but most seem to be looking for T-shirts and ice-cream cones. But Lancaster's saving grace happens each July, when for one glittering month of Ohio summer, the town turns into a performing arts mecca, courtesy of the Lancaster Festival.

Lancaster is a historic town filled with restorable Victorian mansions that can be picked up for $75,000. Schools, downtown shops, and city parks are within easy walking distance of the town's tree-shaded neighborhoods. As a result of Lancaster's love affair with regional malls that stripped the community's major retailers, downtown is filled with two-story structures ripe for transformation into artists' live and work spaces. Local schools are way behind the national curve on using art education programs as curriculum enhancers, and Lancaster is still stuck in the "art-cart" mode.

Arts Scene

Many of Ohio's most prominent visual artists live in Lancaster, but they don't have much of a local profile because their only local venue is at the Lancaster Festival. Some of these artists teach at Ohio State University in nearby Columbus, some teach at Ohio University's campus in Lancaster or at the main campus in Athens, and others just stay in their studios and crank out work for galleries in Chicago, New York, and Pittsburgh. Of the few commercial galleries in town, one exhibits the work of the region's top visual art talents, while another's reputation is in traditional crafts. Two other exhibition sites exist at the library and at the local branch of Ohio University. Lancaster is slowly turning its nineteenth-century Reese-Peters House into a visual arts center, one targeted toward children's classes as well as invitational and touring exhibitions.

The rules that apply to the town's compact visual arts scene during the other 11 months of the year are thrown to the wind during July's festival, when Lancaster turns into the Aspen of the Midwest, sprouting galleries the way an Ohio cornfield sprouts cornstalks. More than three dozen temporary gallery sites are pressed into service during the festival weeks. Bank lobbies, restaurants, law offices, classrooms, and public buildings are plastered with art, most of it for sale.

Performing arts rule the roost here, which isn't surprising considering the enormous economic impact the Lancaster Festival has on the community's artists, art businesses, retailers, restaurants, and bed and breakfasts. Theatre Lancaster and the Lancaster Chorale run their seasons from September to May, at Ohio University and at local churches, respectively. When the festival is in full swing, the town swarms with classical musicians, country performers, reggae bands, contemporary dance companies, performance artists, jazz combos, and opera singers. Any and every possible venue—from the Elk's Club to the Ohio University amphitheater, to several downtown bars and restaurants, to the bandstand on Zane Square—is wired for sound, hung with spotlights, and filled with folding chairs. Free family performances occur at the mall and the county fairgrounds, and tons of late-night fun can be had at any place pouring drinks. This is also the time for locals to do their biggest entertaining of the year, and caterers' trucks from Columbus swarm over town like fireflies. In all, more than 75 musical and performing arts events are scattered around Lancaster during the festival's run.

Alternatives

Besides the dozen or so performance venues that are pressed into service during the festival, Lancaster's visual artists exhibit at places like the Four Reasons Deli, Tavern at the Mill, and the Georgian.

Art Perspectives

Maggie Sobataka, a painter and ceramicist, says that the challenge for Lancaster artists is to develop markets outside the area. "If you're living from your work, you've got to have a professional approach to marketing. This community is supportive of the arts, and one of the reasons I moved here was due to the way people in Lancaster get enjoyment from participating in the arts. Our downtown is positioned to be revived with galleries. It's a gem waiting to be discovered, but we need more of a year-round focus on Lancaster's arts, and not just to be known as a great place to visit in July. A fine arts center would help to build the town's long-range reputation, as well as give the community more exhibition space."

Details

Population: 36,400

Important Arts Events: Lancaster Festival and The Artwalk in July, Zane Square Crafts Festival in August

Must-See Art Galleries: Hammond Gallery, Ohio University Gallery, Studio B

Local Arts Agency: Lancaster Festival
P.O. Box 1452
Lancaster, OH 43130
614/687-4808

Natural Food Store: Sage Advice

Farmer's Market: Saturday mornings in downtown parking lot

National Public Radio: WOSU - 98.7 FM

Bookstore: One is needed—any takers?

Chamber of Commerce: P.O. Box 2450
Lancaster, OH 43130
614/653-8251

Guthrie, Oklahoma

Location

This former frontier boom town is today close enough to Oklahoma City to practically be one of its suburbs, but the 40 miles between OKC and Guthrie's 10,500 residents are more than enough to give this historic town plenty of wide-open spaces and quiet streets.

Great Outdoors

The Cimarron River runs right past Guthrie, adding a measure of interest to what otherwise is a flat landscape crosshatched with country roads that run arrow-straight from one end of Logan County to the other. Two nearby lakes, McMurtry and Carl Blackwell, are Guthrie's summer recreation magnets. Most of Oklahoma's best parks and lakes are located near the state's eastern border, so Guthrie residents are used to two-hour drives to the parks around Muskogee and Tahlequah, the capital of the Cherokee Nation. Winding Stair Mountain National Recreation Area is an enormous stretch of forested hillsides laced with campgrounds, nature trails, marinas, and rivers perfect for canoeing. The closest ski areas are in northern New Mexico, a six-hour drive west.

Lifestyle

Guthrie was once was the state capital. Following Oklahoma's admission to the union in 1907, it was developed to accommodate everything a large city would need, from a Supreme Court to Victorian residences for the state's political elite. After the capital was moved to Oklahoma City, Guthrie went into a tailspin, losing a portion of its historical architecture.

Today, after lots of hard work and investment, what remains has either been restored to its turn-of-the-century glory or at least saved from ruin. Guthrie is now one of the nation's largest National Register Historic Districts, with nearly 400 city blocks bearing this designation. Ornate three-story brick buildings line the streets of the business district, many with upstairs industrial lofts that artists would give their eye-teeth for. The town's neighborhoods brim with Victorian homes that go begging for buyers at $50,000, dream palaces that were built with rare woods, huge porches, and enormous basements. Guthrie has, as one artist told me, an unlimited potential to develop into one of the region's most hospitable places for artists who want great studio and living space, but need to do it all on a shoestring.

Being less than an hour north of Oklahoma City means that art museums and theater are practically on Guthrie's doorstep. But in town, Guthrie's economic development and political leaders are being challenged to formulate the types of artist-inducement plans that have worked economic miracles in other towns. Guthrie's schools have won awards for the excellence of their art education programs, which tend to consist of traditional visual arts, music, and theater offerings. The community lacks a place where children or adults can take visual arts classes, although the Pollard Theatre offers some measure of theater involvement for local kids on a case-by-case basis, and also coordinates a subsidized ticket program to increase access to performances.

Arts Scene

Guthrie has what few communities its size have: a year-round, professional theater. The Pollard Theatre, a one-time vaudeville house now owned by the Guthrie Arts & Humanities Council, presents its performances on two stages—a 280-seat main stage and an 80-seat black box that's used for new plays and readings by Oklahoma playwrights. The Pollard stages ten productions during each of its seasons, and since its start several years ago, has earned a strong reputation among Oklahoma City's theater crowd. Little wonder then that the Pollard has become one of the mainstays of the area's cultural tourism economy. On performance nights, not only is the theater itself full, so are many of the town's restaurants and bed and breakfasts. The Pollard has added an orchestra pit that will permit the theater's company of resident actors and actresses to present more musical productions, just the kind of mainstream fare that could draw large audiences from the nearby city. Downtown Guthrie benefits from the Pollard's recognition of the power of theater to contribute to cultural and economic revival.

While a number of professional visual artists live in Guthrie, their main challenge is getting their work into galleries in Eureka Springs or Santa Fe. A few Guthrie businesses exhibit and sell locally created works of art along with the rest of their merchandise, but without a professionally run community arts center, the Guthrie visual arts scene has had difficulty defining itself.

Alternatives

A few local restaurants, including Granny Had One, the Harrison House Inn, and George's exhibit the work of local artists.

Art Perspectives

Betty Bowen, an artist working in mixed media paper, says, "You can sense the community's support for the arts. The businesses consider arts to be a welcome addition to what goes on in Guthrie. The Western artists and the contemporary artists are working together to develop a ten-year cultural plan for the town, and that's going to produce some very positive results. Our biggest need is for a decent place to exhibit our work."

Details

Population: 10,500

Important Arts Events: Sand Plum Festival in June

Must-See Art Galleries: Kaleidoscope Gallery, Naked Buffalo, Oklahoma Territorial Museum

Local Arts Agency: Guthrie Arts & Humanities Council
P.O. Box 38
Guthrie, OK 73044
405/282-7242

Natural Food Store: Garden of Health

Farmer's Market: Farm stands

National Public Radio: KOSU - 90.1 FM

Bookstores: McVickers, Sunlight

Chamber of Commerce: P.O. Box 995
Guthrie, OK 73044
405/282-1947

$\mathbb{A}$ shland, Oregon

Location

Oregon's southwest corner isn't plagued by the soggy weather that dominates the western half of the state—here it can be sunny and mild while on the same day Portland is blasted by a direct-from-the-Arctic storm. That combination may be rare, but Ashland's climate is certainly better than that 100 miles north; it's just perfect for outdoor theater.

Great Outdoors

Ashland is perfectly placed to enjoy Oregon's wealth of natural treasures. The state's best beaches, at Boardman State Park, are a 90-minute drive west. Alpine skiing is at Mt. Ashland (in the Siskiyou Mountains at the edge of town), or at larger areas in the Cascades, about an hour's drive. Crater Lake National Park and 14,000-foot Mt. Shasta are each an hour's drive away. To the south are the Rogue River and Klamath National Forests; the latter teems with remote state parks, redwoods, campgrounds, wilderness areas, and trout streams. North of Ashland the Rogue River National Forest offers lakes, soaring peaks, and the Pacific Crest Trail.

Lifestyle

Ashland's 17,000 residents live in one of America's most diverse and energetic theater communities. Today Ashland supports a half-dozen theater companies as well as performances staged by Southern Oregon State College drama department. The town's cultural tourism lure is strengthened by the recent development of a visual arts scene; now Ashland offers year-round gallery openings, art walks, and studio tours that allow visual artists to support themselves.

A few art galleries in the neighboring commercial center of Medford are starting to do well, but the surprise has been the rapid arts-scene growth in nearby Jacksonville. Jacksonville's historical and children's museums, bed and breakfasts, and annual Peter Britt Music Festival have become major events on the Northwest's music and cultural tourism circuit—all of which help the town's art galleries to flourish.

Ashland derives half of its ticket- and art-buying income from Californians, especially those from the Bay Area, but in recent years Californians relocating to Ashland have turned the real estate market upside down. The community is struggling with issues of growth and affordable housing. It's becoming increasingly less likely to find a two-bedroom place for $135,000.

Art education in Ashland covers basic visual arts, drama, and music, and the Arts Council of Southern Oregon coordinates a regional artist-in-residence program. But the main arts education opportunity is the Oregon Shakespeare Festival, the town's nationally famous performing arts gem. The festival visits the region's public schools and actively recruits onstage and backstage interns—an incredible opportunity that gives Ashland one of the nation's most dynamic performing arts educational programs.

Arts Scene

Ashland is a theater town, through and through. The Oregon Shakespeare Festival, operating from a downtown three-theater complex, draws thousands of spectators as well as the actors, administrators, and technical staff who run the festival's nine-month, 11-play season. It has also generated a talented group of full-time-resident theater pros who have connected with all aspects of the region's arts scene, including the Peter Britt Festival in nearby Jacksonville, the Ashland Community Theatre, and SOSC's theater arts department. Ashland's theater wizards have also started two more thriving professional companies: Oregon Cabaret Theatre is a nightclub dinner theater and comedy revue, while Off Bardway Actors Theatre performs year-round in its own playhouse. Ashland Armory hosts other performing arts groups such as the Rogue Valley Symphony and Ashland Ballet, which presents free summer performances in downtown Ashland's Lithia Park. In winter, touring classical-music soloists and chamber orchestras perform in SOSC's music-building auditorium.

Ashland's visual arts scene owes much of its success to the continued efforts of SOSC's arts faculty, for training local visual arts pros and for exhibiting and selling their own work in the town's galleries. For years SOSC's Schneider Museum of Art has brought first-rate art exhibitions to town and has continuously offered community art education classes. Commercial galleries in Ashland are very healthy, though local artists must find representation in Portland and Seattle to support themselves. The Hanson-Howard Gallery is Ashland's best commercial space, exhibiting nearly 50 painters and craftspeople, most of whom live in the Northwest. Blue Heron Gallery offers an outstanding mix of photography and paintings, and Graven Images is strong in ceramics and prints.

Alternatives

Most of Ashland's restaurants and cafés exhibit local art, especially the 4th Street Gallery & Café, Geppetto's, Plaza Café, and the Ashland Bakery & Café.

Art Perspectives

Denise Kesler, painter and printmaker, says, "Ashland's becoming known for the quality of its visual arts, and things have gotten a lot better here. There are more sales and a lot more people on the Friday night art walks and studio tours. You can make a surprising amount of sales just by keeping your studio open."

Details

Population: 18,000

Important Arts Events: Oregon Shakespeare Festival from February to October, A Taste of Ashland in March, Peter Britt Music Festival from June to September

Must-See Art Galleries: Blue Heron Gallery, Graven Images Gallery, Hanson-Howard Gallery, Schneider Museum of Art, 4th Street Gallery & Café, Websters Handspinners

Local Arts Agency: Arts Council of Southern Oregon
33 N. Central Avenue, Suite 308
Medford, OR 97501-5939
541/779-2820

Natural Food Store: Ashland Community Food Store

Farmer's Market: Tuesday mornings on Water Street

National Public Radio: KSOR - 98.6 FM

Bookstores: Bloomsbury Books, Blue Dragon Bookshop

Chamber of Commerce: P.O. Box 1360 Ashland, OR 97520
541/482-3486

Joseph, Oregon

Location

Oregon's northeast corner is dominated by spectacular natural beauty, from the vistas over-looking the depths of Hell's Canyon to the heights of the Wallowa Mountains, sights that inspire residents of the isolated town of Joseph to call it the Switzerland of America. The town is home to 1,100, a number that includes one of the country's highest concentration of sculptors and all the technical expertise needed to create bronze statuary.

Great Outdoors

Joseph is flanked on two sides by the 10,000-foot peaks of the Wallowas, and on a third by the rugged wilderness of the Hell's Canyon National Recreation Area. There's only one road in and out of town, and even that bumps you up against the Wenaha–Tucannon Wilderness stretch of the Blue Mountains. Hunting and fishing are popular pursuits throughout the region, from Snake River's steelhead and sturgeon to the kokanee salmon in pristine Wallowa Lake. Locals access back-country wilderness areas on horseback using mules or llamas to haul supplies for week-long trips into the mountainous terrain. Many roads in and around Joseph are impassable to vehicles in winter, hence Wallowa County's extensive system of groomed snowmobile trails. Alpine skiing is right in town on Mount Howard, which features a tram running to the top.

Lifestyle

A few years ago, three lumber mills closed their doors to much of the Wallowa Valley's work force, and the region's agricultural and ranching sectors couldn't absorb the fallout. Fortunately, at the same time the area's tourism industry has seen fantastic growth, due mainly to its mounting reputation as a hotbed of bronze sculpture.

Fifteen years ago, the valley's notions about sculpture were limited to something a logger might do in his off-hours with a small chainsaw and a six-pack; but times have changed drastically, and today everyone in the region knows a thing or two about the sculpture process. In fact, artists can now trade their bronze sculptures for services such as plumbing and electrical work, or they can trade a bronze of a horse to a rancher for a live animal. Everyone is suddenly into the arts. That's not to say that the economy has completely recovered. Things are certainly better in Joseph than they've been in quite some time, but the neighboring town of Enterprise is still hurting.

Arts Scene

Valley Bronze, Joseph Art Castings, Parks Bronze, and Age of Bronze—these are the foundries that are bringing Joseph its national arts reputation. They are also part of the reason why the entire end of the valley is riding the crest of an economic resurgence, built on outdoor recreation, second-home buyers, and cultural tourism.

Summers here are a mad, bronze sculpture collecting frenzy, with visitors returning year after year to load up on increasingly larger sculptures at steadily increasing numbers. Valley Bronze, which started the movement in 1982, operates a gallery in Joseph and one in the coastal community of Cannon Beach. The Joseph gallery outsells the other by a three-to-one margin. Its foundry is the area's largest, employing 60 highly skilled technicians and casting bronzes for artists from Alaska to Texas. The other Joseph foundries are also doing well serving a similarly diverse group of artists, from the top realist sculptors of Santa Fe to wildlife sculptors across the nation. Joseph now has a dozen galleries thriving from this unique economic miracle of cultural tourism and sculpture fabrication. An unusual aspect of the surge in gallery openings is that none have gone out of business in the past five years. Meanwhile, galleries in Scottsdale, Santa Fe, Sun Valley, and Aspen are not having the same luck.

Art instruction in local schools is weak, which makes the artist-in-residence program coordinated by the Wallowa Valley Arts Council crucial for children. The council produces an energetic performing arts series using nearby Enterprise's O.K. Theatre for its annual concerts. The concerts feature touring classical, ethnic, and folk musicians, as well as contemporary dance companies from the coast and an annual children's theater production. During summer, an outdoor western melodrama is staged in a local park; in winter months there's a film series at the theater.

Alternatives

Even the convenience store in Joseph has a few bronzes, but be sure to check out the Bank of Wallowa County lobby as well as restaurants such as Cactus Jack's, Vali's Alpine Deli, and the Wagon Wheel.

Art Perspectives

Dave Jackman, a foundry owner, notes, "Artists will either move into the valley to be close to their foundries, or they'll come into town for a couple of weeks to work on one piece. We're four hours from anywhere, but the shipping costs in and out of the valley are surprisingly low."

Gallery owner Donna Butterfield notes, "People living here don't want to see the town grow into a big deal, but it's changing. Our town needs a design review committee. But we have no concepts or plans, nor do we have a budget to do anything about growth."

Details

Population: 1,100

Important Arts Events: Fishtrap Literary Conference in July, Joseph Arts Festival in August

Must-See Art Galleries: Joseph Art Castings, Manuel Museum & Studio, The Art Angle, Valley Bronze, Wallowa Lake Gallery, Wildhorse Gallery

Local Arts Agency: Wallowa Valley Arts Council

P.O. Box 306
Enterprise, OR 97828

Natural Food Store: The Common Good

Farmer's Market: Saturday mornings in Enterprise

National Public Radio: KPBX - 89.5 FM

Bookstores: Bookloft, The Book Corner

Chamber of Commerce: P.O. Box 13
Joseph, OR 97846
541/432-1015

Newport, Oregon

Location

Near the midpoint of the state's western oceanfront and sheltered by Yaquina Bay, Newport enjoys a cultural tourism economy and easy community access to a wide range of visual and performing arts groups. Together, they make for a flourishing art scene in this town of 9,000

Great Outdoors

Oregon's coast is spectacular, from the massive hulk of Haystack Rock at Cannon Beach to the 50-mile stretch of Oregon Dunes National Recreation Area. Surf casting's a favorite way to spend a day at the beach, and sportfishing's an important part of the coastal economy. Siuslaw National Forest wraps around Newport's stretch of the central Oregon coast, offering many state parks and wilderness areas filled with hiking trails, white-water rafting sites, and ocean-side campsites. Within Newport itself are three state parks, Yaquina Bay State Park and Lighthouse, South Beach, and Beverly Beach. Both South Beach and Beverly Beach have campgrounds. The tidal pools at Devil's Punch Bowl State Park and Yaquina Head are great places for kids. Within a two-hour drive of Newport is alpine skiing in the Cascades.

Lifestyle

Swept by wind, soaked by rain, shrouded in fog, or darkened by overcast skies—this is the Pacific Northwest. Artists move here because they're inspired by the ocean, and Newport's strong arts community is the cultural nugget that tips the scale in its favor over other coastal towns.

Newport still maintains a small fishing fleet, but Coos Bay to the south harbors most of the serious commercial fishers. If you want access to the town, but need a windbreak before you, visit Toledo, about ten miles inland. Several artists have renovated this historic town's old commercial buildings and opened studios and galleries.

Newport's schools, like the rest of Oregon's, have suffered from cutbacks in state funding. Visual arts, music, and drama classes are taught by both arts-trained teachers and through the state-funded artist-in-residence program. Newport is exceptional among small art towns for its First Resort education program that tracks artistically gifted high school students into a special arts-centered curriculum. Newport's also home to a pair of marine science institutions, The Oregon Coast Aquarium and the Hatfield Marine Science Center. Home prices have escalated sharply in recent years; it's now tough to find a place for less than $100,000.

Arts Scene

The town's visual arts scene is dominated by the exhibitions and arts education programs taking place at the Newport Visual Arts Center. The center rotates local and regional work in its two exhibition galleries and holds classes year-round in its three studio spaces. The center also operates a photo lab and an arts resource library. The Yaquina Arts Center is the home base for Newport's more traditional seascape painters, and on occasion it exhibits historical work on loan from other institutions. It also exhibits the art of its members.

Newport's cultural tourism economy supports a number of commercial gallery spaces, some of which specialize in typical seashore watercolors that you can find from Maine to Alaska, while others try to do something different and contemporary. Oceanic Arts has a strong reputation for exhibiting fine crafts, and both the Freed Gallery and Patricia Williams Gallery are worth a look. North of Newport, the town of Glendenen Beach has the area's best commercial gallery, the Salishan Lodge, as well as a few other strong galleries. Nearby Toledo has sprouted several good art galleries, especially the one operated by renowned landscape master painter Michael Gibbons.

Just a few short blocks from the visual arts center, across the street from a public sculpture garden and Newport's Vietnam Memorial, is the Newport Performing Arts Center, a facility that presents an incredible range of music, theater, dance, lectures, and literary readings in its 450-seat Silverman Theater and its 125-seat Studio Theater black box. The Yaquina Orchestra performs on the mainstage, while chamber groups use the Studio Theater. The center presents many touring musical acts, from ethnic and blues to classical musicians; touring dance companies form an important component of the center's mainstage presentations. Children's theater and comedy make their way onto the mainstage as well, along with a foreign film series during the winter months. Newport's two theater groups, the Porthole Players and the Red Octopus Theater Company, use the center for Porthole's mainstream performances and Red Octopus' experimental work. Newport's main music event of the year is the Ernest Bloch Festival, which brings contemporary composers, visiting orchestras, and chamber musicians into town for a series of shows at the Performing Arts Center and at outdoor venues.

Alternatives

Artists exhibit their work at restaurants all over town, but especially at places like Canyon Way, Bayfront Brewery, and Whales Tale.

Art Perspectives

Christina Platz, painter and printmaker: "There are always lots of artists moving into and out of town. They say they move here for the ocean, then they say they leave here because of the weather. What do they expect?"

Details

Population: 9,000

Important Arts Events: Paper Arts Festival in April, Art Bridge in summer, Ernest Bloch Festival in July, Give Art in November

Must-See Art Galleries: Cedric Brown Gallery, Freed Gallery, Michael Gibbons Gallery, Newport Visual Arts Center, Oceanic Arts, Patricia Williams Gallery, Yaquina Arts Center

Local Arts Agency: Newport Visual Arts Center
839 N.W. Beach Drive

Newport, OR 97365
503/265-6540

Natural Food Store: Oceana

Farmer's Market: Saturday mornings in Performing Arts Center parking lot

National Public Radio: KLCC - 90.5 FM

Bookstores: Canyon Way Books, Sylvia Beach Hotel, The Bookend

Chamber of Commerce: 555 S.W. Coast Highway
Newport, OR 97365
503/265-8801

Carnegie, Pennsylvania

Location

The Pittsburgh borough of Carnegie is a nondescript but affordable community with a small-town feel. In recent years Carnegie and its industrial neighbors have been losing residents and looking for ways to pull up their economic bootstraps. Pittsburgh has transformed itself into a modern and livable city; now Carnegie is hoping to become its artsy alternative community.

Great Outdoors

Pittsburgh's parks, zoo, arboretum, and riverfront bicycle trails are within easy reach of Carnegie. But if you want something other than an urban outdoor experience, you've got to drive some distance to find it. Carnegie is a couple of hours from any significant state park, national forest, or ski area. The closest beaches are several hours distant, and the closest lakes are very crowded during the warm summer months.

Lifestyle

Although Carnegie residents put up with some of the city's problems (crime, airport noise, rush hour traffic), they benefit from living so close to Pittsburgh. Opera, professional sports, nightlife, fantastic libraries, and art museums, including the Andy Warhol Museum, are right in their backyard. And Carnegie is affordable—nice homes can be found for well under $80,000. While a Carnegie address is not yet considered desirable, things are changing. Artists from Pittsburgh are quietly moving to its downtown area, where industrial loft studio space is affordable and available. In fact, second-story studio development is one of the real success stories taking place in Carnegie's small business district.

Arts Scene

Long-time residents are amazed at the transformation taking place in Carnegie: it's turning into an arts town. Public art works—bizarre benches and planters designed by local artists—have become fixtures along the community's downtown streets, and an even more extensive public arts project is in the works. Galleries have opened along Carnegie's downtown streets, drawing people for exhibition openings. But Carnegie's revival as an arts community has been so sudden that in many ways local government is trying to play catch-up.

Each September the town stages the Arts and Ethnic Heritage Festival, which focuses on traditional Irish, Scottish, and Ukrainian dance and music. The community's visual artists participate by exhibiting works at the local Ukrainian Orthodox Church.

Performing arts are staged in the Andrew Carnegie Free Library's 850-seat auditorium, a miniature version of New York's Carnegie Hall. The local theater company, Stage 62, and the Pittsburgh Civic Orchestra use Carnegie Music Hall for their performances. One of the arts council's pet projects is a summer residency for a Russian ballet company, which moves into town to perform at the Carnegie and offers classes for children.

Alternatives

With a major art market right at their doorstep, Carnegie's artists need not travel far to find galleries, museums, and alternative exhibition spaces for their work. While coffeebars and restaurants in Pittsburgh are snatching up the work of talented Carnegie artists, local places have yet to catch on. If you're in Carnegie at night, duck into PaPa J's, the Pour House, or Red Hots and you'll always find an artist or two hanging out.

Art Perspectives

Ron Desmett, a sculptor and painter involved in Carnegie's public art project, says the community's potential lies in its ability to continue renovating its downtown. "Carnegie's on the brink. Once it completes what it wants to do with its streets, retail storefronts, and public art, it could become one of the country's greatest public art sites. For a little town to have such broad vision is unique. Carnegie is fortunate to have so many creative people who are willing to help rebuild the community."

Philip Salvato, a painter whose gallery and studio spaces occupy a three-story building in downtown Carnegie, says the community's arts awareness is on the upswing. "Just having the artists here in town, walking down the city streets, changes the attitude of the entire community. The sales we're making from the gallery have really surprised us. We came here just expecting to run a business and now we're finding ourselves in the middle of rebuilding a community. People are coming here from across the state because they've heard about the arts experience in Carnegie."

Details

Population: 9,500

Important Arts Events: Candlelight Arts Auction in May, Arts and Heritage Festival in September

Must-See Art Galleries: Black Swan Gallery

Local Arts Agency: Carnegie Area Revitalization Effort
311 East Main Street
Carnegie, PA 15106
412/279-8822

Farmer's Market: Saturday mornings at post office parking lot

National Public Radio: KQED - 90.5 FM

Bookstores: In nearby malls

Chamber of Commerce:
986 Brodhead Road
Moon Township, PA 15108
412/264-6270

Easton, Pennsylvania

Location

From Easton's perch along the eastern edge of Pennsylvania, most of the Northeast's cultural resources are within easy reach. Philadelphia is an hour south, Manhattan is just 90 minutes east, Washington, D.C. is three hours south, and the Jersey shore is just an hour away, if you hurry.

Great Outdoors

Easton is on the fringe of a metro region that includes Allentown and Bethlehem, and is downriver from the Delaware Water Gap National Recreation Area, one of the nation's most spectacular natural resources. With campgrounds, part of the Appalachian Trail, fishing holes, and bike trails, the Gap is a favorite place for an extended outdoor experience. Two nearby lakes, Beltzville and Nockamixon, are the best alternatives for summer water sports if you can't make the drive to the Jersey shore. During winter months, there's skiing in the Pocono Mountains, about an hour's drive west.

Lifestyle

Easton hit tough economic times in the late 1960s and '70s, and if not for hometown hero and heavyweight boxing champ Larry Holmes, there wouldn't have been anything to cheer about for almost 30 years. Today the community feels its future is bright, even though the economy still has much of the Lehigh Valley in shambles.

Downtown Easton was once a prosperous place, and much of its commercial infrastructure is still intact, even if many of its retailers have moved into regional malls. For the past five years or so, dozens of artists, fed up with the city life in Soho and Philadelphia, have relocated to the industrial loft space of their dreams in Easton's plentiful, empty, turn-of-the-century, brick commercial buildings. One of Easton's largest employers, Binney & Smith—the company that makes Crayola crayons—is opening a visitors center geared to children's science and art exhibits. Easton's economic development leaders are hoping that the Crayola center and the presence of a fast-growing community of artists will bring other arts-oriented businesses into town. A National Heritage Corridor visitors center is going in across the street from Crayola, and a block away there's the Hugh Moore Historic Park, a canal museum and horse-drawn canal boat ride exhibit that's part of the heritage corridor project.

Living in Easton is not a terribly expensive proposition, with average-sized homes going for $100,000. Loft spaces cost about half that, although there is some worry that those prices will increase once the downtown redevelopment project takes off.

Arts Scene

A number of commercial gallery spaces are opening in Easton, but the community's premier exhibition space is the Williams Arts Center Gallery on the campus of Lafayette College. The gallery exhibits a top-shelf range of contemporary work, as well as touring masterworks exhibitions, contemporary craft shows, and international master artists who participate in the campus artist-in-residence programs. Occasionally, Easton's State Theatre exhibits visual arts in their gallery space, but the downtown scene is focused mainly on two types of presentations: the in-studio, semi-private shows that the new artist community stages in their upstairs lofts, and the downtown commercial gallery shows. Some of Easton's more popular galleries include The Gallery, Connexions, Cascadia, Karl Stirner, the Sign of the Carpenter, The Frame, and Blue Easle

Easton is well-endowed in the performing arts realm, primarily due to Lafayette College's energetic programming in its 400-seat Williams Art Center Theatre, and the popular music and comedy programs that take place at the State Theatre. The State Theatre, a restored, 1500-seat Vaudeville, promotes acts ranging from B.B. King and Michael Feinstein to touring Broadway shows and the occasional opera. The Williams Theatre's shows include all types of acts, from classical and jazz music to touring contemporary dance companies, plus student theater productions and a New Horizons festival that pulls in experimental urban work from across the nation. During the summer months, the town sponsors a series of free outdoor concerts in its Riverside Park Amphitheater, and occasionally there are performances at Eddyside Park. Also in the summer, Allentown hosts an outdoor Shakespeare festival.

Alternatives

Pearly Baker's Alehouse is Easton's favorite hangout and local arts alternative exhibition space Bethlehem Bagel Co. also displays the work of Easton artists, as does Weidbachers, a new microbrewery. Todd's Café and Ferry St. Café are also involved in the Easton arts scene-

Art Perspectives

Michiko Okaya, director of the Williams Arts Center Gallery: "I'm meeting more and more artists who are moving into town, and that's great. Easton's off to a positive start, and even though things are moving more slowly than we would like, change is taking place in a very positive way. For us to become a thriving arts center, we need more artists."

Chris Camacho, a sculptor, credits Easton's beauty for his move here. "I live in the College Hill neighborhood, which is by Lafayette College, and it's just beautiful here. People are restoring these old Victorians, and the town's really starting to look great. It's going on one building at a time, but nonetheless, its going on all over town."

Details

Population: 26,000

Important Arts Events: Canal Festival in June, Riverside Amphitheater music series in June and July, Heritage Days in July, Pet Parade in August

Must-See Art Galleries: Cascadia, Connexions, Karl Stirner Gallery, Williams Art Center Gallery

Local Arts Agency: State Theatre Center for the Arts
453 Northampton Street

Easton, PA 18042
610/252-3132

Natural Food Store: Nature's Way

Farmer's Market: Upstream Farm

National Public Radio: WDIY - 88.1 FM

Bookstore: The Quadrant

Chamber of Commerce: 157 South Fourth Street
Easton, PA 18042
610/253-4211

Westerly, Rhode Island

Location

An out-of-the-way town with a strong arts community and tremendous potential for cultural tourism, Westerly is just a few minutes' drive from both the Block Island Sound to the south, and the Connecticut border to the east. In the southwest corner of Rhode Island, the town is two hours from New York City and an hour away from Boston.

Great Outdoors

Recreationally speaking, this part of New England leans toward the ocean, enticed by the string of public beaches and the vacation retreat of Block Island, a short ferry ride offshore. Some of the beachfront has been ruined by development, but untouched stretches still remain to keep tourists and locals happy. Skiing and white-water kayaking are a long drive away in western Massachusetts. Winters are mild by New England standards, with ice storms more common than blizzards.

Lifestyle

Westerly was once famed for its thriving community of Italian stone masons. Those talented artisans left behind an enduring architectural legacy and a local population that's nearly as homogenous as a Tuscan village. In fact, 67 percent of Westerly's residents are Italian Americans, and there are more pizza parlors in this town than there are lawyers—a sign of civic health if there ever was one! Westerly has several fraternal organizations dedicated to promoting the cultural and social identity of this dominant ethnic group.

A rural community of 22,000, Westerly is almost as much a part of Connecticut as it is Rhode Island. But taxes are lower and homes are more affordable on the Rhode Island side; the average residence sells for about $100,000. Westerly was down on its luck not too long ago, leaving many vacant storefronts in the downtown area. The situation and its potential caught the attention and imagination of dozens of artists from Providence, the Rhode Island School of Design, and from out of state. Their arrival reanimated what, up until that point, had been a fairly hidebound, working-class town. Now, word about Westerly's affordability and attractive natural setting has piqued the interest of even more artists, this time from New York, New Haven, and Boston. More artists, more ideas, more energy, and more promise for the future all seem to be converging in Westerly at the same time, making this a small art town worth keeping your eye on.

Arts Scene

Westerly's performing arts are surprisingly strong. The Colonial Theatre draws thousands of visitors during its mainstage season from April to September. During the last part of July, there's a free Shakespeare production in Wilcox Park, an 18-acre blanket of green that also hosts the Summer Pops Concert (and huge fireworks show) sponsored by the Chorus of Westerly. The Chorus programs most of its events during the winter and spring months, using its own auditorium as a venue. Musica Dolce, which also uses the Chorus Performance Hall, presents a series of classical music and chamber concerts through the winter, and Jazzman Productions stages the Industrial Trust series of concerts in the studios of sculptor Lowell Reiland.

The town's main visual arts venues are the Artists' Cooperative Gallery and the Hoxie Gallery inside the public library. Both exhibition spaces focus on local artists, and the recently established Westerly Arts Network publishes a calendar listing their events. The community is working to establish a summer festival of performing and visual arts, as there's not yet a major arts weekend on Westerly's calendar to attract buyers to the town's galleries. For now, most artists open their studios by appointment. The challenge to living here is locating out-of-area markets for art, as Westerly's visual arts reputation is still developing. One gift shop sells a photographer's work, and a frame shop sells some originals, but Westerly could use some gallery entrepreneurship to further its cultural tourism economy.

Alternatives

Woody's Café is the most popular daytime hangout because the food's great and local artists hang their work on its walls. After spending the earlier part of the evening at the Colonial, most of the creative types repair to the Haversham Inn or Stillwater Tavern for theatre or some other arts event. Vocatura's Pizza is either the best or second-best in town, depending on who you're talking to.

Art Perspectives

Sylvia Severance, a children's book illustrator, moved to Westerly from Manhattan several years ago. One of the brightest spots on the local arts map, she says, is a recent commitment by the Rhode Island School of Design to offer extension art classes in a local school building.

"The Arts Network has gone a long ways in pulling the local arts community together, and now we're starting to coordinate our plans and plan our events so as not to overlap with each other's . . . What we need to do in the near future is improve the involvement of the locals in events taking place in the arts community. There's a need for more enthusiasm, which would help to raise attendance levels at exhibitions and at the Colonial Theatre."

Details

Population: 22,000

Important Arts Events: Twelfth Night Celebration in January, Summer Pops Concert in June, Shakespeare in the Park in July

Must-See Art Galleries: Hoxie Gallery, Industrial Trust Studio Gallery, Westerly Artists Cooperative Gallery

Local Arts Agency: Westerly Artists Cooperative
12 High Street
Westerly, RI 02891
401/596-2020

Natural Food Store: Sandy's Fruits & Vegetables

Farmer's Market: Saturday mornings downtown

National Public Radio: WCTY - 89.9 FM

Bookstore: Bookworks

Chamber of Commerce: 74 Post Road
Westerly, RI 02891
401/596-7761

Beaufort, South Carolina

Location

Beaufort, a historic town that's been ruled by nearly every European colonial power with a respectable navy, fronts on the Intracoastal Waterway just 20 miles inland from the Atlantic coast. This town of 10,000 residents sits in what once was the nation's rice-growing center, the Lowcountry of South Carolina. Summer seems to last all year, punctuated by occasional hurricanes and winter chills. Charleston and Savannah are about an hour away.

Great Outdoors

This is boating country, and water sports from sailing and canoeing to deep-sea fishing attract people who have a few hours or a weekend to kill. South Carolina's beaches are legendary for their beauty, and in this part of the state they're also blissfully uncrowded. The Beaufort region offers state parks, campgrounds, lighthouses, golf courses, wildlife preserves, and even a few freshwater lakes for the bass crowd. Even during the chilliest parts of winter you can do almost everything outdoors that you can do in summer, but without having to worry about mosquitoes.

Lifestyle

Beaufort has always been prosperous, first from its cotton and rice economies and more recently from its association with the two military bases just outside of town. Charleston and Hilton Head are both within driving distance, boosting cultural tourism and giving Beaufort artists additional prospects for sales and arts festivals. Beaufort schools are outstanding examples of how progressive administrators and teachers can integrate arts education into all grade levels, and the town's arts education is a source of civic pride. String instrument programs, dance instruction, drama (full-time dance and drama teachers are in all middle and high schools), choral singing, piano, and visual arts programs all start in kindergarten. Upon reaching high school, Beaufort students have been studying fine arts and performing arts for ten years; and high school offers a broad range of professionally-taught arts programs—programs so sophisticated they put many university arts departments to shame.

Housing costs in Beaufort are very affordable ($60,000 starters, abundant rentals), and taxes are reasonable, especially when you consider the kinds of schools, parks, and access to the arts that come with living here.

Arts Scene

Beaufort has everything: a strong arts council plugged into every corner of the region's arts scene; a dynamic local university with serious programs of visual, performing, and music events; a popular community theater company; a dance company that stages its own productions and presents top national acts; an African American arts center (Penn Center of Sea Island) offering visual and performing arts; a 474-seat performing arts center (at the University of South Carolina at Beaufort) that hosts the community's dynamic arts groups; and a months-long series of free concerts in the town's Waterfront Park. There's also a history museum at the Beaufort Arsenal, and one of America's finest gospel choruses at the First

African Baptist Church. All arts programming in Beaufort is geared toward community-wide cultural celebration and enrichment, and it all makes a point of including Beaufort's indigenous (Gullah) African American population.

With so much going on in the performing arts, you might expect a negligible visual arts scene. The community is not yet able to call itself a gallery center, but Beaufort offers the right combination of living conditions and cultural connections that make it attractive to relocating artists. The town's growing reputation as a great source for visual art is also enabling an increasing number of artists to support themselves by selling their work locally. Nearly thirty of Beaufort's visual artists operate their studios as galleries, and several commercial galleries also represent successful regional artists. As in most seacoast communities, local landscapes are the big sellers; but several Beaufort galleries also represent the region's African American basketry traditions. Many contemporary African American artists call Beaufort home, and their work covers an intriguing range of paintings and sculpture. The only things Beaufort lacks are an energetic artists' cooperative gallery and a sophisticated, nationally connected commercial gallery. The university art gallery hosts touring exhibitions as well as regular one-artist shows by the Lowcountry's top professionals.

Alternatives

In the kind of town where everyone from the mayor to commercial fishermen are enthusiastic about the arts, everything is an alternative, and nothing is an alternative—precisely because in Beaufort, art is everywhere. Restaurants feature local art on their walls, as do bank lobbies. Plum's, Emily's, and Blackstone's Café are the favorites among the artsy crowd.

Art Perspectives

Suzanne and Eric Longo moved here from New Orleans to open a gallery and pursue their art careers. "Our work is contemporary, so its a little out of sync with what you normally find here," says Suzanne. "But word's getting out that all sorts of art is being created here, and people are coming into town to take a look. Out-of-town people are very surprised when they come into our gallery, and their impression is that art here is a very good value."

Details

Population: 10,000

Important Arts Events: Beaufort Art Association Spring Show in March, Gullah Festival in May, Water Festival Fine Art Show in July, Penn Center Heritage Days in November

Must-See Art Galleries: Frogmore Frolics Gallery, Gallery One, Red Piano Too, The Craftseller, University of South Carolina at Beaufort Gallery

Local Arts Agency: Arts Council of Northern Beaufort County
801 Carteret Street

Beaufort, SC 29902
803/521-4144

Natural Food Store: The Herb Pantry

Farmer's Market: Tuesday, Thursday, and Saturday at Waterfront Park

National Public Radio: WJWJ - 89.1 FM

Bookstores: Bay Street Trading Co., Firehouse Books

Chamber of Commerce: 1006 Bay Street Beaufort, SC 29901
803/524-3163

Mitchell, South Dakota

Location

The southeast corner of South Dakota is the most densely populated section of the state. In many ways, the area thinks of itself as an extension of eastern Nebraska. Mitchell is strongly influenced by the regional population center of Omaha, a four-hour drive from town.

Great Outdoors

Mitchell prides itself on being the pheasant hunting capital of South Dakota. Between October and January, the ringneck season brings thousands of hunters to the area, along with substantial profits for the region's tourist-dependent hotels, restaurants, and gun shops. More than 200 of the region's farmers work with the local Conservation Reserve Program to provide food for starving pheasants during the winter months.

The focal point for the region's summer recreation is the Missouri River. The state parks are popular as well, strung along the banks of Lewis and Clark Lake. The lake is known for its fishing, which includes bass, walleye, bluegill, and perch. Ski areas in the Black Hills, 300 miles west of Mitchell, are the most accessible winter recreation areas, unless you count the beginners' hills along the Minnesota border two hours east.

Lifestyle

Mitchell is home to Dakota Wesleyan University, which supports a few student-oriented bars and restaurants, notably Cisco's Deli and the Cottonwood Canyon Coffee House. Once a prosperous farming town, Mitchell's economy now merely survives during the roller coaster cycles of the agricultural industry's ups and downs. But the infrastructure created by the good times is still in place, including the community's 14 parks, the Lake Mitchell recreation area, the Corn Palace, and several museums.

Located just across the street from the Enchanted World Doll Museum, the Corn Palace is a multi-purpose agricultural exhibition hall, convention center, and performing arts building. It's Moorish exterior is decorated with mosaics made from thousands of bushels of corn cobs, rye grasses, straw, and wheat.

On the Dakota Wesleyan campus is the Museum of American Indian and Pioneer Life, with a gallery dedicated to the works of the region's master artists. Mitchell's Boehnen Museum, located on the grounds of an ancient Native American settlement. It exhibits historical artifacts and some contemporary Native American work done using traditional techniques.

The most unusual exhibition space in town is the Soukup & Thomas Balloon Museum, South Dakota's version of the National Air and Space Museum. It covers everything from French hot air ballooning in the eighteenth-century to videos of the Hindenburg crash.

Arts Scene

Mitchell's visual arts community revolves around the Oscar Howe Art Center, a red granite structure with three gallery spaces, classrooms, a WPA mural by Oscar Howe, and a permanent collection of his work. The center devotes half its annual exhibitions schedule to art created by Native American painters, sculptors, potters, and basketmakers. Because South Dakota is home to the Sioux, showing the Sioux's culture and talents in the center's exhibition space is only natural. The rest of the visual arts in Mitchell revolves around the historical work exhibited in the town's museums and the town's Summer Solstice Art Festival.

Mitchell's performing arts groups use several spaces, including the Corn Palace, the Oscar Howe Art Center, and the 900-seat Historic State Theater—a partially restored art deco landmark. The Area Community Theater uses the State Theater for its four yearly productions, as does the town's annual Community Concert Series, which brings in touring orchestras and chamber music performers during the winter. There's an effort in Mitchell to have the local arts groups and municipal government take over the theater and turn it into a self-sustaining performance center, a far-sighted plan that could turn Mitchell into a dynamic arts community.

The Community Theater also runs a children's theater program that presents one play annually. Mitchell's public schools do a mediocre job of exposing local children to innovative art education programs, but the Oscar Howe Art Center, located in what once was Mitchell's Carnegie Library, holds children's art education classes year-round, exhibiting their creations in one of the center's three galleries.

Alternatives
Folk and jazz performances are held every weekend at the Cottonwood Canyon Coffee House. Cottonwood also hangs local art on its walls, as does Cisco's Deli.

Art Perspectives
Jeffrey Morrison, an installations artist, feels his work has been influenced by the Midwestern landscape. He believes that Mitchell is a good place to launch an arts career: "I don't know why it is, but in the past two years we've been seeing art dealers and gallery owners from New York and Washington, D.C. come through town looking at local art. Maybe they want something that's rural, that's completely American—and there's plenty of that here. To survive in Mitchell, I've had to develop gallery contacts in Omaha, Minneapolis, and Sioux Falls. When you live in South Dakota you learn how to view the entire state as one, sprawling small town. That's why we think nothing of driving 200 miles to attend another artist's show."

Details
Population: 14,000

Important Art Events: Summer Solstice Arts Festival in June, On Common Ground Agricultural Art Exposition in September, Tour de Corn in September

Must-See Art Galleries: Case Art Gallery, Oscar Howe Art Center galleries, Patton Gallery

Local Arts Agency: Mitchell Area Arts Council
Oscar Howe Art Center
P.O. Box 1161
Mitchell, SD 57301
605/996-4111

Natural Food Store: Wayne & Mary's

Farmer's Market: Casey's farm stand in summer and fall

National Public Radio: 91.1 - KTSD FM

Bookstore: The Reader's Den

Chamber of Commerce: 601 North Main Street
Mitchell, SD 57301
605/996-5567

Woodbury, Tennessee

Location

While less than an hour's drive from the Nashville airport, Woodbury seems as isolated and rural as places several hundred miles from a metro area. The peaceful, low hills of central Tennessee have hundreds of years of crafts traditions, but in the past few years a new generation of artists has moved into the Woodbury area, attracted by its low cost of living, moderate climate, and easy way of life.

Great Outdoors

If there's one drawback to this community, it's the somewhat long distances you have to travel before reaching lakes, parks, and back-country campgrounds. That's not to say there aren't wide open spaces. The 2,300 residents are so spread out, it's a wonder they're able to keep in touch with each other. During the warmer months (April to October), Center Hill Lake in neighboring De Kalb County is the closest place to hoist a sail or cast a line.

Lifestyle

"Every business in town uses the Cannon County Arts Center in its marketing—it's a real source of pride to the people here," says Donald Fann, the center's astute and well-connected director. And indeed, living in Woodbury means being part of what happens at the center, a 13,000-square-foot facility housing classrooms, visual arts exhibition spaces, a 250-seat hall, and even a sculpture park (featuring contemporary three-dimensional work, no less!) on its manicured grounds. The region's school district has embraced the center's and Fann's innovative programs for kids, turning Woodbury's schools into one of the state's up-and-coming bright spots for comprehensive arts education.

Before the arts center was even a dream, Woodbury already had a claim to national fame in its white oak basketry and chair-making traditions. These traditional yet elegant craft forms are among the nation's most sought-after, and today Woodbury craftspeople are no strangers to art dealers and gallery owners from across the nation who journey here to discover new talent and buy everything in sight at local crafts shows.

Life here is quiet, studious, and completely family oriented—perfect for the dedicated crafts professional who wants to live and work in affordable tranquility. Homes in Woodbury on wooded, two-acre parcels are easy to find in the $70,000 range. The college town of Murfreesboro is just 20 miles to the west, providing Woodbury's residents with all the pizza joints and shopping centers they could ever desire.

Arts Scene

Everything here centers around activities at the arts center, which programs events ranging from Woodbury's annual Black History Celebration to local dance and choral performances to the annual gathering of the Sons of Confederate Veterans. By opening itself to all of Woodbury's residents, the Cannon County Arts Center makes itself a model of community inclusiveness; everyone can participate. There's no snootiness, no rivalries, and no limits on who can do what for how long and at what time.

While several accomplished painters live in the Woodbury area, fine crafts remain the primary draw on the local arts scene. Everyone around here freely acknowledges the debt Woodbury owes to its traditional artisans, and in large part the arts center's recent expansion stems from the need to instruct a new generation of craftspeople. The nearby community of Smithville is home to the Appalachian Center for Crafts, a branch of Tennessee Tech that programs a year-round series of classes and workshops bringing master artisans into Smithville to teach local artists crafts ranging from wax molding for jewelers to hot glass sculpting to fiber arts to ceramics. For professional artists living here, the arts center gives them an important and accessible vehicle for contributing to Woodbury's civic life. While local sales outside of the annual crafts festival are minimal, the arts markets of Nashville, Atlanta, St. Louis, and Charleston are important sales outlets.

Alternatives

In a way, everything in Woodbury is an alternative. If it's big-name entertainment or pro sports you're looking for, Nashville is in easy reach. Murfreesboro has interesting historic museums. In Woodbury, Joe's Place and the Main Street Deli both feature local art on their walls.

Art Perspectives

Arlene Knaak, a sculptural ceramicist, learned her craft at the Appalachian Center for Crafts. "We're just 20 miles from Smithville, so it's easy to drive over there and learn from the great artists they get to teach classes. . . . You can go to buy supplies, to show your work in a gallery, and to meet the other artists living around here.

"Our arts center in Woodbury has made all of us aware of the strong arts traditions that are already here, even if in years past these crafts were done for practical, as opposed to artistic, reasons. The art center's playhouse is important, the art classes are important, and what happens over there helps to make all of us better at what we're doing. Woodbury's small, quiet, and safe. It's a great place to live."

Details

Population: 2,300

Important Arts Events: White Oak Country Crafts Fair in August

Must-See Art Galleries: Appalachian Center for Crafts Gallery, Cannon County Arts Center Gallery

Local Arts Agency: Cannon County Arts Center
P.O. Box 111
Woodbury, TN 37190
615/563-2787

Farmer's Market: Many farm stands throughout the region

National Public Radio: WPLN - 90.3 FM

Bookstore: Williams Booksellers, in Murfreesboro

City Hall:
102 Tatum Street
Woodbury, TN 37190
615/563-5021

Albany, Texas

Location

Once a military outpost on the Texas frontier, the small, 2,000-resident art town of Albany sits on the broad, flat plains of the state's north-central region, about two hours from Dallas to the east and the Hill Country to the south.

Great Outdoors

If you're standing at the top of Albany's Shackelford County Courthouse, the only thing that blocks your view is the flat horizon. Hubbard Creek Reservoir, outside Albany, is a 15,000-acre magnet for bass fishermen, water-skiers, and campers from across the state. Possum Kingdom State Park, just east of Hubbard Creek Reservoir, is the region's most popular campground. Fort Griffin State Historical Park, an 1860s military installation north of Albany, is filled with the remains of its brick buildings and serves as Albany's annual excuse for the Fort Griffin Fandangle, the local version of Mardi Gras. Gulf Coast beaches at Corpus Christi are a half day's drive south, and New Mexico's mountains are a longer drive west.

Lifestyle

Imagine you live in a small town in the middle of Texas. You need a little brain stimulation, some culture, something to broaden your horizons and make life more interesting. You've always wanted to check out a Thomas Hart Benton, or a Modigliani, or even a Miró, and you don't want to spend the time and money to get to the Kimbell Art Museum in faraway Fort Worth. So whatcha gonna do? In Albany, all you do is stroll down to the town's 1878 jail and ask to be incarcerated in art heaven. With the help Albany's oil- and ranching-rich civic leaders, the old limestone structure has been transformed into The Old Jail Art Center, a unique outpost of Asian, American, European, and pre-Columbian art smack in the middle of town. The privately supported institution, soon to expand to 14,000 square feet, has turned Albany from a forgotten spot on a straight two-lane blacktop into a must-see on any cultural tourist's Texas itinerary.

When it first opened as an art museum in 1980, the Old Jail's main purpose was to give local millionaires a place to show off parts of their art collections. Soon, a friendly competition developed to see who could spend the most on a painting or sculpture by an internationally famous artist. And since this is Texas, the only honorable way to deal with a spectacular art acquisition was to give it to the Old Jail. The museum's collection became so large that the only sensible thing to do was to solicit donations to finance an expansion project, creating—you guessed it—so much new space that as soon as the last brick settled into place, local well-moneyed art patrons stampeded (by Lear jet) to Christie's next round of art auctions. The Old Jail benefits from this cordial rivalry, and so does everyone who walks through its doors.

Art Scene

Ten years have passed since the Old Jail's last expansion project, and an Albany art-collectors' catastrophe has been narrowly avoided with the 1996 start of a new, 7,000-square-foot expansion project. With 1,300 masterworks in its present permanent collection, the Old Jail's four existing galleries will add three new galleries as well as a new art library, video production and viewing center, and learning center for its expansive education programs. Much of the new wing is dedicated to art storage facilities

The Old Jail Art Museum has now become the Old Jail Art Center, and its horizons have changed as well. In addition to its permanent collection, the center also organizes an energetic schedule of one-artist and touring national and regional shows by painters, sculptors, and fine craftspeople. Most of this work is contemporary and quite different from what you would expect to see in a small art town's museum. The Old Jail also plays a central role in Albany's arts education programs, coordinating an ongoing lecture series that brings in top curators from around the Southwest. It sponsors everything from Family Art Hour to classes in kite-making and community field trips to Texas art museums. The Old Jail offers a July art camp for elementary schoolkids, an in-school art appreciation program called "My Dog Could Do That" for high-school students, and in-school artist residencies for middle school and high school art classes. The community also awards scholarships to Albany high school seniors who want to pursue art education in college.

Alternatives

Albany's gloriously restored 1927 movie house, the Aztec Theatre, is this can-do community's latest point of civic pride. Local business and civic leaders raised the money needed to revive the 285-seat Aztec, and it's now used for everything from historical lectures to classical music recitals and kids' theater shows. The Fort Griffin Fandangle is an outdoor summer theater pageant produced by an all-volunteer local committee and staged at Prairie Theatre, a natural amphitheater. The Fandangle's six evening performances draw thousands to Albany every June

Art Perspectives

Jolien Magoto, the director of the Old Jail Art Center, says, "There aren't too many artists in town, but we bring a lot of visiting artists in for programs. Our largest audience comes in from Abeline. We're developing more performing arts here in Albany, and the museum is now stepping out in front as co-sponsor of some performances at the Aztec."

Details

Population: 2,000

Important Arts Events: Exhibition opening nights at Old Jail Art Center, Fort Griffin Fandangle in June

Must-See Art Galleries: The Old Jail Art Center

Local Arts Agency: The Old Jail Art Center
Rt. One, Box One

Albany, TX 76430
915/762-2269

Farmer's Market: Farm trucks park along Main Street in summer months

National Public Radio: KERA - 90.1 FM

Bookstore: The Lynch Line

Chamber of Commerce: P.O. Box 1581 Albany, TX 76430
915/762-2525

Alpine, Texas

Location

The spectacularly beautiful Big Bend region of Texas is unlike any other part of the country. It's still very cowboy yet quite Mexican as well. Filled with enormous, empty vistas, it somehow attracts an off-kilter group of artists who come here either to earn their living from the local tourist market or to just do their own creative thing in peace.

Great Outdoors

Alpine's 6,200 full-time residents and 1,200 college students live at the edge of Big Bend National Park. Its 1,250 square miles of rugged desert terrain are bounded on the south by the Rio Grande River and Chihuahua, Mexico's sparsely populated ranching state. Inside the park's boundaries, the Chisos Mountains are filled with hiking trails winding their way up 7,000-foot mountains. To the north are the Davis Mountains, a surprisingly green, forested region whose 8,000-foot peaks are the home of the historic Ft. Davis and its Buffalo Soldiers' memorial. Nearby, the Chihuahuan Desert Research Institute is a unique nature center with hiking trails, a desert arboretum, and a shop selling cacti. The region's old U.S. Cavalry outposts at Forts Lancaster, Leaton, and Stockton remind us that Big Bend's frontier days are not long past.

Lifestyle

Once a mining region whose major industry shifted to ranching in the 1930s, Big Bend is still very much a cattleman's kind of place. But national and state park tourism has diversified the economy, giving local galleries and artists access to cultural tourism's cash flow. Each of the Big Bend region's small towns accommodate at least a couple of art galleries, some representing local work, others importing art from cultural hotbeds like Austin and San Antonio. Interestingly enough, it all sells.

Alpine's largest employer is Sul Ross State University, a small college that prides itself on having the appearance and reputation of a private school. The college's Museum of the Big Bend is both an historical institution and an art museum. Its visual art exhibits are popular enough, but schoolchildren go berserk over its Texas Pterosaur. Now in fancy new digs, the museum draws lots of children bussed in from a huge swath of West Texan desertscape.

Alpine's schools do a basic job with art education, and some local artists voluntarily teach within the system. Several local artists also instruct out of their studios—but that's it.

Arts Scene

Museum of the Big Bend's active exhibition calendar is broadly based, well-attended, and solidly financed. Regional invitationals and one-artist shows for local painters comprise a big chunk of the schedule, with the rest devoted to other Texan, Santa Fean, and some national artists.

The biggest arts surprise in the Big Bend—outside of the crowd at Ojinaga's La Estancia drive-in bar—is the eye-popping and mind-warping experience at the Chinati Foundation in nearby Marfa. A former Army airfield that once housed Nazi POWs, it became the focal point of international mega-artist Donald Judd's attentions in the early 1980s. Judd converted the hangars and barracks into gleaming high-tech exhibition spaces for his own work and that of several prominent others on the international contemporary art circuit, including sculptor John Chamberlin.

Alpine has developed a healthy commercial gallery scene in the past few years, and surprisingly, many local artists can make it here. Twenty-five miles east in Marathon, two commercial spaces, the James Evans Gallery and the Chisos Gallery, exhibit lots of work by Austin artists, while a new cooperative gallery in the ghost town of Terlingua shows art by the painters, photographers, jewelers, and sculptors who live along the rim of the national park. Terlingua Trading Company is another fine place to spot Big Bend art, both visual and fine craft.

Performing arts in the town are in good shape, thanks to the college's programming. Marshall Auditorium contributes a year-round fine arts series of classical music, theater, chorale, Shakespeare, and contemporary dance. The biggest yearly event is the Texas Cowboy Poetry Gathering, filling every possible campus venue with dozens of cowboy and cowgirl poets. Thousands of poetry lovers descend upon Alpine for this wild weekend bash, turning this former cow town into the Florence of West Texas, if only for a little while. Alpine's community theater group, the Big Bend Players, stage summer shows at the Alpine Civic Center.

Alternatives

Everyone's favorite bar is the Cinnabar, which hangs local art in its Rio Grande Room. Right behind it is Railroad Blues, a great music joint that doesn't hang local art, but should. Another pleasant surprise is Terlingua's Starlight Nightclub, a wonderful music club and hangout drawing some of the top names in Austin's music scene.

Art Perspectives

Artist Charles Bell notes, "Alpine's the kind of place that forces you to be organized. Out here, you've got a sense of the vastness of the land. We've had a number of artists move in, but a certain number just come and go. The ones who stay tend to be pretty isolated from each other."

Details

Population: 6,200

Important Arts Events: Texas Cowboy Poetry Gathering in March, Trappings of Texas Art Show in March, Marfa Lights Festival in May, Alpine Gallery Nights in July and December (16th of September in Ojinaga)

Must-See Art Galleries: Bill Chappell Gallery, Chinati Foundation, James Evans Gallery, Kiowa Gallery, Mescalero Gallery, Museum of the Big Bend, Terlingua Trading Company

Local Arts Agency: Museum of the Big Bend
Sul Ross State University

Alpine, TX 79832
915/837-8143

Natural Foods: Monthly deliveries by local food co-op

Farmer's Market: Once monthly at Alpine Community Center

Bookstores: Front Street Books, Ocotillo Enterprises

Chamber of Commerce: 106 North Third Street
Alpine, TX 79832
915/837-2326

Kerrville, Texas

Location

Kerrville sits smack in the middle of Texas' Hill Country. The town's 19,000 residents include a number of the nation's foremost Western realist painters and sculptors—one of the reasons why the Cowboy Artists of America Museum is located here. San Antonio is a 60-minute drive southeast.

Great Outdoors

Kerrville's location on the Guadalupe River not only means a year-round supply of freshwater, but also a landscape of beautiful valleys with towering cypress, cottonwoods, and lush farmlands on the river's upper stretches. Kerrville and its surrounding communities are home to many of the nation's top pro rodeo cowboys and cowgirls; a short drive outside of town leads you into ranchland and smaller towns where the dominant structure is the rodeo arena. There aren't many lakes around, but the region's rivers are loaded with swimming holes fed by underground springs. Just a few hours' drive southeast lands you on Gulf Coast beaches.

Lifestyle

A recent spurt of growth has turned Kerrville from a sleepy little wayside into a bustling place where new homes and commercial buildings are sprouting all over. (You can still find a nice home in Kerrville for $90,000.) Some folks say "howdy" to the newcomers, but others—those who knew the Kerrville of the early 1980s and wanted peace, safety, and neighborliness—are worried. Lots of the newcomers are retirees whose needs are few, but whose interest in Kerrville's quality of life is high. One of the things they've supported is the Hill Country Arts Foundation, which is located six miles from Kerrville in nearby Ingram but serves the entire region. Just down the road from the foundation's building is a nearly full-scale replica of Stonehenge, public art of an enlightening sort.

The art education programs in local schools are basic, but getting better. The Hill Country Arts Foundation's programs have classes year-round for adults and kids. The foundation's adult classes employ regional as well as national artists and have developed a Southwestwide reputation for their strength. These are master classes for serious artists, people who travel long distances to do some heavy-duty career development. But the foundation also presents a number of programs for beginners and intermediates that better serve local needs.

The Cowboy Artists of America Museum, a gleaming, contemporary structure overlooking Kerrville, is the home of one of the country's most outstanding collections of masterworks by twentieth-century Western artists. The museum rotates many exhibitions by its member artists and emerging Western realist painters and sculptors. Two historical institutions, the Texas Heritage Music Museum and the Hill Country Museum, are at Kerrville Schreiner College. This private college is in the process of developing a new performing arts and visual arts center that will make a positive impact on Kerrville's cultural tourism economy as well as enhance the community's access to arts events.

Arts Scene

The Cowboy Artists of America Museum is the region's leading nonprofit visual arts exhibi
tion space. Schreiner College's visual arts faculty and students exhibit work at the college's
library. The Duncan-McAshan Gallery at the Hill Country Arts Foundation's 17-acre facility
is the home of a permanent collection of work by regional artists and exhibition space for the
area's fine craft, contemporary, traditional, and young artists. This gallery varies its calendar to
cover regional invitationals, one-artist shows, juried national exhibitions, and some touring
shows in its 1,800-square-foot space. There are several commercial art galleries in Kerrville and
the surrounding area—as well as art fairs, music festivals, and craft fairs nearly year-round.

Performing arts revolve around the Hill Country Arts Foundation's Smith-Ritch Point
Theatre, a 722-seat tiered amphitheater on the banks of the Guadalupe River. The theater's a
venue for the foundation's two summer productions and one in early autumn, a repertory of
musicals, family theater, and Shakespeare. During the rest of the year, the foundation presents
plays as well as some music performances in its small space. The Kerrville Performing Arts
Society uses the community's municipal auditorium for its fine arts series of touring classical
and popular music groups. A new local drama company, the Shoebox Theater, stages new plays
and experimental work in the Arcadia Theater, Kerrville's renovated downtown movie house

Alternatives

The small art town of Fredericksburg, a half hour's drive northeast of here, has great German
restaurants and a brew pub exhibiting local art.

Art Perspectives

Carolyn Quinn-Hensley, painter and art professor, says, "Kerrville's open-minded about contemporary art, and my work has been well received. It's a small community, a place where what's traditionally been shown in galleries is the tried-and-true, but there's a positive attitude about where
the town's heading in the future, and I think that's been very positive for the arts community."

Details

Population: 19,000

Important Arts Events: Kerrville Folk Festival
in May, Texas State Arts & Crafts Fair in May,
Texas Heritage Music Festival in October

Must-See Art Galleries: Artisans Gallery,
Cowboy Artists of America Museum, Duncan-
McAshan Gallery, Woodstone Gallery

Local Arts Agency: Hill Country Arts
Foundation
Hwy. 39 West
Ingram, TX 78025
210/367-5120

Natural Foods Stores: New Life Health
Foods, River Valley Health Foods

Farmer's Market: Wednesday afternoons at a
barn on G Street

National Public Radio: KSTX - 89.1FM

Bookstores: The Main Bookstore, Mystique
Books

Chamber of Commerce: 1700 Sidney Baker
Street
Kerrville, TX 78028
210/896-1155

Rockport, Texas

Location

Texas' Gulf Coast is so tropically beautiful it could fool you into thinking you were in south Florida or on a Caribbean island. The small art town of Rockport, which for decades has been a winter retreat for artists from across the Midwest and Southwest, is less than an hour's drive north of Corpus Christi, and just a few hours from the Mexican border.

Great Outdoors

The name of the outdoors game in this part of the country is fishing—deep sea, surf casting, bottom fishing, anything that involves a hook, line, and sinker. In exchange for your time, the sea delivers tarpon, flounder, marlin, ling cod, sailfish, and bonito. If you want to reach the ripe old age of 90, buy yourself a rod and reel, and you just may discover the secret of eternal youth.

Rockport adjoins the Aransas National Wildlife Refuge, a 55,000-acre waterfowl and migratory bird sanctuary best known as the wintering home of North America's Whooping Crane population. But more than 300 species stop here on their journeys north or south, an incredible abundance of wildlife that's made Rockport an attractive destination for birders, especially during the winter months. The refuge has several walking trails that let you get up close to the "whoopers" in their natural environment. Nearby Goose Island State Park's 307 acres are located on a gorgeous peninsula shaded by ancient oak trees, one of which is said to be 2,000 years old.

Lifestyle

Local residents come in two varieties: winter Texans and year-rounders. The winter folks come here for Rockport's fantastic beaches and mild climate, and it's largely been their word-of-mouth about the town and the wildlife refuge that has made Rockporters so gung-ho about eco- and cultural tourism. The winter Texans also leaked out another of Rockport's secrets: its ridiculously low cost of living. Considering that the Gulf of Mexico is right on their doorstep, many artists have found that the $60,000 cost of an average home in this beautiful small art town is almost too attractive to pass by. Rockport has two museums: the turn-of-the-century Fulton Mansion historical museum and the Texas Maritime Museum, focused on the state's fishing, transportation, and naval histories.

Local schools take a standard approach to arts education, but the Rockport Center for the Arts offers year-round art classes as well as art-related activities for kids, including a month-long summer arts camp. The Rockport Art Association also helps fund an art teacher for the elementary grades.

Arts Scene

The Rockport Center for the Arts, housed in a fin-de-siècle Victorian structure with views looking out on two bays, is the region's nonprofit art exhibition showcase. Inside the center are two galleries: a 2,500-square-foot main exhibition space and an 800-square-foot Rockport Art

Association member's gallery, plus a 1,000-square-foot demonstration/studio workshop. The art center's exhibitions explore a wide range of the regional arts scene, with lots of contemporary shows as well as one-artist exhibitions for local and Texan artists. The association's members focus on traditional seascapes, marshlands, and wildlife painting—much of it very accomplished. Rockport's ten art galleries show mostly the typical art found along oceanfronts from Deer Isle to Homer, fine-tuned to appeal to local buying tastes. Galleries that manage to break out of that mold include the Estelle Stair Gallery, Rockport Artists Gallery, Frame of Mine Gallery, Tejas Gallery, and the Austin Street Gallery.

Rockport is home to the Alpha-Omega Players, a three-company touring troupe under the banner of the Repertory Theater of America. Alpha-Omega companies perform as many as four different shows in their touring repertory. The Players' forte is taking their acts out on the road for months at a time, hitting small and medium-sized town art centers, college theaters, fraternal clubs, and anyplace that's willing to stage a play. Rockport Center for the Arts lines up the Alpha-Omega Players for its twice-yearly Dessert Theatre shows. The center also presents occasional performances by regional folk singers and classical musicians, plus literary readings by local authors and playwrights.

Alternatives

Several restaurants display Rockport art, but one of the few that sponsors rotating exhibits is The Duck Inn. Catch some local color at Hu Dat, a Vietnamese/Cajun/Chinese café.

Art Perspectives

Jimmie Bouldin, owner of the Estelle Stair Gallery, notes, "This little town is like an art colony. Artists love coming here to paint the whooping cranes and other wildlife, and winter Texans just like to play around with the idea of painting. My gallery sells sculpture, some abstract painting, some of lots of things. I look for strong artwork, stuff I haven't seen in the other galleries around here—that's what I bring into town, and that's what sells."

Details

Population: 4,000

Important Arts Events: Fulton Oysterfest in February, Rockport Art Festival in July, Fiesta en Playa in September, Rockport Seafair in October

Must-See Art Galleries: Estelle Stair Gallery, Rockport Artists Gallery, Rockport Center for the Arts

Local Arts Agency: Rockport Center for the Arts
902 Navigation Circle

Rockport, TX 78382
512/729-5519

Farmer's Market: Jimmy Wood's Produce

National Public Radio: KKED - 90.3 FM

Bookstores: The Book Shelf, The Book Worm, Culpin Booksellers, Pat's Place

Chamber of Commerce: 404 Broadway
Rockport, TX 78382
512/729-6445

Round Top, Texas

Location

The east end of Texas' Hill Country will surprise anyone who thinks this enormous state is one big, flat desert. Round Top, population 81, is set into a rolling green landscape that could pass for western Massachusetts. Round Top was settled by German and other European immigrants. Its town square and surrounding streets are lined with beautiful wood frame homes. Houston's a two-hour drive to the southeast.

Great Outdoors

The landscape here is either farmland or thick forest, with lots of streams and lakes. The long growing seasons are a perfect tradeoff for the hot, sticky summers. The closest large recreation area is at Somerville Lake, about 20 miles north—an 11,000-acre reservoir with campgrounds on its north and south shores. Largemouth black bass are the catch of the day, as they are at Fayette Lake, just a short drive south of town.

Lifestyle

Over the past several years, Round Top has developed a national reputation for its enormous antiques fairs. These twice-yearly events have become so massive that when Round Top stages its fairs in April and October, so do the surrounding communities. Emma Lee Turney, an antiques impresario formerly of Houston, is the wizard behind the Round Top shows. Her success has spilled into neighboring towns and communities who capitalize on the influx of cultural tourists for Turney's blowouts. Because Round Top's fairs have been around for some time, they attract sharp dealers and buyers who know the difference between fine antiques and old junk. It's Turney's own eye that has maintained the shows' quality, even if the fairs in other area towns are caveat emptor.

Round Top itself is a gorgeous little place, built around a square that looks like it was airlifted in from the set of a Frank Capra movie. It has a couple of places to eat, a couple of craft stores, and all the rest of what makes small-town America run. Homes in Round Top can be expensive. Prices in the $100,000s for average-sized residences are the norm.

On the outskirts of Round Top, the University of Texas operates the Winedale Historical Center, a 215-acre step back in time that's built around a mid-1800s mansion. A wealthy Houstonian, Ima Hogg, bought the place and gave it to the university. Over the years, the university has purchased other historic structures in the area and moved them onto Winedale's grounds, using them as museum and conference center. Today Winedale hosts week-long seminars on traditional frontier crafts such as spinning, weaving, and rug-making, as well as a twice-annual crafts festival and Shakespeare festivals during the spring and summer.

Arts Scene

The International Festival Institute at Round Top is one of America's classical music treasures. Located on 200 spectacular acres of Hill Country right in Round Top, in a complex of elegant structures known as Festival Hill, the institute is the brainchild of internationally known classical pianist James Dick. This talented visionary has made Festival Hill's rise to international prominence an important part of his life's work. Nowhere else in America will you find a state-of-the-art, 1,000-seat performing arts theater in a village of fewer than 100 residents.

The institute draws nearly 100 gifted young musicians from all over to Round Top for a summer-long education and performance program that teams them with professional classical musicians, many of whom are from Texas-based symphony orchestras and university music departments. The institute boards 'em, teaches 'em, and performs 'em in a series of young musicians concerts that are part of the summer season. The concert series also features institute instructors and visiting soloists.

Festival Hill's activities extend beyond the summer months. There's a spring festival of Baroque music, a monthly concert series during the autumn and winter months, a film series, a lecture series, a series of dinner party performances, and even a year-round slate of herb gardening seminars and an annual herb festival. Festival Hill is truly Round Top's arts center in that many of its performances and programs are offered free to anyone who wants to attend. Even the festival performances themselves charge an astoundingly low $8 as a way of saying, "Come on down, y'all."

It is clearly Mr. Dick's classical music leadership and Ms. Turney's antiques fairs savvy that are the twin engines driving the entire region's cultural tourism economy. And it's worth noting that their success has had everything to do with entrepreneurship and little to do with government funding.

Alternatives

Karganov's Café, on the Festival Hill grounds, displays local art and serves a mean cappuccino. If you visit during the spring or fall antiques fairs, be sure to visit the barbecue pits outside of Emma Lee Turney's fair tents. You may even bump into a famous Texan or two.

Art Perspectives

Emma Lee Turney, an antiques impresario, says, "Round Top's a perfect place for what I do because we've created an aura and an ambiance, and we have more than 2,000 Houston families living in the four-county area. They want to decorate their ranches, farms, and restorations in traditional styles, and that's what our focus is on . . . Americana."

Details

Population: 81

Important Arts Events: Round Top Antiques Festival in April and October, summer season at Festival Hill in June and July, Summer Shakespeare Festival at Winedale in July and August

Local Arts Agency: Festival Hill
P.O. Drawer 89
Round Top, TX 78954
409/249-3129

Farmer's Market: Farm trucks parked along Round Top roads

National Public Radio: KUHF - 88.7 FM

Chamber of Commerce: Round Top Merchants Association Information
P.O. Box 41
Round Top, TX 78954
409/249-4042

Moab, Utah

Location

Southeast Utah's red rock landscape is a region unlike any other in the nation, not just for the ochre tint of its rugged terrain but also for the massive formations of sparsely vegetated rock canyons, mesas, mountains, and dry riverbeds. An outdoor-oriented town of 4,500, Moab is spread across a narrow valley of the Colorado River and is a four-hour drive southeast of Salt Lake City.

Great Outdoors

Flanked by two national parks and the towering 12,000-foot La Sal Mountains of the Manti-La Sal National Forest, Moab's landscape inspires people to do crazy things—like mountain-bike far into the Colorado Plateau badlands or take death-defying white-water rafting trips down the Colorado River's Cataract Canyon. Canyonlands National Park and Arches National Park are both just a short bike ride from town. The Colorado River cuts through both parks, and meets up with the Green River in the Canyonlands, deep at the bottom of a red rock canyon. In recent years both parks have become top sites for the nation's mountain bikers.

Moab's climate is mild through most of the winter, but can be broiling in the summer. Locals make a point of enjoying their town from October through April, before the hordes of summer tourists arrive. Many residents head to the La Sal Mountains in the summer to modest vacation homes that have spectacular Canyonlands views. A three-hour drive east into Colorado takes you to Aspen, so on many days people wake up in the 70-degree warmth of Moab and are on the alpine slopes by lunchtime.

Lifestyle

Moab was a depressed community when artists started moving into town a decade ago. The mine had closed, businesses had shut down, and Main Street had plenty of empty storefronts. What a difference a decade makes! Since its discovery by legions of mountain bikers and its resurrection as a Southwest center for outdoor recreation, Moab has gone through an economic boom that is today causing havoc. The town is now filled with hotels and restaurants, as well as a number of hip coffee bars, ready to serve the many tourists (including Europeans) who come here looking for the American outdoor recreation dream. Real estate speculators from Salt Lake City have bought up lots of the town and are raising rents as fast as they can. Local real estate prices have tripled . . . at least! Where small houses once sold for $25,000, today they cannot be touched for less than $80,000. For the long-time locals who bought when prices were low, the town is still a laid-back place to live.

Arts Scene

Moab's main nonprofit visual arts exhibition space is the upstairs gallery at the Dan O'Laurie Museum, a place that doesn't get much tourist traffic because it's on a quiet side street. The museum does a great job of organizing one-artist shows for Moab's growing community of fine artists, and its regional invitationals have developed a strong reputation among gallery owners as a great place to spot emerging Utah talent. The town's other primary nonprofit space is in the lobby of the Moab Post Office. As unlikely as it seems, it has proven to be a great place to make sales.

Commercial galleries range from good to awful, with the awful ones filled with junk art from Mexico that's intended to look as if it were created in the Southwest. Moabilia shows contemporary work by local artists, as does One Shot Gallery, a funky little place run by an artist couple that exhibits a wild and inexpensive range of work by some very talented local painters, sculptors, photographers, and jewelers. Mark Two Gallery exhibits a more traditional range of regional landscape work, as does the Moab Mercantile and Home on the Range. One of the most exciting commercial gallery developments taking place in Moab is the visual arts gallery that's been added onto the Moab Community Co-op, the town's natural foods store. If you're in Moab and you want great art at amazingly low prices, this is the place to find real treasures.

The town's two theater companies, Community Theater and Tributary Theater, perform at different venues around Moab, as does the community chorus. During the summer months there is an annual performance by members of the Utah Symphony in one of the natural amphitheaters along the Colorado River

Alternatives

Local artists exhibit (and sell) their work at Eddie McStiff's Brewpub, Honest Ozzie's Café, Mondo Café, and the Center Café.

Art Perspectives

Bob Walker, painter and printmaker comments, "Moab's not yet developed into a great art market, and if you want to survive as an artist then you need a couple of jobs. Artists like living here because we like the balance of working on our art, playing in the outdoors, and doing things with our friends. It's too nice a place to leave during the winter months, but summers are totally out-of-hand, just madness   ."

Details

Population: 4,500

Important Arts Events: Moab Arts Festival in May, Moab Music Festival in September

Must-See Art Galleries: Dan O'Laurie Museum, Moab Community Co-op Gallery, Moab Post Office, One Shot Gallery

Local Arts Agency: Canyonlands Arts Council P.O. Box 1441

Moab, UT 84532
801/259-8431

Natural Foods Store: Moab Community Co-op

National Public Radio: KUER - 90.3 FM

Bookstores: Back of Beyond, B. Osborn's

Chamber of Commerce: 805 N. Main St.
Moab UT 84532
801/259-7814

Springville, Utah

Location

Springville's valley setting ten miles south of Provo gives it easy access not only to the art museums and performing arts events at Brigham Young University, but also to Salt Lake City. Any of Springville's 18,500 residents can hop into a car and drive less than an hour north to see the NBA's Utah Jazz play on their new Salt Lake City home court.

Great Outdoors

Everything from soaring Rocky Mountain peaks to searing Southwestern deserts are within an easy drive of Springville. Like the rest of the communities in this part of the state, Springville is framed on one side by the Wasatch Range and on the other by water—in this case, the 50-square-mile Utah Lake, a favorite summer recreation center. Nearby Strawberry Reservoir, a mountain lake ringed by campgrounds and hiking trails, offers some of the state's best sport-fishing. The Uinta National Forest is filled with hiking trails, hunting areas, and campgrounds. To Springville's south is the Mt. Nebo Wilderness and to the north, the Mt. Timpanogos Wilderness, a favorite place for day hikes. The Union Pacific Rail Trail starts at Echo Reservoir and continues 28 miles to the small art town of Park City. Both Park City and nearby Sundance, in Provo Canyon, offer world-class downhill ski resorts.

Lifestyle

Springville promotes itself as "Utah's Arts City," and with its large art museum and eight commercial galleries, the name fits. Nearby Provo is experiencing a stunning period of growth, and there are plenty of jobs in the area with lots of well-educated professionals who buy the art exhibited in Springville's galleries. Neighborhoods are characterized by modest homes on tree-lined streets and by many city parks. The average home costs $75,000 or so, but if you drive a short way toward Salem, prices drop dramatically.

BYU's arts and theater departments are legendary. A new Museum of Art on the BYU campus brings national touring exhibitions into Provo, and two smaller museums in the school's fine arts center show a range of contemporary and traditional work. Also on the BYU campus is the Museum of Peoples and Cultures. The school hosts an impressive performing arts series, and the dance department's productions are highly regarded. Sundance is the home of a summer repertory theater company staging musicals from June to September.

Arts Scene

The Springville Museum of Art's 20,000 square feet of exhibition space is a tremendous asset to this town's arts community. In operation since the mid-1930s, the museum has evolved into one of the most influential forces in the Western arts scene. The museum's dozen galleries house a permanent collection, as well as national and international touring exhibitions ranging from Impressionist paintings to Soviet realism. The museum also serves Springville as an exhibition venue for local and regional artists, with many one-artist exhibitions, student art invitationals, and fine craft and sculpture exhibits. The museum's arts education program buses in the region's school children to tour shows, and provides teacher training on everything from art history to technique.

In the past few years, several famous sculptors have moved to Springville to be close to the new Baer Bronze foundry, and their presence is reflected in the many public works of art that have been installed around Springville by the Sculptures to Live By project. The town's commercial galleries exhibit a mixed bag of art, from Western realism to the fabulous landscape paintings coming out of both the faculty and students of BYU's arts department.

Springville's main performing arts event is the annual Springville World Folkfest, a summer dance spectacular hosting a dozen or more international dance companies who perform at Spring Acres Art Park and downtown at the art museum. The Folkfest dancers come from Asia, Africa, India, Europe, and Latin America, treating the town to a festival of national significance. A classical music concert series takes place at the art museum through the winter months, with performances primarily by soloists associated with BYU's music department. Springville has two community theater groups performing during the winter months—Springville Playhouse uses the Springville Civic Center's Theater in the Round while the Arts City Community Theatre stages its plays in a renovated downtown movie house.

Alternatives

In just three years, the Sculptures to Live By project has installed nearly 20 sculptures of various media, by leading national sculptors, all over downtown Springville. Central Bank also exhibits sculpture in its lobby.

Art Perspectives

Mike Baer, owner of Baer Bronze, says, "I wanted my foundry to be part of an arts community, and after looking all over Utah, I settled on Springville. It's a town that's excited about art, not in the sense of being a market for art, but rather of being a place where art's appreciated for art's sake. Springville's growing as an arts community, and the long-term prospects for someone who wants to be part of an arts community's growth are just right."

Details

Population: 18,500

Important Arts Events: Spring Art Salon in April, Art City Days in June, Springville World Folkfest in June

Must-See Art Galleries: The Art Shop, Sculptures to Live By installations, Springville Museum of Art

Local Arts Agency: Springville Arts Commission
50 South Main Street
Springville, UT 84663
801/489-2726

Natural Foods Store: Dr. Christopher's Herb Shop

Farmer's Market: Saturday mornings on North Main Street

National Public Radio: KBYU - 89.1 FM

Bookstore: The Book Mark

Chamber of Commerce: P.O. Box 293
Springville, UT 84663
801/489-4681

Burlington, Vermont

Location

You've got to have a sense of humor to live an hour's drive from the Canadian border. Winters are tough, growing seasons are brief, and the cost of California-grown produce is enough to convert diehard vegetarians. A mecca for the performing arts and music, Burlington puts on a happy face by calling itself the "West Coast of New England" and turning its best natural asset, the shores of Lake Champlain, into a focal point for much of its cultural and artistic life.

Great Outdoors

Half of the state's best ski areas are within an hour's drive, and Stowe and Stratton are even closer. Winter rolls into town in early November and doesn't leave until April. Summer and fall are glorious. Twelve-mile-wide Lake Champlain is lined with city parks, running trails, marinas, and ferry docks. White-water canoeing and kayaking are wildly popular with locals, but some of the better river stretches are very crowded on weekends.

Lifestyle

Burlington, the state's largest city, is a magnet for technology companies, so there are plenty of jobs when the economy's strong. Fortunately, even when it isn't, the cost of living is manageable on low salaries, and employers take advantage of this. Burlington is a safe community with a strong commitment to multiculturalism. Lower-income neighborhoods are an intriguing blend of aging hipsters, college students from the University of Vermont, Tibetan refugees, hungry artists, and Mexican laborers. Community services are well funded, and public transportation actually works.

Middle-income neighborhood homes on maple tree–lined streets start in the $100,000 range, but ambitious do-it-yourselfers can pick up a shack for half that price and turn it into a palace. The public schools take art education seriously, and many local artists participate in residencies. The city employs other artists through its mobile arts academy project for community centers. Public art has become an integral part of the city's landscape, with murals scattered about town and a public sculpture garden on its busy waterfront.

Arts Scene

Burlington's annual arts calendar is jammed with professional and amateur theater, dance, jazz, chamber music, and kids' theater. The Flynn Theatre for the Performing Arts presents an eight-month main stage. The city's summer jazz festival is a week-long bash featuring the nation's best jazz musicians. First Night packs nearly 100 acts into 20 downtown venues—and offers free trolley shuttles and fireworks on the waterfront. The classical music series presented by UVM at the campus recital hall and chapel includes everything from San Francisco Opera to the Harlem Spiritual Ensemble. During the summer, the Waterfront Stage resounds nearly every night with free and paid concerts, Shakespeare-by-the-Lake moves into Hauke Auditorium at Champlain College, nearby Stratton Mountain presents the usual summer touring music acts, and the Vermont Mozart Festival graces St. Paul's Cathedral.

The visual arts scene is not so robust. City Arts, Burlington's far-reaching urban arts orga nization, operates the nonprofit Firehouse Gallery for contemporary and traditional Vermont artists. The gallery is an anchor of the Church Street Marketplace, a downtown pedestrian mall. The Marketplace also houses a crafts gallery operated by the Vermont State Craft Center, and the Robert Paul Gallery, one of the city's few commercial exhibition and sales spaces. Arts Alive, a co-op, runs the Union Station Gallery for contemporary artists and presents the June Festival of Fine Arts on the Marketplace, three days of exhibitions in storefronts along with a street fair. If you want to see the latest in foreign films, catch the Vermont International Film Festival each October.

Alternatives

Besides the nonprofit art spaces operated by City Arts and Arts Alive, there are dozens of cafés, restaurants, and public buildings where visual artists exhibit their work and make a surprising number of sales. Daily Planet is one of the best, as is Leunig's and the Red Onion Deli. There's an art gallery in city hall, at the airport, and at Chittenden Bank, as well as local art hanging at most of the downtown restaurants. At night the Marketplace is a magnet for Burlington's creative set, with rock 'n' roll shaking the Club Metronome, blues acts crooning at Halvorson's, and folkies strumming at the Burlington Coffee House.

Art Perspectives

Katharine Montstream has made Burlington her home for more than a decade. She works in a renovated industrial building that has been turned into studio spaces with views of Lake Champlain. "Artists here have a sense of community and do a surprising number of projects together," she says. "There are no billboards, no natural disasters, great ski areas, and a feeling of safety. I'm a painter, so for me having a visual connection with the lake is an important influence in my work. If you want to make a living from your art, you've got to be flexible here There are galleries all over the state that you should be selling in, and then you've got to sell outside the area as well."

Details

Population: 40,000

Important Arts Events: Discover Jazz in June, Festival of Fine Arts in June, Vermont Mozart Festival in July and August, Summer Music Series at Battery Park, Vermont International Film Festival in October, First Night on December 31

Must-See Art Galleries: Firehouse Gallery, Fleming Museum on UVM campus, Robert Paul Gallery

Local Arts Agency: Union Station Gallery, Burlington City Arts
149 Church Street

Burlington, VT 05401
802/865-7158
Newsletter: Art Beat ($20/yr. membership)

Natural Food Stores: The Onion River Co-op, Origanum

Farmer's Market: Saturday mornings in City Hall Park

National Public Radio: WVPR - 107.9 FM

Bookstore: Chassman & Beam

Chamber of Commerce: 60 Main Street Burlington, VT 05402
802/863-3489

Johnson, Vermont

Location

Johnson is in the heart of northern Vermont's Lamoille Valley, a spectacular river plain bounded by 4,000-foot-high mountains, the Green River Reservoir, and verdant rolling farm lands. Johnson's 3,000 residents live an hour from the small art town of Burlington, and less than an hour's drive from the Canadian border.

Great Outdoors

Although there isn't a ski area right in Johnson, Stowe and Smuggler's Notch are less than 30 minutes from town. Snowfalls in northern Vermont are legendary, coming early in autumn and piling up to depths of several feet by the end of November—perfect not only for groomed downhill slopes but also for cross-country skiing and snowmobiling. Mt. Mansfield State Forest, a few minutes' south of Johnson, encompasses two state parks, Underhill and Smuggler's Notch, each with campgrounds and hiking trails.

Canoeing the Lamoille River, which runs along the edge of Johnson on its way to Lake Champlain, is a popular summer activity, as is canoeing the Gihon River, which bisects Johnson. Lake Champlain's parks and beaches can be reached in less than an hour. Mountain biking has become a summer industry in this part of the state. But the main summer outdoor activity is still fly-fishing for smallmouth bass and rainbow trout. There's summer recreation of a different sort at Ben & Jerry's ice cream plant in nearby Waterbury.

Lifestyle

Johnson's largest employer is Johnson Woolen Mills. Historically a working-class town, Johnson is the kind of place where several generations of a family work at the mill. The town's other main employer is Johnson State College, a branch of the University of Vermont. Average homes in Johnson sell for around $115,000.

Ten years ago a new business came to town in the form of the Vermont Studio Center, a fledgling artist-in-residence program with an art instruction component. Since then, the center has grown from a nine-week program accommodating 75 artists to a 50-week program attended by 525 artists. This success is all the more impressive when you factor in the center's unwavering commitment to contemporary art. The center offers a resident-artist program of unprecedented size for such a small town, taking in as many as 75 artists monthly and housing them in typically quaint and historic residences scattered along the banks of the Gihon River.

Local schools do an adequate job with arts education programs, but state funding cut-backs have forced them to focus their resources elsewhere. Parents who want more for their kids link up with the year-round programs at Helen Day Art Center in Stowe or the Wolcott Children's Ballet, a dance program just ten miles from town.

Arts Scene

Corporate and private support pours into the Vermont Studio Center, funding its extensive programs and attracting artists not only from the United States and Canada, but also from

Japan, Mexico, France, and points in between. The contemporary work created at the center is exhibited in its nonprofit Red Mill Gallery space. Johnson State College's art department, which offers an MFA program through the studio center, exhibits mostly student and faculty work at its nonprofit Scott Gallery. Under new leadership, the gallery has started broadening its focus to include more regional and even some national exhibitions.

The main commercial galleries in the area are at the Stowe ski resort, which attracts vacationing folks who have some bucks to burn. Clark Gallery in Stowe is known for the strength of its traditionalist work. The area's co-op gallery is the Jacob Walker Gallery, which displays the full range of what's created in this part of the state. The Helen Day Art Center rotates its local/regional shows with an intriguing range of exhibitions that cover everything from touring fine crafts to photography.

Performing arts take place at the Johnson State College's Dibden Auditorium, a 1,400-seat venue that hosts a winter series, a weekly foreign film series, touring kids' theater, productions by the college's music and theater departments, and a summer dance residency program. Hyde Park Opera House, just a few minutes' drive from town, is home to the area's community theater company, which stages four winter shows in their 150-seat playhouse. Other performances take place through the year at the Helen Day, while summer's Vermont Mozart Festival brings top classical musicians into the Trapp Family Lodge for a series of open-air concerts.

Alternatives

Local art rotates on the walls of Johnson's restaurants, so check out French Press Café, Tuscany, Plum & Main, and Long Trail Tavern.

Art Perspectives

Jonathan Gregg, president of Vermont Studio Center and a guiding force in its growth and national renown, says, "We're beginning to see a lot of international artists come to the center, and we've arrived at a point where people take us quite seriously. What we're always trying to do is intensify the caliber and quality of the art being created here; we don't have an interest in tourist art."

Details

Population: 3,000

Important Arts Events: Stowe Student Art Exhibit in May, For Art's Sake in August, Fall Foliage Festival in October

Must-See Art Galleries: Blue Heron Gallery, Clark Gallery, Helen Day Art Center, Red Mill Gallery, Scott Gallery, Jacob Walker Gallery

Local Arts Agency: Vermont Studio Center
P.O. Box 613
Johnson, VT 05656
802/635-2727

Natural Food Store: Roo's Natural Foods

Farmer's Market: Roadside stands, Rankin's Farm

National Public Radio: WVPR - 107.9 FM

Bookstores: Bear Pond Books, French Press Cafe, Johnson State College Bookstore

Chamber of Commerce: P.O. Box 445
Morrisville, VT 05661
802/888-7607

Middlebury, Vermont

Location

West-central Vermont isn't as mountainous as other parts of the state, but the rolling hillsides surrounding Middlebury are as typically bucolic New England as anywhere. There are more farms here than in other parts of Vermont, yet great ski areas are within a 30-minute drive. Lake Champlain is only a 15-minute drive west.

Great Outdoors

"We've got lots of lakes, lots of canoeing, and lots of parks nearby. Our quality of life is high, but so are our taxes," one artist told me. Oh well, someone has to pay to keep the place looking great. Outdoor recreation opportunities are everywhere, and what's not right outside your back door is just a short drive away. Middlebury borders Green Mountain National Forest, an accessible and lightly populated outdoor sports haven. During summer the beach at Lake Dunmore in nearby Branbury State Park attracts the region's sun slaves, while Middlebury College's Snow Bowl ski area a few minutes outside town is the sort of low-key, family operation where local folk can bump into each other on the lift lines.

Lifestyle

Middlebury is a college town, so the community has stores and bars a place its size normally couldn't sustain. The college is the area's largest employer, but home-based businesses are a huge component of the local economy. The business community was hit hard by the region's recession over the past few years, but has recovered nicely. Downtown retailers are especially happy about a new tourist-train service that runs twice daily between Burlington and Middlebury, dumping hundreds of spenders into the heart of town for a few hours, then sweeping them off the streets by dinnertime. It's still possible to find homes for under $100,000 in the area, but they're ten miles or so outside the city limits.

Local schools take arts education seriously, with instruction starting in elementary schools and expanding to multidisciplinary programs in high school. A main education site in the area is the Vermont State Craft Center at Frog Hollow, a converted mill building that's filled with exhibition spaces, classrooms, a state-of-the-art pottery studio with visiting master artists throughout the year, and a sales gallery representing the state's most prominent fine craft artists.

Arts Scene

Middlebury College's new Center for the Performing Arts has infused the creative community with excitement about the performances that can now take place in Middlebury rather than in Burlington. Local theater groups will still perform at the high school, but the new center should free up other campus venues that have been used mostly for student productions. The college's art museum focuses primarily on traditional nineteenth- and twentieth- century works, but occasionally hosts traveling and invitational shows. The Vermont Folklife Center has a small craft gallery and larger exhibition spaces showing the state's folk art and traditional crafts. Frog Hollow, the state craft center, attracts artists from across the Northeast for its year-round schedule of master classes by potters, woodcarvers, painters, weavers, and basket makers.

Visual arts are less prominent in Middlebury than are fine crafts, a situation painter Woody Jackson says needs correction. "We need a really good visual arts gallery here, run by people who know more about selling art than just how to hang things on a wall. There are probably 15 serious painters living in Middlebury year-round and lots of New York artists who own vacation homes around the area. But right now, because there's little opportunity to make a living here, your marketing needs to be done outside the area," he says. The community's visual arts scene is fairly supportive, primarily because the college museum exhibitions and Frog Hollow classes tend to keep artists in regular contact with each other.

Alternatives

You can watch foreign films year-round at the college's continuing film series in Sunderland Hall. The walls of Woody's Restaurant on Bakery Lane are a sales and exhibition opportunity for local artists, and the Storm Café on Mill Street. has regular shows as well. One favorite meeting place for the artsy crowd is the Otter Creek Brewery, but since this is a working brewery and not a brew pub, you really don't want to be seen hanging out in the parking lot.

Art Perspectives

"I like the fact that you have to sell your work in local restaurants and the alternative spaces around town," says painter and children's book illustrator Phoebe Stone. "I was a little disappointed at first, but then I found out that, amazingly enough, this is how people buy art around here. Things really sell from the walls of restaurants.

"Having the college in town means people living in Middlebury avoid intellectual stagnation. There are lectures and exhibitions up there all the time, and the teachers are mostly artists who are part of our community. Middlebury's beautiful, quiet, and a great place to live for artists who want to build their careers slowly."

Details

Population: 8,000

Important Arts Events: Festival on the Green in July, Vermont Handcrafters Annual Show in October, Vermont Symphony's July 4th concert.

Must-See Art Galleries: Danforth Pewterers, Great Falls Collection, Holy Cow, Middlebury College Museum of Art, Red Clover Rugs, Sheldon Museum, Vermont Folklife Center, Vermont State Craft Center at Frog Hollow

Local Arts Agency: Vermont State Craft Center at Frog Hollow
1 Mill Street

Middlebury, VT 05753
802/388-3177

Natural Food Store: Middlebury Natural Foods Co-op

Farmer's Market: Saturday mornings at the Marble Works

National Public Radio: WVPR - 107.9 FM

Bookstore: The Vermont Bookshop

Chamber of Commerce: 2 Court Street Middlebury, VT 05753
802/388-7951

Woodstock, Vermont

Location

A hundred years ago, the main industry in this part of Vermont was timber, and the architectural legacy of that economy survives in the many mill houses and brick warehouses that have been converted into retail and residential spaces. The Ottauquechee River courses through Woodstock's town center, and steep hillsides frame both sides of town. Burlington's airport is 90 minutes north.

Great Outdoors

From late spring through mid-summer, the Ottauquechee offers respectable white-water stretches, as does the nearby White River. Silver Lake State Park and Quechee State Park are the closest beach and sailing havens, and the trout streams in this part of the state are legendary. Woodstock's Suicide Six ski area was one of the first in the states to build a rope tow in the early 1930s. Because it's just three miles from the historic town green, the slopes are used like a park, filled with kids and families all winter long. Woodstock also has public pools, tennis courts, a golf course, and an equestrian center.

Lifestyle

For several years, Woodstock has basked in the favor of travel writers, which has led to a proliferation of B&Bs, restaurants, and shops. Fortunately, Woodstock also values the arts, so as it has grown it has expanded its financial support for community arts organizations such as the Pentangle Council on the Arts, the Vermont Institute of Natural Science, the local historical society, and the Billings Farm & Museum.

Woodstock isn't an inexpensive place to live. The influx of upwardly mobile urbanites has jacked up housing costs to the point where a $100,000 home is the norm—15 miles out of town. You'll pay two or three times that to live in town. On the other hand, these same newcomers are buying local art and contributing to performing arts groups.

Arts Scene

The Pentangle Council on the Arts owns and programs the Town Hall Theatre, a 300-seat venue for theater, dance, and music performances from September through May; year-round, people can catch first-run and occasional foreign films here. Pentangle also sponsors an impressive in-theater kids' arts education series. The Woodstock public school system has both full-time arts education instructors and a comprehensive program of artist-in-residence engagements coordinated through Pentangle and the state arts council. Keeping in mind that only 4,000 people live here, Pentangle's ambitious programming is a tremendous asset to the local arts scene.

The Briggs Opera House 15 miles east in White River Junction offers year-round performances. Local companies such as the New Woolhouse Players and the Coffeehouse Concert Series use the Little Theatre, a 150-seat space in a converted riverside mill building. During the summer months, folks enjoy a Down by the River picnic concert series at one of the parks along the Ottauquechee, a series of chamber music concerts called Maybe Mozart, and a brown bag concert series on the library lawn.

Visual artists are able to sell their work through some of the local galleries and craft shops· The town lacks a visual arts center, and the local arts community does not operate the sort of co-op gallery that has opened up sales for contemporary artists elsewhere The local sales opportunities for craft artists who don't want to pay a gallery commission are much stronger than they are for painters, especially at the Pentangle Crafts Fair in July and at the Apples & Crafts Fair in October One of the best visual arts events in the area is the annual Wildlife Art Show held in September at the Vermont Institute of Natural Science

Alternatives

Rachel's Kitchen is one of the few local restaurants exhibiting anything but banal regional landscape scenes. Bentley's Cafe is a favorite hangout for local creative types who want some semblance of a nightlife, but the real action after dark is 15 miles away at the Skunk Hollow Tavern in Hartland.

Art Perspectives

Charlet Davenport, a local sculptor who opens her rural home to invitational sculpture shows during the summer months, says that the arts community here is in a state of transition. "There used to be a lot more artists living in Woodstock, but when homes cost nearly $300,000, people find other places to live Studio space isn't hard to find in some of the converted mill buildings, as long as you can drive to one of the nearby towns that are more affordable. Some of the town's commercial spaces that in other towns are rented by artists stay vacant in Woodstock, because the artists can't afford them and landlords won't lower their rents. The way I look at it as an artist is that if you can get artists into these spaces other business will be encouraged as well, but landlords don't seem to get it.

"Our local galleries are struggling and only the ones selling prints seem to be doing well. For local artists there's nowhere else to look but outside the state. You've got to be selling your work somewhere else."

Details

Population: 4,000

Important Arts Events: Pentangle Crafts Fair in July, Riverfest in Wilder in August, Wildlife Art Show in September

Must-See Art Galleries: Gallery on the Green, North Wind Artisans, Stephen Huneck Gallery, Woodstock Gallery of Art

Local Arts Agency: Pentangle Council on the Arts
1 High Street
Woodstock, VT 05091
802/457-3981

Natural Foods Store: 18 Carrots

Farmer's Market: Saturday mornings on Route 12 North

National Public Radio: WVPR - 89.5 FM

Bookstores: Shiretown Books, The Yankee Bookshop

Chamber of Commerce: 18 Central Street
Woodstock, VT 05091
802/457-3555

A bingdon, Virginia

Location

This small town sits in the southern Appalachian mountains at the intersection of Virginia, North Carolina, and Tennessee. Surprisingly, Abingdon is closer to both Atlanta and Indianapolis than to Washington, D.C. With over a foot of snowfall each year, winters can be tough here. Spring comes late and the gardening season is shorter than you might expect.

Great Outdoors

Abingdon's 7,000 residents live in rural splendor, nestled into forested hillsides in a historic community near lakes, mountains, rivers, and abundant golf courses. South Holston Lake's 20 miles of shoreline are just ten minutes from Abingdon's historic district/business area. Nearby White Top Mountain (5,729 feet) shelters part of the Appalachian Trail inside a national recreation area. Several spectacular natural resources—the Great Smoky Mountains, New River Gorge, and Cumberland Gap—are within easy driving distance. Ski areas are south in North Carolina's Appalachians; larger West Virginia resorts are about a three-hour drive.

Lifestyle

Abingdon is beautiful, historic, artistic, and affordable. Homes can be found in the $75,000 range, and homes with acreage in surrounding Washington County are astoundingly cheap. There are eight colleges and universities within the region, which includes Kingsport and Johnson City, Tennessee, as well as Bristol, Virginia. Abingdon promotes itself as a cultural tourism center, and each year thousands of visitors pour into town for visual and performing arts programs. Local school arts programs have yet to match the community's arts awareness, which increases the importance of the roles played by the area's three fine arts groups: William King Regional Arts Center (affiliated with the Virginia Museum of Fine Arts), Depot Artists Association, and Holston Mountain Crafts Cooperative. Besides the programs available in Abingdon, events in the three larger nearby cities are essentially at residents' doorsteps.

Arts Scene

For visual artists inspired by nature, Abingdon offers a spectacular Southern setting without the heat and humidity common to much of the region May through October. The William King Regional Arts Center's 4,000-plus square feet of visual arts exhibition space includes four galleries as well as classrooms for adults' and kids' programs, studio spaces rented to local artists, and a new performing arts space. Exhibitions here present everything from emerging contemporary Southeastern artists to historic touring shows from museums nationwide. Abingdon itself has seven commercial businesses that exhibit art as part of their retail mix, but no dedicated commercial gallery space yet

Emory & Henry College operates the 1912 Depot Gallery in the adjacent community of Emory and presents an ambitious slate of performing arts events throughout the school year, as does Abingdon's Virginia Highlands Community College. Some of Abingdon's visual artists exhibit their work at the artist-run Arts Depot Gallery, while others hang their work on the walls of the Starving Artist Café (owned and operated by an artist), which features deli sandwiches named after famous painters from Monet to Andrew Wyeth.

Abingdon's historic, 400-seat Barter Theatre presents nine months of top-notch theater. The Barter (which, as the State Theatre of Virginia, receives partial funding directly from state government) programs mainly to please the cultural tourists who flock into town to attend plays such as *Forever Plaid*, *Amadeus*, and Tennessee Williams standards. To its credit, the Barter also uses its black-box facility, the Barter Stage II, to present new works such as *Wrong Turn at Lungfish* and *Greater Loesser*, a children's theater series during summer, cabaret shows, and even an annual Halloween thriller.

Alternatives

Recognizing the importance of the arts to the economy, many downtown restaurants and cafés hang local work on their walls. Foremost among these is the Starving Artist Café, which functions as both an emotional and nutritional filling station for the fast-growing community of artists, actors, and authors. P.J. Brown's is another popular venue that sells a surprising amount of art. Alison's, the Hardware Lounge, and Addison & Company are other places artists like showing their work—and when night falls, they drink their profits at The Tavern. An interesting project in progress at the local arts center is the construction of a 22-acre sculpture park, intended to attract not only exhibiting artists but also sculptors willing to relocate to this corner of the state.

Art Perspectives

John Sauers, a landscape painter, finds inspiration in the area's beauty. "The seasons here are very different, with early frosts the norm and spring arriving late, but in a very big way when it finally gets here. And our humidity is so low most of the time that the nights here are absolutely opaque.

"The artists and businesses in Abingdon cooperate on almost everything, which helps everyone stay in touch and builds the integrity of the work being created here. Artists have been gravitating in this direction for several years, and today the levels of expertise I'm seeing at local shows really surprises me—it goes from abstract Impressionism to beyond realism, and a lot of it's very good."

Details

Population: 7,000

Important Arts Events: Barter Theatre season from March to December, Virginia Highlands Arts & Crafts Festival in August

Must-See Art Galleries: 1912 Depot Gallery, Arts Depot, Main Street Books & Crafts, The Marketplace, P.J.Brown's, Starving Artist Café, William King Regional Arts Center Gallery

Local Arts Agency: William King Regional Arts Center
415 Academy Drive

Abingdon, VA 24212
540/628-5005

Natural Food Store: Whole Health Center

National Public Radio: WETS - 89.5 FM

Bookstores: Bookends, Main Street Books & Crafts

Chamber of Commerce: 179 East Main Street
Abingdon, VA 24210
540/628-8141

Charlottesville, Virginia

Location

Beautifully framed by hillsides that roll toward nearby Shenandoah National Forest and the Skyline Drive, Charlottesville is in the northwest part of the state, a two-hour drive from the museums and art galleries of Washington, D.C.

Great Outdoors

Charlottesville has something for everyone, from snowboarding and downhill at nearby Wintergreen ski area to white-water kayaking and hiking in the Shenandoah National Forest, Virginia's 450-mile stretch of the Appalachian Trail. A two-hour drive west deposits you in the middle of West Virginia, where first-class white-water adventure and challenging ski runs await you. On summer weekends, the Atlantic seashore is just three hours away, and Lake Monticello, much closer, beckons with sailing, swimming, and bass fishing. The climate here tends to favor long, humid summers and brief, New England-esque autumns. Charlottesville is dusted with snow a few times each winter.

Lifestyle

Charlottesville has natural beauty, a strong local economy, a prestigious university, funky bars and barbecue joints, and an exemplary arts conscience. The artists relocating here range from established folks who exhibit in galleries in Washington, D.C., New York, Atlanta, and Richmond, to progressive young artists taking advantage of the low cost of living and accessibility to major markets and regional hot spots on the summer arts fair circuit. In attractive, close-in neighborhoods, you'll pay about $125,000 for an average-sized home, about $95,000 in the fast-growing communities throughout Albemarle County.

Charlottesville's one of those rare small towns that actually has a nightlife. Some of the region's most creative chefs in nouveau Southern/American cuisine ply their trade at several great restaurants. Crankin' bars draw top talent in rock, alternative, blues, and jazz. An incredibly ambitious UVA performing arts series showcases the best in national and international classical, dance, and new performing arts. And several movie houses show foreign films.

Arts Scene

An eclectic, multidisciplinary group of artists calls this town home, including eminent literary figures, Broadway actors, and Hollywood producers. Music and theater are taken quite seriously at the UVA arts department, and that attracts talented instructors and visiting performers. Two modern theaters on campus handle the performing arts presentations, and there's also a summer repertory group on campus. On the downtown pedestrian mall, two old theaters are in the early stages of being converted into performance venues for theater, dance, and music.

Lots of graduates of the art department have made Charlottesville their full-time home, setting up their studios in one of the two studio centers downtown, BozArts and the McGuffey Arts Center. The McGuffey is located in a converted schoolhouse and has a central gallery space as well as many studios. Charlottesville has nearly 20 galleries, including the nonprofit

Second Street Gallery and a few spaces showing expensive fine crafts. Some of the city's politi cal leaders seem unable to come to terms with the fact that the creative community is burgeoning, and the debate about public art projects frequently degenerates into name-calling.

The local arts council is extremely proactive in promoting arts education in local schools. National education figures are frequently wooed to help the schools develop fully inte grated art programs in school curricula, and, as in most small college towns, the level of expertise in Charlottesville's school district is quite high. The Charlottesville Performing Arts Center is a combined civic center and auditorium that's used by local presenters ranging from kids' theater groups to ethnic dance companies.

Alternatives

The community has a year-round slate of arts events ranging from film festivals to summer opera programs at Ash Lawn, Thomas Jefferson's estate on the outskirts of town. Most of the town's many coffeehouses and restaurants exhibit local art; the best places to show are Spencer's 206 (a music store), the Metropolitan, Brasa, Scarpa, the Coffee Exchange, Continental Divide, and the Prism Coffee House. The Vinegar Hill Theatre shows foreign and art flicks; local musicians can make a decent living playing the region's surprisingly active college circuit.

Art Perspectives

"There's getting to be a strong community of visual artists in this town," says local calligraphic artist Roz Casey, "and they're congregating in places like the downtown mall, which in turn is bringing a lot of good restaurants into that area. We've got lots of people living here who can make a living in the visual, performing arts, and music. For visual artists the sales are much easier if you keep your work recognizable to the buyers. Contemporary's still a tough sell and does much better elsewhere.

"Our local theater group, Live Arts, is very professional, and they're indicative of the kinds of good artists who are moving into Charlottesville. The McGuffey Arts Center is a great working environment, a magnet that's helped to give all the artists here a sense of who each other is and what our broader impact in this town can eventually be."

Details

Population: 43,000 plus 20,000 college students

Important Arts Events: Children's Dance Festival in April, Summer Festival of the Arts in July, Court Days in October, Virginia Festival of American Film in October, First Night in December

Must-See Art Galleries: Fairweather Gallery, Second Street Gallery, UVA Art Museum

Local Arts Agency: Piedmont Council for the Arts
P.O. Box 2426
Charlottesville, VA 22902
804/971-2787

Natural Foods Stores: Integral Yoga, Rebecca's

Farmer's Market: Saturday mornings in the city parking lot on Water Street

National Public Radio: WTJU - 91.1 FM

Bookstores: New Dominion Books, The Quest Bookshop, Williams Corner Bookstore

Chamber of Commerce: P.O. Box 1564
Charlottesville, VA 22902
804/295-3141

Fredericksburg, Virginia

Location

Living here is like living within a city but without the hassles and crowds. Fredericksburg is a well-preserved historic community an hour south of Washington, D.C., and an hour north of Richmond. Most of the region's nightlife takes place in the northern Virginia suburbs, which are even closer

Great Outdoors

This 21,000-resident art town is surrounded by Civil War battlefields, haunting sites that local residents prize. A drive of slightly less than three hours lands you in Virginia Beach, and Cape Hatteras is just another hour away. While winter snows are not uncommon, downhill skiing is at least a two-hour drive away. Sailing and canoeing on the nearby Potomac River are popular year-round. Boaters also put in at nearby Lake Anna, a 13,000-acre freshwater fishing hole and summer recreation center.

Lifestyle

Each weekend Fredericksburg residents have the option of heading into D.C. for events at the Kennedy Center for the Performing Arts, exhibitions at the Smithsonian, and pizza at Vesuvio's. Of course, being so close to the city also brings with it the specter of commuters, and thus, higher real estate prices. A decent residence runs in the $150,000 range, much more if you want to live in one of the many historic homes in the town center. More than anything, Fredericksburg radiates a sense of the mid-1800s, when the city was rebuilt following the war years. A 40-block National Historic District is loaded with nearly 400 architectural treasures, including the homes of Mary Washington and James Madison. The Rappahannock River cuts right through the middle of town, providing waterfront views and making canoeing one of the favorite ways for surviving those humid southern summer days.

Arts Scene

The Fredericksburg Center for the Creative Arts, part of the Virginia Museum of Fine Arts, is located in the downtown's riverfront area in a home built during the late 1700s—an aesthetic boon but a logistical nightmare of constant repair and renovation. The center stages an annual slate of visual arts exhibitions, ranging from kids' art to invitationals to a successful annual studio tour. Mary Washington College has two first-rate art exhibition areas, one devoted to contemporary work from varying media, and the other focused on more traditional paintings. The town is loaded with antique shops and a dozen or so galleries, most of which display historical or contemporary works centered around Civil War themes. Artists moving into Fredericksburg try to snag studio space in the historic brick buildings along Hanover and Sophia Streets, and many join the Art First Gallery, a 28-member cooperative showing work by artists who are unconcerned with what happened here 150 years ago.

Performing arts are a year-round attraction at Mary Washington College, which uses both the Dodd Auditorium and the Klein Theatre for its frequently free performances of classical music, theater, and dance. The arts center works with the town library to present programs in theater and children's storytelling. The local repertory company is the Rude Mechanics. Classical music, kids' theater, jazz, and ethnic performing arts programs are somewhat ubiquitous, occurring at the college and the Episcopal and Presbyterian churches, the community center, the Colonial Theatre, and the Fredericksburg Area Museum and Cultural Center. Events taking place in D.C or Richmond are also easily reached.

Alternatives

Most of the coffeehouses serve as venues for local artists showing and selling their work. The best are Espresso Grounds, Java Connection, Hyperion, and Merriman's Bar. Fredericksburg has a bronze foundry, Wagner Metal Arts, casting mostly realistic sculpture for artists on the East Coast. It's not uncommon to find established artists from other areas dropping into town for a week or two to work on their works in progress. The local library shows an occasional foreign film, but with Richmond and D.C. nearby, nobody's lacking in cultural input.

Art Perspectives

Rob Gassie, a fine art and commercial photographer, says that the Fredericksburg art festivals are important venues for local artists selling their work. "We've got lots of people coming in here from D.C. and Richmond, and they're the ones who buy the art that's made by our artists. It would be very helpful if the city would put some of the energy it devotes to promoting Fredericksburg as an antiques center into promoting the arts and artists who live here.

"The past few years I've noticed a lot more artists and novelists moving into the area, and many younger artists who have experimental ways of looking at what can be done in visual arts and theater. .. These artists, who come here for the low rents and pretty scenery, have ideas that are energizing the entire town and will turn us into an arts center, whether or not the city fathers get behind us."

Details

Population: 21,000

Important Arts Events: Annual Fine Arts Exhibit in March, Fredericksburg Art Festival in June, Heritage Festival in July, Children's Art Expo in August, Studio Tour in October, First Night in December

Must-See Art Galleries: Art First Gallery, Dan Finnegan Gallery, Eyeclops Studio, Fredericksburg Center for the Creative Arts Gallery, Premier Gallery, Ridderhoff Martin Gallery and the duPont Gallery at Mary Washington College, Wagner Metal Arts

Local Arts Agency: Fredericksburg Center for the Creative Arts

813 Sophia Street
Fredericksburg, VA 22401
540/373-5646

Natural Food Stores: Healthway, Pantry Shelf

Farmer's Market: Daily in summer and fall at Hurkamp Park

National Public Radio: WAMU - 88.5 FM

Bookstore: Collective Books

Chamber of Commerce: P.O. Box 7476 Fredericksburg, VA 22404
540/786-7080

Anacortes, Washington

Location

If towns were restaurants, and location were "everything," Anacortes would have it made. Drive 90 minutes north and you're in Vancouver, British Columbia, one of the continent's most cosmopolitan cities. Drive 90 minutes south and you come to Seattle. Home to about 12,000 people, Anacortes sits at the tip of an island loverooking the beautiful San Juan Islands.

Great Outdoors

Living in the natural splendor of Anacortes is living surrounded by incredibly beautiful islands, wetlands, and secluded coves easily reached by paddle—which is why ocean kayaking is such a popular sport and canoeing comes a close second. Puget Sound gives up some of the biggest and baddest salmon in the Pacific; to live here is know exactly when the fish are biting and where. Anacortes has several public parks, the largest of which is Washington Park, a forested reserve known for its hiking trails.

The San Juan Islands and nearby Whidbey Island are chock-full of state parks, recreation sites, and boat launches. Campgrounds are abundant and, outside of some peak summer weeks, usually near-empty. In the summer, hikers and campers head into the North Cascades National Park, one of the most remote national park wilderness areas. If you don't have the time for an overnight trip, there's always the Washington State Ferry System, which maintains a terminal in Anacortes. You can catch a football-field-size ferry for a trip through the San Juan Islands to as far as Vancouver Island, Canada.

There's great downhill skiing at Stevens Pass, a resort a couple of hours from town. On your way to the Pass you can stop in at the Pilchuk School, a mecca for fine art glassmakers.

Lifestyle

Fidalgo Island separates Anacortes from the mainland, but bridges and highways connect it to interstate highways so close that some folks commute to jobs in Seattle. The big local employers are two oil refineries, who also happen to be major contributors to Anacortes' arts scene. This hip little town attracts plenty of artists and writers who, tired of the daily Seattle grind, have opted instead for a more sedate, affordable lifestyle in a place that's still within driving distance of the Pike Place Market. Homes here start in the $100,000 range, but you can find less expensive fixer-uppers in nearby towns like Burlington, a 15-minute drive away. Local schools take a comprehensive, if conventional, approach to arts education, offering visual art, drama, and music instruction as well as inviting regional artists to their artist-in-residence programs. Most kids with an interest in arts find their way to the after-school and summer classes provided by Anacortes Youth Arts, a nonprofit arts education group.

Arts Scene

Although Anacortes has a 35-year-old arts-and-crafts fair, the idea that artists from Seattle would move here to live and work was considered absurd until a few years ago. Galleries started popping up in the elegant downtown brick buildings, and artists started opening studio spaces on the spacious second stories of those same historic structures. The community's visual arts scene centers around the Depot Arts Center run by the Anacortes Arts Foundation. Trains don't stop here any more, but visual arts are rotated monthly in the Depot's exhibition gallery, and a resident dance company uses part of this renovated 1911 building as its rehearsal and performance space. The arts foundation holds art classes in the Depot, and there's a move underway to swipe a few freight cars from a Burlington Northern yard, move them to the Depot's rail siding under cover of night, and turn them into more classroom and art studio space.

While many performing arts and music events take place at the Depot Art Center's small space, the Anacortes Community Theatre presents its six annual plays in a former church building. Touring classical music acts and orchestras perform at Brodniak Hall on the high school campus; literary readings and poetry slams are held at How It Works, a combined gallery and performance space. Two popular ethnic music groups, Vela Luka Croatian Dancers and the Celtic Music Group, use the Depot for performances, as does International Folk Dancers, an Anacortes nonprofit that presents touring dance companies. Nearby Mount Vernon's Lincoln Theatre is a regional center for foreign films.

Alternatives
Watermark Books and the Anacortes Brew House both display and sell visual art created by Anacortes artists, as does How it Works. Favorite local hangouts are the Port-in-a-Storm Juice Bar, Gere-a-Deli, and the Courtyard Bistro.

Art Perspectives
"Anacortes is friendly, safe, Scandinavian, and affordable," says Anne Martin McCool, a contemporary painter. "I work in an incredibly beautiful downtown studio that looks out onto the Cascade Mountains and the Puget Sound, and when I open my windows, the studio's filled with fresh ocean air. The town has a working-class feel, yet it supports the arts. Attitudes are changing, artists are moving in, and Anacortes is developing into a great place to live."

Details

Population: 12,000

Important Arts Events: Waterfront Festival in May; Downtown Art Walks in June, September, and December; Anacortes Arts & Crafts Festival in August

Must-See Art Galleries: Cabiri Gallery, Northwest Departures Gallery at the Depot Arts Center, Serendipity Gallery

Local Arts Agency: Depot Arts Center/Anacortes Art Foundation
P.O. Box 635
Anacortes, WA 98221
360/293-3663

Farmer's Market: Depot Arts Center on Saturdays

Bookstores: Pelican Bay Books, The Business, Watermark Books

National Public Radio: KUOW - 94.9 FM

Natural Foods Store: Anacortes Health and Nutrition

Chamber of Commerce: 819 Commercial Avenue, Suite G
Anacortes, WA 98221
360/293-7911

Coupeville, Washington

Location

Whidbey Island, a scenic refuge at the mouth of Puget Sound, is linked to the mainland by ferries to its south and west, and by a bridge from the north. If you hit the ferry on time and miss mainland traffic, the drive into Seattle takes less than an hour.

Great Outdoors

Halfway up Whidbey Island, Coupeville is nestled into an elbow-crook of land that follows the shores of Penn Cove. Ebey's Landing National Historic Reserve sweeps around the cove, taking in not only this historic community, but also thousands of acres of shoreline, forests, and farmland. Within an easy bike ride of downtown are two waterfront state parks, Fort Casey and Fort Ebey, each offering campgrounds and vast stretches of undeveloped rocky beachfront. The 17,000 acres of Ebey's Reserve are almost completely privately owned, but the government maintains many historic structures, scenic roads, and hiking trails throughout the reserve. The waters around Penn Cove are very popular with scuba divers, crabbers, and commercial oyster cultivators, so the ecological integrity of the cove is carefully maintained. This priority is typical of the mindset that has limited Coupeville's commercial growth and preserved the town's integrity. Sportfishing is a favorite pastime, along with kayaking and clamming. The closest ski area is a two-hour drive and a ferry ride away, on the northern end of the Olympic Peninsula.

Lifestyle

The lower end of Whidbey Island is close enough to Seattle to have attracted steady growth over the past few years, while the northern end is dominated by the naval air station at Oak Harbor. In between, tiny Coupeville survives as a quiet place attractive to retirees and a growing number of artists. Real estate prices are average by Washington standards—a small home in the area will run about $125,000. The schools are quite good but limited in the art classes offered. Local artists sign up for artist-in-residence programs through the school's Arts Alive program.

A breathtaking range of classes is offered by the Coupeville Art Center, and although most of the center's classes during the school year are geared toward adult artists, motivated high schoolers are also admitted. The center also operates an innovative and comprehensive summer series of youth art classes for all ages, covering literary arts, fine crafts, and watercolors.

Arts Scene

Coupeville's claim to small art town fame is founded on two pillars: a mind-boggling array of education programs and a national reputation as the most dynamic fiber arts community north of Crownpoint, New Mexico. The Coupeville Arts Center sponsors several education tracks, offering beginning to advanced instruction in several artistic disciplines. The "Let's Begin" track covers nearly two dozen entry-level classes in fields from beadwork to weaving to pottery to painting. "Palettes Plus" brings nearly two dozen established painters from across the nation to Coupeville to teach advanced painting techniques. The "Photo Focus" track hosts a dozen or so professional photographers to teach all levels of photo classes. The "Needleworks" track brings a dozen top national artists into Coupeville for a week-long seminar and classroom series at the nearby Camp Casey Conference Center. Add to this mix the kids' summer classes, a series of classes in "City & Guilds Embroidery" (a medieval English form of fabric art) and the center's biggest national show, the annual Fiber Forum, and you have to conclude that this tiny town's arts center could holds its own against any in the nation.

Though the Fiber Forum is a decade old, it has risen to the top of the nation's annual conferences for the promotion, education, exhibition, and collecting of fiber arts. Two dozen of the nation's foremost weavers, embroiderers, dyers, historians, designers, and ethnic fabric arts authorities are brought into Coupeville for a week of intermediate to advanced activities in this increasingly popular form of fine craft. Because of the Coupeville Arts Center's dynamic approach to arts education, a number of the nation's best fiber artists have relocated here.

The visual arts in Coupeville are certainly strong, as evidenced by the rapidly expanding series of master classes held in conjunction with Palettes Plus. The one thing that's missing in Coupeville is first-rate exhibition space, and this is one town that has demonstrated tenfold its ability to fill an art gallery with exciting artwork from all media—work that would fly out the door were it properly presented. There are several commercial galleries on the island, including the very fine Penn Cove Gallery on Coupeville's gorgeous Front Street. Certainly in a state like Washington, which values and invests in the arts, some funding source can be found to endow this great art town with the exhibition, sales, and educational facilities it needs.

Alternatives

Several Coupeville area restaurants as well as the cafés in nearby Langley and the small art town of LaConner exhibit local art work. Be sure to check out the Artist's Cooperative Gallery in Langley and Christopher's, a Coupeville restaurant.

Art Perspectives

Madelyn van der Hoogt, a fiber artist and writer, says, "The artists here all know each other through the network created by the art center. We live in a beautiful, peaceful place that's quite rural, but is actually very concerned with the cutting edge of what's happening in the world of fiber arts."

Details

Population: 1,300

Important Arts Events: Needleworks in March, Photo Focus in April and May, Coupeville Arts & Crafts Festival in August, Fiber Forum in September

Must-See Art Galleries: Childers/Proctor Gallery, Coupeville Arts Center, Museo Piccolo Gallery, Penn Cove Gallery

Local Arts Agency: Coupeville Arts Center P.O. Box 171

Coupeville, WA 98239
360/678-3396

Natural Foods Store: Sassafras Farm

Farmer's Market: Weekends on Main Street

National Public Radio: KUOW - 94.9 FM

Bookstores: Book Bay, The Moonraker, Warm Winds Books & Music, The Wind & Tide

Chamber of Commerce: 5 South Main Coupeville, WA 98239 360/678-5434

Metaline Falls, Washington

Location

The sparsely populated far northeastern corner of Washington is a landscape rich with natural beauty, though cold as a polar bear's nose from Halloween through Easter. Metaline Falls is packed to its rafters with 215 in-town residents—and just a couple thousand more if you count every living being within a 25-mile radius. The closest place to get a pastrami sandwich is the small art town of Nelson, British Columbia, an hour's drive north, or Spokane, 90 minutes south.

Great Outdoors

Around this neck of the woods, you're never more than ten minutes from spectacular fishing and hunting grounds. People around here know how to do the one-two trick of tying a fly and casting a line, either into the raging waters of the Pend Oreille River, which cuts through the middle of town, or Sullivan Lake, a five-mile finger of trout-fishing paradise just a short drive from the edge of town. Anyone with an urge to commune with nature can walk north, south, east, or west from the front of the Cutter Theatre, and within a few minutes find themselves in either the Colville National Forest, the Kaniksu National Forest, or the Salmo-Priest Wilderness. If you want to hike the rugged glacial terrain of the Canadian Rockies, Kokanee Glacier Provincial Park is 90 minutes north, along with the spectacular, fjord-like splendor of Kootenay Lake The closest ski areas are in Nelson, BC and Sandpoint, Idaho, where the burgeoning giant of Schweitzer Ski Area takes on all comers.

Lifestyle

Tiny Metaline Falls absorbed some enormous financial hits a few years ago when its largest employer, a cement plant, killed its operations about the same time the forestry industry slowed to a trickle, stranding hundreds more workers and forcing some to leave the region in search of jobs. But even if Pend Oreille County remains right at the top of the state's unemployment list, there's a glimmer of light on Metaline Falls' horizon. The economy has stabilized, and largely through the spirited transition that gave the community its first performing arts center, folks have started to hold their heads high. Metaline Falls' 80-year-old downtown has been spruced up, although there are still a few vacant retail storefronts. Average-sized homes in wooded neighborhoods sell in the $50,000 range, less than half of what they'd go for closer to Spokane, the region's fast-growing economic center.

Despite the tough times, the town's schools have maintained their commitment to arts education. Grade school kids get visual arts classes, while middle- and high schoolers choose among visual arts, music, and drama electives. Those who want more can join the drama classes taught at the Cutter Theatre or enroll in the after-school art classes offered by an accomplished painter who also happens to be the town's mayor.

Arts Scene

Four years ago the state pumped nearly $1 million into renovating the Cutter Theatre. The old high school building is now a 167-seat performing arts space, arts education center, branch library, artists' studio space, visual arts exhibition space, community mental health center, and even banquet facility with a catering kitchen. The Cutter Theatre embodies Metaline Falls' hopes for a bright future. While serving the community's creative spirit, this amazingly diverse facility provides the entire town with a slice of the cultural tourism pie it's never before tasted.

The Cutter Theatre Players, Metaline Falls' community theater group, stages five productions annually. So strong is its regional reputation that shows regularly sell out to audiences from small communities in southeast British Columbia, northeast Washington, and northern Idaho. Amateur theater troupes from Spokane, newly aware of the market for their acts in Metaline Falls, now rent the Cutter for their road shows. Regional artists show their work in the Cutter's exhibition space, while the high school uses the theater for its student productions. The Cutter's renaissance has also inspired a library lecture series, bringing academics and public figures from Spokane and the surrounding area into town. Meanwhile nearly 200 residents have signed on as either volunteers or enrollees in the theater's many educational programs. Through the theater's programs, the community has found its direction. What started with the renovation of one building has turned into an astounding and far-reaching transformation.

Alternatives

If you're in Metaline Falls, wander over to the mayor's office in the lobby of the Washington Hotel (she owns the place). If you can get her to put down her paintbrush for a few minutes, ask her how much money she needs to renovate the downtown. Maybe she'll take you over to Katie's Oven for a cinnamon roll.

Art Perspectives

Teen McGowan, mayor/oil painter/hotel owner puts it bluntly, "Winters are long and rents are cheap. The word's starting to get out about Metaline Falls, and artists are moving in, so you better get your rear end over here, fast!"

Details

Population: 215

Important Art Events: Affair on Main Street in September, Deck the Falls in December

Must-See Art Galleries: Cutter Theatre Gallery

Local Arts Agency: The Cutter Theatre
P.O. Box 133
Metaline Falls, WA 99153
509/446-4108

Natural Food Store: Ione Co-op

National Public Radio: KPBX - 91.1 FM

Bookstore: Book Depot

Chamber of Commerce: Washington Hotel
P.O. Box 277
Metaline Falls, WA 99153
509/446-2211

Olympia, Washington

Location

The south end of Washington's Puget Sound is a region of tremendous natural beauty, where dark blue waters cut through forested islands, and narrow, steep land formations separate one fjord-like waterway from another. The 37,000 residents of Olympia, the state capitol and a great art town, live less than a two-hour drive south of Seattle.

Great Outdoors

Olympia's big outdoor recreation is fishing, especially for salmon and steelhead trout, but also for Dungeness crab. Olympic National Park, less than an hour's drive from town, is surrounded by wilderness areas and a national forest—all filled with hiking trails, hot springs, campgrounds, and streams. Mt. Rainier National Park and Mt. St. Helens National Monument are also nearby, with the same great outdoor recreation resources. Around Olympia are several great parks, bike trails, running trails, and nature reserves, including Nisqually National Wildlife Refuge. Ten miles south of town, Millersylvania State Park has nearly 200 campsites.

Lifestyle

Olympia's work force is very stable, hooked in as it is to the agencies, courts, and contractors that make the state government work. The local population is well educated and tends to buy art, which makes this community's arts scene larger than you might expect in a town this size. Olympia is a beautiful place to live, especially in the historic neighborhoods surrounding the capitol. Average-sized homes in most parts of town start in the $100,000 range.

Arts education is just starting to hit high gear in Olympia's public schools, but it's taken the schools years to offer much more than basic classes and matinee outings at the Washington Center, a downtown Olympia performing arts venue. An artist-in-residence program has begun in most schools, but in many instances these artists are fighting the school dis-trict's lingering "art-cart" mind-set.

The presence of the Washington Center means that local residents need not drive wet roads to Seattle to see great shows, and Evergreen State College has generated a thriving alternative music scene in town. Evergreen, which offers credit courses in body piercing and tie-dying, is a magnet for students so creative (or just odd) that they don't fit into the environment of a "normal" college. After graduation, many of these students remain here and become the performers and audiences that drive the local music scene.

Arts Scene

Olympia has an active, but divided, visual arts scene. Arts Olympia, with younger contemporary artists, uses the nonprofit lobby exhibition space in the Washington Center, while the Artist Co-op Gallery, the town's arts establishment, has its own exhibition and sales space elsewhere. The groups have not yet joined in pushing for a community center to provide the kind of exhibition, arts education, and small performance space needed. Olympia's commercial gallery situation is healthy, with several galleries selling the local work and a few developing regional reputations for their quality. Childhood's End Gallery, State of the Arts Gallery, Site Line Gallery, The Gallery, and Thompson Gallery are all in this latter category. Olympia's largest arts festival is the Olympia Arts Commission's twice-annual Arts Walk, a one-night affair that turns nearly 100 of the town's retail stores, neighborhood bars, bookstores, studio buildings, and street corners into gallery spaces; Art Walk draws over 10,000 people into town for an evening of fun, and the visitors buy art by the armfuls.

Olympia's performing arts scene revolves around the Washington Center for the Performing Arts, a nearly-new, 800-seat space that can present a dozen different acts each month without skipping a beat: from Broadway musicals and Olympia Symphony performances to ethnic music and contemporary dance. The center's black box, a 125-seat facility, is constantly busy with community theater groups, kids' theater groups, and classical music recitals. At the Olympia Center, a smaller performing-arts venue, are poetry readings, local ballet, folk music, and some classical music performances. During summer Olympia's own Shakespeare company stages an evening festival at Sylvester Park; otherwise it performs at the Washington Center. The Olympia Film Society shows foreign flicks at the Historic Capitol Theatre and produces an annual fall film festival.

Alternatives

For starters, check out Olympia's music scene. The town has lots of bands, several venues, its own college radio station, and recording companies. On any weekend, a half-dozen or more acts are hitting the stage. Visual artists exhibit their work all over town, and places such as Batdorf & Bronson's, Dancing Goats, The Spar, Ben Moore's, Smithfield's Café, and The Fish Bowl Pub sell it as well.

Art Perspectives

According to Tom Anderson, mixed media artist, "To survive here you've got to sell in Seattle and Portland, but the town's becoming conscious of the numbers of artists living here and moving into town. Artists who have lived here a while have found themselves in the middle of a wonderful community revival, and the downtown atmosphere's changing for the better, largely because of the booming music scene that's developed."

Details

Population: 37,000

Important Arts Events: Spring and Fall Art Walks, Shakespeare Festival in July

Must-See Art Galleries: Artist Co-op Gallery, Arts Olympia Gallery, Childhood's End Gallery, State of the Arts Gallery

Local Arts Agency: Olympia Arts Commission
222 North Columbia
Olympia, WA 98501
360/753-8380

Natural Foods Store: Olympia Co-op

Farmers Market: Thursday through Sunday at Farmers Market

National Public Radio: KPLU - 88.5 FM

Bookstores: Browsers Book Shop, Orca Books, Four Seasons Books, Fireside Books, Pathway Books

Chamber of Commerce: 521 Legion Way
Olympia, WA 98507
360/357-3362

Walla Walla, Washington

Location

As the saying goes, "the town's so wonderful they named it twice." Actually, Walla Walla means "many waters" in a regional Native American tongue. The name is still appropriate for this community set in Washington's southeast corner.

Walla Walla River flows along the edge of town. Spring runoff from nearby Blue Mountains feeds several streams and rivers, all of which end up joining the Columbia River 30 miles west of town. Walla Walla is known for its mild climate, with the early springs and late Indian summers an agricultural region thrives on. There's even sunshine 300 days each year, which sets this place apart from gloomier sections of the state. The town is home to three colleges: Whitman College, Walla Walla College, and Walla Walla Community College, each of which programs a range of visual and performing arts programs.

Great Outdoors

Walla Walla features dozens of parks and recreation sites, from pocket-sized Heritage Square downtown, to 200-acre Fort Walla Walla Park. Heritage Square is best known as a rallying point for the arts community, which a few years ago teamed up with a local bank to relocate the ornate sandstone façade of the town's Odd Fellows Temple to the side of a brick commercial building near the park. Dismantled and reassembled brick by brick, the historic façade is a monument to Walla Walla's artistic side.

Fort Walla Walla Park, filled with bicycle trails, nature areas, and dozens of campsites, is the site of the community's 1,300-seat amphitheater, which is filled during the summer months with audiences attending the community college's annual musical. From Walla Walla's location on the Washington-Oregon border, the Blue Mountain Range that runs across both sides of the state line can be seen from town. Once in the Blue Mountains, you can follow the 200-mile trail system of the Wenaha-Tucannon Wilderness area (on the other side of which is Joseph, another great small art town). Hell's Canyon National Recreation Area, with the deepest canyon on the continent, has campgrounds, back-country hiking, incredible views, and Indian petroglyphs, most of which are within a three-hour drive from Walla Walla.

On the Washington side of the border, it's just a short drive to Juniper Dunes Wilderness, or to breathtaking Palouse Falls, or to McNary National Wildlife Refuge on the shores of the Columbia River. Ski Bluewood and Spout Springs are two small downhill skiing areas nearby, while larger areas in Idaho, Oregon, and Washington are about three-hour drives

Lifestyle

Walla Walla was once an outpost along the Oregon Trail. It was a gold mining boom town, but once the Klondike began to heat up, Walla Walla settled down to what it does best—farming. Much of the town's turn-of-the-century architectural legacy has been restored to its original grandeur, and today these structures house many of the businesses that fill Walla

Walla's compact, prosperous downtown. One such building is Fort Walla Walla Museum, which features restored log and wood structures that once were the town's schoolhouse, railroad depot, and trading post. Nearby is Whitman Mission National Historic Site, dedicated to Protestant missionaries who lost their lives here during the Indian Wars in the mid-1800s

The main employers in the region are agricultural (the Walla Walla sweet onion and Maui's sweet onion wage an annual war), beef processing, and the forestry industries. One of the big surprises here in recent years has been the growth of the region's wine industry There are now a half-dozen vineyards among the rolling, green hills characteristic of Walla Walla's landscape. The college students in town also support a range of oddball clothing and skateboard shops.

The Carnegie Art Center, a converted, 1905 Carnegie Library, is Walla Walla's local nonprofit art exhibition space and art education facility. Carnegie's art classes are especially important to the community—thanks to the decidedly unimaginative approach to art education programs taken by the city's schools· The schools rely on state-funded artist-in-residence programs to supplement regular art, music, and drama classes.

Walla Walla is a community of quiet neighborhoods, with treelined streets and inexpensive homes Much of the town is within walking distance of downtown, and bicycle trails link outlying communities such as College Place with the rest of Walla Walla.

Arts Scene

The local colleges' art departments give Walla Walla a head start in the visual arts, not only for its art-educated graduates, but also by bringing well-known artists into town to teach. The community college's art gallery focuses on local and regional visual arts, while Whitman's Sheehan Gallery and Walla Walla College's Harris Gallery mix traditional and contemporary work in their exhibition calendars. Local artists occasionally exhibit their work through these galleries' invitational shows, but their best local opportunities are at the Carnegie Art Center, which rotates work through three gallery spaces.

Walla Walla's commercial gallery scene has done well for itself in the past few years, with art-savvy cultural tourists having made this town a must-stop on the northwest art collector's itinerary. Paula Ray Gallery is a modern exhibition space that exhibits the work of an exceptionally strong group of contemporary landscape artists, along with bronzes and figurative work. Sicyon Gallery and the Fenton/Stahl Gallery are able to sell contemporary work, while Mill Creek Gallery and Wheatland Gallery are more traditional in their choice of artists.

One of the most interesting visual arts exhibition venues in Walla Walla isn't an official gallery. The Walla Walla Foundry attracts huge crowds to its site whenever it throws one of its impromptu opening celebrations for works of contemporary sculpture bound for major metropolitan art centers. The Foundry is a bronze-pouring operation employing nearly two-dozen skilled craftspeople Its casting operation creates three-dimensional art for some of the nation's most popular names in the contemporary art world. Unlike the foundries in Loveland or Joseph (both wonderful art towns), which owe much to the realism school of sculpture, the Walla Walla Foundry has made its reputation in the realm of contemporary abstract work. On occasion, when the crew completes some massive, mind-bending assemblage that's headed for some faraway place, the foundry throws a party to celebrate, throwing its doors open to anyone and everyone connected to the Walla Walla arts scene. Crowds of 500 are common.

Walla Walla's visual arts scene exceeds the expectation you'd customarily have for a community of this size, which is the direct result of having a performing arts department and three area colleges at its disposal. For instance, the community college has a multi-use sports and entertainment complex used for the town's larger events, such as jazz festivals, rock concerts, and an occasional theater department presentation. Walla Walla College has its own fine arts center performance space used by the school's theater and music departments.

Whitman College has the community's two most heavily used performance spaces, the 1,500-seat Cordiner Hall and the smaller Chism Auditorium. The college also has a small amphitheater used for summer concerts. Cordiner is the home of the Walla Walla Symphony, which presents six concerts during its October–April season. Chism serves as the venue for visiting classical music acts such as chamber orchestras and soloists. Whitman's highly regarded dance department uses Chism for its school-year performances and for shows connected with its annual summer dance camp. Walla Walla also has community choral and jazz societies. With a thousand or so college students in town, Walla Walla is also able to support a few live music nightclubs that mix alternative, rock, and folk music into their calendars. The most popular of these clubs are the Blue Mountain Tavern and J.P.'s on the Green.

Walla Walla theater is as strong as its visual arts and music. It is headed up by the Little Theater of Walla Walla, an adept community theater company that presents four annual productions between August and February. The Little Theatre recently launched an expansion project aimed at doubling its seating capacity.

Walla Walla's colleges present their own drama productions in their respective spaces, but the programming at Whitman College is especially worth noting. Using the Harper Joy Theatre as its main stage, the school's theater department presents ten or so productions a year, ranging from mainstage one-act operas to Shakespeare. Experimental productions and new plays premier in the theater's Freimann Stage black-box setting.

Alternatives

Several of Walla Walla's restaurants and cafés exhibit the work of local artists, but there are a number of downtown establishments that don't and should be informed of the commissions they're losing. Pangea Coffeehouse on the edge of the Whitman campus exhibits and sells local art and provides an open mike for the touring folk acts on weekends. Merchant's LTD and Merchant's Second Feature are two downtown alternative exhibition spots and hangouts for local artists.

Art Perspectives

Wayne Chabre, a sculptor working primarily in hammered copper constructions, says, "For a sculptor, having a foundry in town helps me feel connected to the rest of the art world. It's a great resource I can use for problem solving. I like living here. I grew up here and moved back to Walla Walla after working in the Peace Corps. Here you can smell the cottonwoods and hear the sounds of meadowlarks—the kind of stuff that goes right to my solar plexus. Walla Walla's arts community has a lot of people working here for art's sake, and I know most of them. We're a community that is trying to keep the quality of our life high and make this town as pretty as it can be."

Mark Anderson, managing director and owner of the Walla Walla Foundry: "We like working with artists who are trying to create personal statements. Lots of artists are from the Bay Area, lots from L.A. We have a niche in the contemporary art world, and I try to hire my staff locally. I'd rather train someone who grew up and lives in this area than bring in someone from outside. Eventually, though, I'd like to see more artists moving into town."

Details

Population: 29,000

Important Arts Events: Balloon Stampede in May, Walla Walla Sweet Onion Festival in July, Whitman Mission Pow-Wow in July, Summer Concert series in Heritage Square

Must-see Art Galleries: Carnegie Art Center, Fenton/Stahl Gallery, Harris Gallery, Paula Ray Gallery, Sheehan Gallery, Sicyon Gallery, Walla Walla Foundry

Local Arts Agency: Blue Mountain Arts Alliance
P.O. Box 2192

Walla Walla, WA 99362
509/525-1126

Natural Foods Stores: Andy's Market, Vitamin Cottage

Farmers Market: Farm stands all over the region

National Public Radio: KFAE - 89.1 FM

Bookstore: Earth Light Books

Chamber of Commerce: P.O. Box 644
Walla Walla, WA 99362
509/525-0850

Berkeley Springs, West Virginia

Location

The 840 residents of tiny Berkeley Springs live in the easternmost end of West Virginia, less than a two-hour drive from Washington, D.C. The Potomac River, a white-water rafting mecca, is just six miles from town center. Weekend day-trippers from the nearby metropolis have allowed artists here to make a decent living from their work.

Great Outdoors

Berkeley Springs' residents have the best of both worlds: mountainous terrain and great ski areas a short drive to the west, and Atlantic beaches a slightly longer though still easy drive to the east. West Virginia has a first-rate state park system, and Cacapon State Park on the town's outskirts has a championship golf course in addition to its river, lakes, and recreation areas. In fact, this community was originally named Bath, after the thermal springs that for centuries have lured travelers seeking its healing waters. Today many local businesses offer therapeutic treatments ranging from new-age healing to Swedish massage, along with long soaks in the many springs sprinkled around town. One of the community's largest employers is a manufacturer of homeopathic remedies, while the nearby Coolfont Resort is one of the East Coast's foremost spa retreats. Berkeley Springs State Park sits squarely in the middle of town, from which several mineral baths are only a short walk away.

Lifestyle

Haven to an interesting mix of retirees, physical therapists, visual artists, fine craftspeople, and new agers, Berkeley Springs is still a place where homes can be picked up for well under $100,000, despite their relative proximity to Washington, D.C.'s museums, galleries, and airports. The Morgan Arts Council oversees an Adopt-a-School program giving working artists extended teaching residencies in all of the county's schools. A program is also under way to integrate arts education into the county schools' curricula. Arts have had a major economic impact here. Since the mid-1980s artists and cultural tourism have been responsible for the renovation and reopening of most downtown buildings.

Arts Scene

Berkeley Springs' success as an arts town comes from two sources: cultural tourists cruising its art festivals and galleries, and a ten-year influx of creative professionals hellbent on improving things. Weekend events such as the Apple Butter Festival and the Bath Craft Fair draw thousands of visitors who return to town at other times of the year, buying art, filling B&B rooms, eating at restaurants, and soaking in the town's warm mineral springs. Run by restored movie theater owner Jeanne Mozier, the Morgan Arts Council programs concerts, artist-education workshops, kids' art programs, and theater events throughout the year. The state arts commission and local taxes support these activities, plus a council-published annual artists' directory.

Performing arts exist here but in a small way. The Coolfont Resort is extraordinarily supportive of Berkeley Springs' arts scene, operating an arts foundation that brings classical music performance to its 200-seat theater and underwriting an artists' residency program of free arts classes and lectures. The Star Theatre peppers its roster of first-run releases with an occasional foreign film. The New World Theatre Company is a street-theater organization modeled after the guerrilla groups popular in the U.S. during the '60s and still thriving throughout Europe.

Alternatives

Everything here is an alternative of one sort or another. Some Berkeley Springs artists run their own galleries from their studios in the downtown area (yes, overhead costs and local taxes are quite low), while others exhibit at places like Tari's Café or at the Bath House shop at Cacapon State Park, ten miles south of town. The two art galleries in nearby Hedgesville are great places to find work by local artists.

Art Perspectives

J.W. Rowe, founder and artistic director of the New World Theater, observes that Berkeley Springs is an ideal rural community. "Just from the nature of all the creative people living here, you feel that you're living where the arts are considered important, not just for people's personal reasons but also for the community's economic well-being. There's a large cadre of professional artists here making a living from their work, and because of that, the dialogues about what's important for the community tend to be fairly far-reaching. For example, a lot of us would like to see Berkeley Springs have some sort of a performing arts center as well as a non-profit visual arts exhibition space, so we're dealing with how to financially put something like that together. It also shows you how many people around here appreciate, and attend, the performing arts events that come to town."

Details

Population: 840

Important Arts Events: Summer Concert series at Berkeley Springs State Park, Apple Butter Festival in October, Bath Craft Fair in November, Classical Music Series at the Coolfont Resort

Must-See Art Galleries: Amingo Glass, Coolfont Resort, The Country Inn, Heath's Studio Gallery, Mountain Laurel Crafts, Tari's Café Gallery, Whisperwood Studio

Local Arts Agency: Morgan Arts Council
Route 3, Box 191
Berkeley Springs, WV 25411
800/447-8797

Natural Food Store: Tonoloway Foods

Farmer's Market: Saturday mornings in the Courthouse Square parking lot

National Public Radio: WVPN - 88.9 FM

Bookstores: The Bath House, Mountain Laurel Crafts

Chamber of Commerce: 304 Fairfax Street
Berkeley Springs, WV 25411
304/258-3738

Location

Framed on three sides by the Monongahela National Forest, this 8,500-resident art town in east-central West Virginia is several hours' drive from Washington, D.C., Pittsburgh, and Charleston. The closest airport is in Clarksburg, an hour's drive.

Great Outdoors

As is true of many rural communities, Elkins' isolation is also its greatest asset when it comes to natural resources. Lakes, hiking trails, ski areas, white-water sports, and back-country wilderness are all within a short drive of town. Winters can be difficult, but the skiers who traipse through Elkins in mid-February provide an important economic boost. Unlike other parts of the state, forestry and not mining built this region. The area is a magnet for competitive mountain bikers who enjoy the region's old logging roads, and several of the east coast's toughest biking events are held here. For those with an aversion to scraped knees, the state stocks nearly 200 nearby rivers and streams with brook and rainbow trout.

Lifestyle

Elkin's tremendous wealth in the early part of the century resulted in the growth of Victorian mansions, ornate downtown retail stores, and large public buildings. Much of this historic legacy has been preserved, and today Elkins is among West Virginia's most beautiful places to visit. It is also an affordable city—$50,000 buys you a respectable-sized home in a leafy neighborhood. If you want land, homes on five-acre lots go for about twice that price.

The local school system is one of the best in the state, reflecting the community's ties to Davis & Elkins College, an outstanding school with a strong influence on the regional arts community. D&E, as it's known, is the site of the Augusta Heritage Center, one of the nation's premier institutions devoted to the preservation and performance of traditional folk arts. Augusta emphasizes crafts and music, from Cajun and blues to Irish and Appalachian. Each summer it presents an incredibly diverse schedule of classes with master artists who come to Elkins for workshops, performances, and lectures, making it a sort of Southern Chautauqua.

Arts Scene

Several years ago Elkins' leaders realized that cultural tourism and outdoor recreation were economic godsends upon which the town could build its future. As a result, they both receive the community's financial and moral support—which means they're here to stay. The Big Daddy of visual arts in Elkins is the fine-crafts field, which attracts artists from points east who not only visit to attend or instruct at an Augusta summer workshop but who also move here.

Craft artists in Elkins live in a supportive community of creative individuals and make their livings selling directly to collectors at regional craft shows and also through fine craft galleries from Washington, D.C. to Atlanta. The community's reputation is so strong that metropolitan-area art dealers prowl Elkins' arts and crafts exhibitions, seeking marketable artists.

The Old Brick Playhouse is home to two arts groups: one of West Virginia's premier children's theater companies and the Artists at Work Gallery, a cooperative loaded with premier fine-crafts artists. The community also has a volunteer theater company, a private music school, a very popular dance society, and access to the many performing arts events at D&E, which include a classical music series at the 1,300-seat Harper McNeeley Auditorium and a summer series of concerts by the Augusta Center in the college's 1,000-seat outdoor amphitheater. Kids who want a taste of performing under the lights can enroll in summer programs at the Old Brick

Alternatives

Elkins is a year-round music center, and many Augusta Center instructors play gigs around the region on weekends. Two of the more popular local bars that have live music are Beander's, known for its jazz, and Pete's Place, a hangout for Elkins' many contemporary folk musicians and occasional touring rock bands. Local visual artists are well-represented in the town's cafés and restaurants, with the Starr Café and C.J. Maggi's being two of the best places to exhibit and sell local art.

Art Perspectives

Fiber artist Michael Davis says that in Elkins he's found an active group of professional artists, great places to enjoy live music, spectacular natural beauty, and even a few good restaurants. "You'll find a lot of informal get-togethers taking place where artists come together for dinners at someone's house or meet somewhere to talk about what's going on around town," he says.

"Augusta's programs are a big reason many artists are moving here; with that kind of programming, living here takes on a quality you'd expect to find in much larger communities. Augusta provides many of us with employment opportunities as well, and the Randolph Arts Alliance is another group that works hard at finding opportunities for the artists living here. Land prices are very reasonable, taxes are low, and studio space is easy to find . . . what else do you need?"

Details

Population: 8,500

Important Arts Events: International Ramp Cookoff in April, Augusta Heritage Center summer concert series in July and August, Augusta Festival in mid-August, Mountain State Forest Festival in October, Fiddler's Reunion in October

Must-See Art Galleries: Artists at Work Gallery, Paull Gallery at D&E, Seneca Trail Artists Guild (changing exhibitions in the post office lobby), Talbot Paint

Local Arts Agency: Randolph Arts Alliance
329 Davis Avenue
Elkins, WV 26241

Natural Foods Store: Good Energy Foods

Farmer's Market: City Park on Wednesday mornings

National Public Radio: WVPR - 88.5 FM

Bookstore: Augusta Books

Chamber of Commerce: 200 Executive Plaza
Elkins, WV 26241
304/636-2717

Amery, Wisconsin

Location
Almost a suburb of Minneapolis, Amery is situated in northwestern Wisconsin, land of lakes, forests, small towns, fishing resorts, and bait shops. Winters are difficult, which is why the town's 2,800 residents think summer starts in late April, about the time everyone is half-crazed with cabin fever.

Great Outdoors
Just about everything you expect from Mother Nature is either right outside Amery, or a short drive away (well, except maybe for palm trees). The hundreds of lakes in this region include a few that practically lap downtown doorsteps, and if you want to throw a line, the fish are waiting. Trout streams are everywhere and include the Apple River, which flows through the center of town. Tubing the Apple is a big-time sport; the season's short but fun. The nearby St. Croix River, which connects with the Mississippi just south of the Twin Cities, is the site of several state parks, including Interstate State Park with 1,300 acres of campsites, cross-country skiing, river gorges, and hiking trails; and Willow River State Park, about twice the size of Interstate. Around here, duck hunting isn't just a popular autumn pastime, it also provides the final tourism boost, an important pocket-filler that helps some folks make it through the long winter. A respectable ski area in nearby Dresser has one of the best winter season night scenes, and the region is thick with cross-country and snowmobile trails.

Lifestyle
Amery's close enough to the Twin Cities to allow for commuting, so on weekday mornings people hit the two-lane blacktop connecting this tiny town to the rest of the world. Amery is attractive but not historic, built on a still-active forestry economy. This is a solid, working-class community that promotes some things other towns take for granted, like good schools and a large public library. Art instruction in the Amery schools, however, hasn't been innovative, which is one of the main reasons why the Northern Lakes Center for the Arts runs a year-round program of kids' art education (called the Northern Lakes School of the Arts) as well as a summer arts camp. Average-sized homes in Amery's quiet, safe residential areas start in the $60,000 range.

Arts Scene
Amery's arts programming is community-based and thoroughly accessible. It takes place at the Northern Lakes Center for the Arts, a turn-of-the-century church that in 1989 was turned into 2,200 square feet of visual arts exhibition space, performing arts facility, classroom and studio complex, and lecture hall. On the visual arts end, the center uses its exhibition space for nearly three dozen shows each year, rotating work by local and regional artists, including an occasional exhibition of Native American contemporary work as well as fine craft, photography, and textiles.

   Classical music performance is handled by the Northern Lakes Chamber Orchestra, an ensemble that splits itself into a string quartet for Amery's October-to-May classical music season. The Northern Lakes Theatre Guild uses the Center's 100-seat theater-in-the-round for its four annual productions, and there's also a professional summer repertory season in nearby St. Croix Falls.

Through the extensive programs offered at the arts school, Amery's kids have every opportunity to learn how to play an instrument (and join the orchestra) or to work in theater (and join the theater guild) or to paint and sculpt (and exhibit their work in annual student exhibitions). In all, what's happening here will make tomorrow's generations of artists and arts audiences much better informed about their place in the arts world.

Alternatives

One of the areas that needs improvement in Amery is the lack of exhibition space in town restaurants and cafés for the region's many fine artists. One of the local banks has tried to lead the way, but Amery artists are having to exert some muscle to elbow out the beer posters on the walls and make room for their artwork. One hopes that places such as the Country Hearth Café and the Camelot Supper Club will see the error of their ways and contact the local arts center for a much-needed infusion of local creative input.

Art Perspectives

David Cysewski, a writer who has lived in Amery for five years, says that the town's awareness of itself as a rural arts center is just starting to make an impact on locals. "What the artists in this town have done is to take matters into their own hands, to do things themselves that needed to be done. Now you see young people in this town excited about things like art exhibitions and classical music concerts, and you also see people from other towns coming into Amery to attend an opening or a performance. The town's business community is catching on to the fact that what's happening at the art center is having a positive impact on Amery's business climate; lots of the local businesses are contributors to the arts."

Details

Population: 2,800

Important Arts Events: Amery Women's Club June Festival of the Arts, Amery Fall Festival in September

Must-See Art Gallery: Northern Lakes Center for the Arts

Local Arts Agency: Northern Lakes Center for the Arts
113 Elm Street
Amery, WI 54001
715/268-6811

Natural Food Store: Natural Foods

Farmer's Market: Mondays in downtown parking lot

National Public Radio: WHWC - 88.3 FM

Bookstore: Amery needs one; anyone interested?

Chamber of Commerce: Amery City Administrator
118 Center Street, West
Amery, WI 54001
715/268-7486

Fish Creek, Wisconsin

Ranked #20

Location

Fish Creek really isn't a town . . . it's more of a post office with a classy name in Gibraltar Township, a municipality about halfway down Wisconsin's Door Peninsula. Only about 300 residents call Fish Creek home year-round; but during the busy summer, the population zooms to somewhere between 10,000 and 15,000, many the sort of cultural tourists small art towns love.

Great Outdoors

When on this narrow strip of land jutting out onto Lake Michigan, you're never more than ten miles from the water. Fish Creek lives for its summers—glorious, celebratory days filled with sailing, beachcombing, fishing, and (of course) the arts. Locals seeking quiet time toss a line into the lake to angle for walleye, brown trout, smallmouth bass, and northern pike. The peninsula is loaded with state and county parks, many perched around its lakefront bluffs and beaches. Peninsula State Park has 3,700 acres of more developed marinas, bike trails, and campgrounds. Newport State Park holds 2,000 acres of hiking trails and campsites.

Lifestyle

Because it is a resort area, prices for a slim selection of homes along the peninsula are much higher than you'd expect in rural Wisconsin. Housing starts in the $80,000 range, but at the foot of the peninsula in nearby Sturgeon Bay, prices drop dramatically. As a whole, places like Fish Creek are friendly, safe, and family-oriented. About the biggest local threat is getting run over by an out-of-control Winnebago driven by a vacationing Iowa farmer. Families take evening bicycle trips together or go out to the Skyway Drive-In for the latest PG flicks.

Art education programs in local schools are surprisingly good because of the many visual and performing artists available for in-school residencies and classes. During summer the Peninsula Art School offers more than 60 visual arts and fine crafts classes for adults and kids, and The Clearing, in Ellison Bay, runs a May-to-October series of adult art education classes.

Arts Scene

The range of visual and performing arts available on the peninsula is amazing. There are three nonprofit exhibition spaces: the Hardy Gallery in Ephraim (ten miles north), the Miller Art Center Gallery in Sturgeon Bay (20 miles south), and the Link Gallery of the Door Community Auditorium in Fish Creek. The Door County Art League also operates its own gallery in Ephraim. The Hardy Gallery hangs work by both the Peninsula Arts Association and local kids, and hosts an occasional classical music performance. The Miller Art Center shows regional work, including an annual show of student art. It also hosts a summer classical music series.

Commercial galleries, many seasonal, line the peninsula from one end to the other. One-artist, fine crafts, contemporary, traditional landscape/lakescape, ceramics and weavings—each of the peninsula's towns seems to have a dozen galleries presenting astounding amounts of work. Cultural tourism is obviously alive and well in this corner of the state.

As good as things are for the region's visual arts, the performing arts have it even better. The abundant offerings encompass new plays by Chicago playwrights, touring classical soloists and orchestras, Shakespeare, and mainstream theater. Fish Creek is home to the Peninsula Players, the country's oldest professional resident summer theater, which performs in its lakefront playhouse from June through October. Other summer performers are the American Folklore Theatre, who present their repertoire of new works at the Peninsula State Park Ampitheater from June through August and the Peninsula Music Festival, which presents an outstanding program of top classical musicians at the Door Community Auditorium in August.

Midsummer's Music Festival is a chamber ensemble that spends its June running from one end of the county to the other performing at every possible venue, while Door Shakespeare holds its month-long season on the grounds of a waterfront estate. Open Door is a theater company presenting avant-garde work at several peninsula venues, and Peninsula Dance, a University of Wisconsin program, presents a summer performance series at the Fish Creek Town Hall.

Birch Creek Music Center is a summer music academy bringing together nationally prominent jazz, classical, and world musicians and several dozen talented high school and college musicians for classes and performances. Blue Circle Theater is Fish Creek's summer theater program for kids. It presents an annual production each August.

Alternatives

On this art-crazy peninsula, practically every business, restaurant, and café hangs local work. Be sure to check out the White Gull Inn, Village Café, the Viking, and the Black Locust.

Art Perspectives

Bob Hastings, visitors bureau director, observes, "This place is what Santa Fe would be like if it had Cape Cod architecture. Several years ago, we decided to build our reputation around the theme of 'culture in the country,' figuring that this would increase our tourism profile and give us a better quality of visitor. It's worked like you wouldn't believe."

Details

Population: about 300

Important Arts Events: Artigras in February, Jacksonport Maifest in May, Waterfront Art Festival in August, Autumnfest in September

Must-See Art Galleries: Blue Dolphin House, Edgewood Orchards Gallery, Fieldstone Gallery, Hardy Gallery, Jack Anderson Gallery, Maple Grove Gallery, Miller Art Center, North Light II, Paint Box Gallery, Water Street Gallery, Woodwalk Gallery

Local Arts Agency: Peninsula Arts Association
P.O. Box 213

Ephraim, WI 54211
414/854-1833

Natural Food Store: The Healthy Way

Farmer's Market: Saturday morning markets in most villages; farm stands all over the peninsula

National Public Radio: WPNE- 89.3 FM

Bookstores: Book World, Passtimes Books

Fish Creek Tourist Information Center
4097 Main Street
Fish Creek, WI 54212
414/868-2316

La Pointe, Wisconsin

Location

The Apostle Islands are an environmental treasure on the western end of Lake Superior. Madeline Island, home to part of the Bad River Indian Reservation and the town of La Pointe, is the one island that is not included in the Apostle Islands National Lakeshore. The closest city is Duluth, an hour's drive west once you ferry to the mainland.

Great Outdoors

On Madeline itself is the Big Bay State Park, 2,300 acres of campsites, hiking trails, and beaches, as well as an 18-hole golf course. Several county parks and public campgrounds (including some on the Red Cliff Reservation on the mainland) fill up with the nature-bound summer tourists, but the most glorious outdoor action takes place around the Apostle Islands. Here, sailboats and yachts from as far away as Toronto can anchor in splendid, deserted coves, spilling their passengers onto island campsites. In this part of the state, fishing's big business.

Lifestyle

Since the late 1960s, the island has been a magnet for second-home types who summer here. If you're one of the 180 people crazy enough to live on this island year-round, you learn to love each and every one of the 2,300 summer residents who arrive in late June and flee in early September. These are the people who make it possible for everyone else to live here, buying local art, attending concerts and theater performances, and patronizing places like Grampa Tony's and the Island Café.

Most months of the year ferries ply the water route connecting La Pointe to Bayfield, the town of 600 that everyone and everything headed for the island has to move through. In grade school, kids attend the island's school. Beyond eighth grade, they commute back and forth to Bayfield High on the ferry—until January, when the waters separating Madeline Island from Bayfield freeze. Then the trek to school requires a windsled or traveling an ice road. If you fret over the thought of your kids walking to school, just think of them zipping across a frozen lake at 50 mph on a windsled. Art classes are very basic in the local schools, so parents give top priority to involving their kids in the drama and visual arts program at The La Pointe Center. Homes on the island range from the very affordable, basic types artists prefer (in the $50,000 range) to the more expensive faux palaces marring the waterfront.

Arts Scene

The State Historical Society controls the Madeline Island Historical Museum, built on the site of what once was a fur trading post. The place is still a bit on the hidebound side, changing exhibits too infrequently and shutting out local artists except in its annual lecture series. The island's cultural headquarters is The La Pointe Center, a year-round, multidisciplinary exhibition, education, performance, and studio facility that attracts large crowds to its summer activities, and a consistent 180 to whatever it does during the winter. Founded in 1988, this multipurpose facility also serves as a conference center, nursery school, movie house, and community garden. The Art Guild exhibits at the center, as well as in its own gallery in La Pointe. Traveling exhibitions, invitational shows, and one-artist shows by the region's leading artists are housed in the La Pointe Center Gallery.

Artists living on the island tend to work in the craft fields, both in traditional and fine craft work. The island's craft gallery, Woods Hall Craft Shop, is the main exhibition and sales venue outside of the regional craft fair circuit. Nearby Bayfield has its own strong community of artists, with three gallery spaces in town: First Street Gallery, The Stone's Throw, and the Bayfield Artist's Co-op Gallery.

Performing arts are a large part of what keeps islanders sane during the winter. The island supports two groups, the Positivity Children's Theatre and the Positivity Players, who move their operations to the 78-seat Pole Barn Playhouse during the summer, a space used by other island groups, including the film society. The Big Top Chautauqua in Bayfield is the area's leading performing arts venue for summer folk music, jazz, and drama.

Alternatives

Most of the island's businesses hang local art on their walls; the Island Café and the Madeline Island Inn are the best sales spots. Occasionally The Clubhouse brings a jazz band over from the mainland.

Art Perspectives

According to Richter Hartig, a founding members of the Positivity Players, "There's a spirit here of trying things, because nobody knows what the local reaction will be to things the artists want to do. Now that things have blossomed and the arts are popular, people living here have more to do than just go to bars."

Michelle Auger, textiles artist notes, "I've learned a lot of my craft through the La Pointe Center's classes, and through the island's artists, who showed me how to sell my work through galleries and art festivals. There's a great spirit of support and cooperation among the island's artists."

Details

Population: 180 in winter, 2,500 in summer

Important Arts Events: July 4th Art Festival, summer performances at Madeline Island Music Camp, Positivity Players summer season at Pole Barn Playhouse

Must-See Art Galleries: Art Guild Gallery, Bayfield Artists Co-op Gallery, Buffalo Art Center at Red Cliff Indian Reservation, La Pointe Center Gallery, Woods Hall Craft Shop

Local Arts Agency: La Pointe Center
P.O. Box 247
La Pointe, WI 54850
715/747-3321

Farmer's Market: Farm stands on island and mainland

National Public Radio: KUMD - 89.9 FM

Chamber of Commerce: P.O. Box 274
La Pointe, WI 54850
715/747-2801

Sheridan, Wyoming

Location

Just before the Great Plains meet the Big Horn Mountains lies Sheridan, nestled into a river valley that's home to 14,000. The days of the frontier West are still very much a part of Sheridan's charm, and despite a recent surge in tourism, this community remains a true outpost of cowboy culture. Winters are absolutely brutal, which is how locals like it.

Great Outdoors

The Big Horn Range outside of Sheridan falls somewhere between spectacular and incredibly spectacular, leaning toward the speechless side of things. Far enough north to get the rainfall needed to keep its foothills a lush green, yet far enough south so that it lacks northwest forests' junglelike ground cover, the Big Horns are as picturesque as can be. They are part of a national forest which contains the Cloud Peak Wilderness. With these resources right in Sheridan's backyard, nobody needs an invitation to head out on a back-country hike or a week-long pack trip. There's a downhill ski area at Antelope Butte, and serious skiers need only drive a few hours west to reach Jackson Hole. Summer's main recreation areas are the Bighorn Canyon and Yellowtail Dam, which forms a spectacular 50-mile lake.

Lifestyle

Cowboy cultured . . . and proud of it! Sheridan celebrates its past in a hundred different ways, from the sophisticated elegance of the King Saddlery shop on Main Street to the fabulous Trail End mansion, a state historic site that doubles as one of Sheridan's important performing arts venues. Cowboy poetry programs here sell out as easily the annual Sheridan WYO Rodeo, a major event on the PRCA circuit.

Settled by English and Scottish cattlemen, Sheridan was a place of range wars between cattlemen and sheepherders earlier in the century, and one of the last frontiers for nineteenth-century Indian wars. Battlefields and monuments are a living part of the culture, and places like Fort Phil Kearny, Sawyer Battlefield, and Fetterman Ridge Monument are just a few of the local treasures. Much of Sheridan's turn-of-the-century architectural legacy has been preserved and restored, and the Sheridan Inn, the Bradford Brinton Memorial, Trail End, and the Main Street district are all National Historic Landmarks.

Arts Scene

Sheridan's visual arts scene is one of the nation's top markets for western traditionalist art, from the absolutely beautiful landscapes exhibited in downtown commercial venues to the touring exhibits hung at Sheridan College's Martinsen Gallery (the art department faculty includes several great artists). Historical western works are exhibited at the Bradford Brinton Memorial, a restored ranch house. Another western collection is shown at Trail End, a Flemish-style mansion once home to the state's governor. In nearby Ucross, the Ucross Ranch Gallery exhibits contemporary work by the fine artists who enter its residency program. The Big Red Gallery, also in Ucross, exhibits many Sheridan and regional artists.

Fine western crafts are also an important component of the Sheridan arts scene. One of the world's premier saddle and leather shops, King Saddlery employs dozens of fine craftspeople to create everything from elegantly tooled saddles to the ropes favored by America's top professional cowboys.

Sheridan's performing arts are centered around the WYO Theatre, a 1920s vaudeville house restored to its art-deco elegance in late 1989. Garth Brooks was one of the first big-name national acts to swoop into Sheridan for a performance or two at the 483-seat WYO. Every year the theater presents an outstanding series of its own, with several children's theater companies, urban jazz, contemporary dance, country music stars, touring theater, classical music, and ballet. Each summer the Civic Theatre Guild performs its Shakespeare in the Park festival on the manicured grounds of Trail End. The rest of the year it uses the Carriage House Theatre, also at Trail End, to present its regular season of comedy, musicals, and drama. The one performance that should not be missed, however, is Sheridan's fantastic rodeo—not an art form in the traditional sense, yet an integral part of Wyoming's cowboy culture.

Alternatives

You can spot Western art all over Sheridan, even in the hotel lobbies. Of special note is the Sheridan Inn's Buffalo Bill Bar.

Art Perspectives

Discussing the development of the WYO Theatre, director Sophie Pelissier notes, "A local corporation and concerned citizens saved the WYO from being destroyed in the early 1980s, and now it's one of the only facilities of its type in the entire state. But it wasn't always easy, and just a few years ago, the place came close to closing down because of its debt. Then we got a call from Garth Brooks' manager saying that Garth wanted to come to Sheridan and do a Christmas show, and could he somehow rent out the WYO? After thinking about it for a half-second, we set the date and announced the show. Sheridan's never seen ticket lines stretching down several city blocks, but that's what we had as soon as the news hit the radio. We were able to pay off our bills, and ever since then we've been operating in the black."

Details

Population: 14,000

Important Arts Events: Leather Trade Show in May, Bozeman Trail Days in June, Prairie Rose Art Festival in July, Don King Days in September

Must-See Art Galleries: Big Red Gallery, Bradford Brinton Memorial Gallery, Martinsen Gallery at Sheridan College, Trail End

Local Arts Agency: WYO Theatre 42 North Main Street

Sheridan, WY 82801
307/672-9083

Natural Foods: Once weekly at local church hall

National Public Radio: KEMC - 89.5 FM

Bookstores: Bighorn Books, Sheridan Book Gallery

Chamber of Commerce: P.O. Box 707 Sheridan, WY 82801 307/672-2485

Small Art Towns

in

Canada

Banff, Alberta

Location

Banff, an extraordinary community of 7,000 residents, is inside the boundaries of Banff National Park, one of the world's most beautiful places. Banff is a one-hour drive from Calgary.

Great Outdoors

Stretching hundreds of miles and flanking both sides of the Continental Divide, Banff National Park and its northern neighbor, Jasper National Park, are filled with 13,000-foot peaks and pristine glacier-fed lakes. Both parks are full of challenging alpine hiking trails, campgrounds, wilderness, and white water. Banff National Park has more than a dozen campgrounds and hundreds of miles of back-country hiking and mountain biking trails. Mountain climbing here is enormously popular.

Nearby Lake Louise, while too cold for swimming, is great for sailing and fishing for brook, cutthroat, and rainbow trout. The hot springs just a short walk from Banff's attractive downtown are irresistible year-round.

The ski areas around Banff are among Canada's best. Sunshine Village and Mt. Norquay are just a few of miles outside of town, and Lake Louise ski area (Canada's largest) is 40 minutes south of Banff.

Lifestyle

In addition to phenomenal natural beauty and outstanding outdoor recreation resources, Banff has a visual arts scene with tremendous strength in both its commercial and nonprofit sectors. Its performing arts scene attracts both local and big-name international talent—names usually seen only in major cities.

Banff is a fun town with a healthy nightlife and dynamite restaurants. Though popular, it has not yet grown too large or too expensive—it's still a place that refuses to put on airs, and still a place that cares deeply about its future.

The Banff Centre for the Arts is a year-round, multidisciplinary arts education center with a focus on classical music, opera, theater, playwriting, literature, and media arts. It is Canada's most prominent non-university arts center and certainly the most spectacularly located facility of this nature anywhere in North America. The Banff Centre's four programs—Centre for the Arts, Centre for Conferences, Centre for Management, and the International Institute for Innovation—attract everyone from contemporary artists to corporate executives. The institution is expanding its outreach, attracting artists from places like Japan and Australia.

Arts Scene

Local art can be found at nonprofit exhibition spaces like the Walter Phillips Gallery at Banff Centre and the Whyte Museum of the Canadian Rockies. The international Phillips Gallery features avant-garde art, while the Whyte's galleries are focused on more popular artistic expressions, mixing some traditional work with a predominantly contemporary focus. The

Whyte presents touring national exhibitions, regional invitationals, and local one-artist shows by the fine contemporary artists living in Banff, Lake Louise, and nearby Canmore.

Banff's commercial galleries exhibit traditional landscape work, executed in watercolor and oil by dozens of very strong realist painters who call the area home. This work sells by the truckload to Banff's cultural tourists, while the contemporary art created here finds buyers through galleries in Calgary, Toronto, Vancouver, and Montreal.

Banff's performing arts scene is in great shape, primarily due to the presence of the Banff Arts Festival, which runs from early June to mid-September. The festival is organized in stages that feature classical music and jazz; opera, theater, dance, and literature; an international string quartet competition; and an international film festival. The Banff Centre's venues range from a 900-seat performing arts auditorium to a 500-seat amphitheater and draw performers from all over the globe.

Visiting or living here during the summer months is like being in the midst of one of North America's performing arts whirlwinds—Aspen, Santa Fe, or Tanglewood. As a matter of fact, were it ranked with the U.S. towns, Banff would have fit neatly between Belfast, Maine, and Olympia, Washington.

A resident summer Shakespeare company performs at one of Banff's large hotels, and Any Space Theater is known for high-quality productions of experimental and new plays. Banff's large community of writers is always staging literary events such as readings and poetry competitions. The Calgary Philharmonic does its summer residency at the Nakiska ski area, where its Mozart on the Mountain festival is one of the year's most popular events.

Alternatives

Being a ski town, Banff has a respectable night scene. Two-steppers head to Wild-Bills, while the blues and jazz crowd goes over to Barnaby Coast.

Art Perspectives

According to Peter Hutchings, publisher, "Our performing arts scene is very diverse, and our tourism focus is international. When people come here they don't just want to look at nature . . . they want to participate in what's going on at different levels."

Details

Population: 7,000

Important Arts Events: Ice Sculpture Competition in January, Mozart on the Mountain in June, Banff Arts Festival from June to September, Artwalk in July, Banff Festival of Mountain Books in November

Must-See Art Galleries: Art of Man Gallery, Canada House, The Gallery, The Quest, Walter Phillips Gallery, Whyte Museum,

Local Arts Agency: Banff Centre for the Arts
Box 1020, Station 17

Banff, Alberta TOL OCO
403/762-6180

Natural Foods Store: Buckwheat and Sage

Canadian Broadcasting Company: CBC - 102.2 FM

Bookstore: Banff Book & Art Den

Chamber of Commerce/Tourism Bureau: P.O. Box 1298
Banff, Alberta TOL OCO
403/762-0270

Chemainus, British Columbia

Location

The inland side of Vancouver Island stretches hundreds of miles, starting from below the Washington side of the U.S.–Canada border and ending around the halfway point to the small art town of Ketchikan. Chemainus, population 4,000 and counting, hugs the island's eastern side. It's about an hour's drive north of Victoria, capital of British Columbia.

Great Outdoors

As you might expect, the fishing's great here. Migratory runs of every salmon species known to the Pacific Ocean cruise right past Chemainus on their way to spawning grounds. At certain times of the year, half the town jumps into anything and everything that floats so that they can haul in their share. The east side of Vancouver Island is one of the few parts of British Columbia where you'll find certifiable beaches, like the one at Qualicum, a short drive north of town. A short drive north of Qualicum is the huge wilderness of Strathcona Provincial Park, with alpine lakes, rain forest, 7,000-foot-high peaks, and a downhill ski resort.

Lifestyle

A little more than a decade ago, Chemainus was about as down in the dumps as a one-horse town can be, primarily because its one horse, the lumber industry, had packed its bags and galloped out of town. Real estate was worth next to nothing, the town's business leaders had no answers, and the future was gloomy. Chemainus' stage was set for the not-atypical sort of rebirth that transforms many depressed mining, logging, and manufacturing communities into thriving small art towns. The existing infrastructure was sound, and commercial and residential buildings were affordable to the creative individuals who started moving in on a shoestring and a prayer.

Perhaps most important, one dynamic local visionary had the courage to pursue a dream Karl Schultz, a railroad worker and millhand, stumbled upon his vision for his hometown while visiting cathedrals in Europe, where thousands flocked to gaze at centuries-old murals. When he told the Chemainus town council that a murals project could be just the ticket for the town's failed economy, nobody took him seriously. Fast-forward to the mid-1990s and the new Chemainus, where downtown real estate values have skyrocketed 500 percent since the early 1980s and the average home price is $135,000.

Arts Scene

What this town is about is public art. Starting in 1982 with a downtown mural painted by two artists from nearby Victoria, the Chemainus murals project has grown to three dozen public works (with more created each year) scattered throughout the business and residential areas. The murals project has become so well funded that internationally respected artists from across Canada and other nations have come to join the group of local and regional muralists. In recent years, sculpture has been added to Chemainus' outdoor art gallery, and now the town's collection of bronzes and carved wood sculpture is growing each year. Since the murals project's start, Chemainus' now-booming cultural tourism economy has launched more than a hundred businesses, attracted 400,000 visitors each year, and opened a new theater. Town leaders are now convinced of cultural tourism's unlimited potential not only for reviving the economy, but for creating a bona fide cultural renaissance. It's little wonder that Karl Schultz now advises an international group of communities eager to duplicate Chemainus' success. Chemainus would come in at number 55 if Canadian towns were ranked with U.S. art towns.

Chemainus is the home of Chemainus Theatre, which presents five dramas and a Christmas musical in its new 275-seat theater. The theater's play selection is a challenging one, and it invites both a resident repertory company and visiting theater pros to take the stage. Chemainus is also planning a multidisciplinary performing arts education center that will collaborate with the Chemainus Theatre. The town's community concert series is an occasional user of the theater on its dark nights. The theater's a must-stop for its art gallery and restaurant, both of which are top-notch. The Gallery exhibits visual arts, fine crafts, and textile arts. Chemainus is very active on the arts festival scene; during the summer months, daytrippers from Vancouver and Victoria can always find a reason to come to Chemainus.

Alternatives

Local artists hang their work in rotating exhibitions on the walls of The Playbill Cafe, which is part of the Chemainus Theater, and also in the Waterfort Restaurant.

Art Perspectives

Karl Schultz, founder of the Chemainus Murals Project, thinks the town's future is bright. "Everyone here thinks that things are just going to get better for Chemainus, and, given the investments people are making in this town, I'd agree with them. The neighborhoods are spruced up and very beautiful, and that's just one of the positive facets of the murals project's success that has spread to the community. Murals projects have worked everywhere I've seen them, but in some communities better than in others, depending on how dynamic the leadership is that's behind the project."

Details

Population: 4,000

Important Arts Events: Foundations Market Day in July, year-round performances of the Chemainus Theater

Must-See Art Galleries: The Gallery, Great West Art

Local Arts Agency: Chemainus Arts & Business Council
P.O. Box 1311
Chemainus, British Columbia
VOR 1KO
604/246-4701

Farmer's Market: Saturday mornings in nearby Duncan

Canadian Broadcasting Company: CBC - 690 AM

Bookstore: The Book & Card Co.

Chamber of Commerce: P.O. Box 1311
Chemainus, British Columbia
VOR 1KO
604/246-3944

Nelson, British Columbia

Location

Southeast British Columbia's Kootenay region is so mountainous that small towns such as Nelson have to sneak their airports right onto the edges of riverbanks. The landscape is spectacular, mountain ranges are separated by lakes, rivers, and narrow valleys. Just a three hour-drive north of Spokane and eight hours east of Vancouver, Nelson's 9,500 residents live in the awesome setting of Kootenay Lake's West Arm, its scenery framed by the glacial peaks of the Selkirk Mountains.

Great Outdoors

Kootenay Lake is a narrow, 70-mile gash in the rugged terrain known as Kootenay Country. Several Rocky Mountain ranges feed their runoff into the lake, which stretches into Idaho and western Montana before winding its way back into British Columbia's southeast corner. Everywhere you look are national parks, provincial parks, regional parks, and endless miles of densely forested wilderness. The lake's West Arm is a pristine refuge for migrating birds, wildlife, and enormous fish. Because it's fed from nearby snowmelt and glacier melt, its waters stay cold enough in summer that wearing a wet suit is always a good idea for water-skiers, even in July.

Bird-watching is just one of Nelson's claims to fame; in late spring thousands of migrating osprey (also known as sea eagles) return to the region after wintering along the coastline of southern Mexico's Oaxaca state, and the summer bird population includes great blue heron, western grebes, and several species of duck. The lake's reputation among Canadian sportfishermen is legendary; during summer the action is fast and furious for rainbow trout and kokanee (a freshwater salmon), with the local rainbow record a 35-pound giant snagged by a Kootenay Lake fisherman! Kootenay Lake's Dolly Varden are the largest in Canada, and it's almost an everyday occurrence to pull in a ten-pounder. But the big fish action is Gerrard Rainbow trout, which run as large as 20 pounds and can be fished almost year-round.

With dozens of parks scattered around the countryside, there's an amazing range of campgrounds and back-country hiking trails within easy reach of Nelson, from Grohman Narrows Provincial Park's easy nature walk to world-class mountaineering at Purcell Wilderness Conservancy's 10,000-foot peaks. The town's parks include miles of mountain-biking trails (competitive biking events are a major summer activity here), nature trails, a lakefront park, and abandoned back-country roads leading to old mines. Kokanee Creek Provincial Park, a short drive east of town, has a dozen or so marked and well-maintained hiking trails of varying degrees of difficulty. Nelson is a great place to live in winter if, like me, you enjoy working half a day and skiing half a day (the trick here is that you have to live very close to a ski area). Whitewater is a great powder-skiing spot 20 minutes south of Nelson. There's world-class downhill action at Red Mountain, about an hour away in Rossland.

Lifestyle

Nelson was a turn-of-the-century boom town that became famous first for its silver mines and then for its forest industry. Ornate structures were erected all over Nelson in those years of fast wealth, many designed by legendary Canadian architect Sir Francis Rattenbury. Almost all of Nelson's architectural heritage has been meticulously preserved, and today the community is known throughout Canada for its treasure trove of 350 designated-historic commercial and residential buildings. Walking tours of the town's historic districts and neighborhoods (home prices average in the $150,000 range) are a main reason why Nelson has developed a strong summer tourism industry. Many homes originally designed and built for silver kings and lumber magnates are today B&Bs catering to visitors who want to immerse themselves in the town's culture and history. The spectacular growth of the town's cultural tourism has diminished the mining and lumber industries' roles in Nelson's economy

Nelson's turn-of-the century wealth is what made it a cultural center for touring opera, vaudeville, and visual artists. As time passed, however, Nelson found less time for the arts; it wasn't until the early 1970s that artists who had graduated from Kootenay School of the Arts began sticking around town (instead of immediately heading to Vancouver), creating and selling work to the region's trickle of tourists. Over the past 25 years, Nelson's artists have come of age. They no longer scratch out livings by selling their work cheap—but that goes hand-in-hand with the fact that these artists have become quite good at what they do. In recent years Nelson has also attracted many strong artists from Calgary, Vancouver, and other towns across the province—professionals who have developed markets from Hawaii to Halifax for their art, and who are masters at placing their work in galleries where it will sell. This powerfully talented community has built for Nelson a Canada-wide reputation as a gorgeous small town where the cultural tourist can find top-rate art in a beautiful setting.

Nelson may not be the Santa Fe of the north, but with all its artists and outdoor treasures, I'd bet even money that it has a great shot at becoming the Jackson Hole of the late 1990s (as long as it avoids the commercialization that has muddied Jackson Hole's waters). Government, both in Nelson and at the provincial level, must recognize that cutting community arts funding would seriously damage the town's economic development and its prospects for cultural-tourism job development, and thus Nelson's best hopes for a prosperous future.

One of Nelson's most interesting arts developments is the Kootenay School of the Arts, which shut its doors in the 1980s at about the time Nelson's lumber mill closed. Entrepreneurial artists reopened the school in a historic downtown building and once again made it a central component of this community's arts scene. Today, renamed the Kootenay School of the Arts, Centre of Craft and Design, the institute has taken a hard look at what the region's arts-based economy needs in order to increase its Kootenay-wide impact. In addition to presenting courses in visual arts, ceramics, fiber arts, jewelry, and literary arts, the school also offers educational programs in fine crafts as well as furniture craftsmanship.

British Columbia's education funding has been sharply cut in the past few years as the province struggles with its economic downturn, a situation that led Nelson's schools to axe much of their arts budget. Artist-in-residence programs still bring local visual and performing artists into the schools for daylong seminars. And the town's restored Capitol Theatre works closely with the Nelson schools to fund touring kids' theater productions as well as field trips to matinee performances by visiting artists. Nelson's two historical museums, the Nelson Museum and The Chamber of Mines, have research libraries and exhibits about the region's past

Arts Scene

Back in the 1980s, when both the town and provincial governments were spending money lavishly, Nelson made a wise investment that has paid off millions in terms of its cultural tourism impact: it found the money needed to restore the 550-seat, former vaudeville house known as the Capitol Theatre. Today the Capitol is nothing less than the performing arts nerve-center for a huge part of the Kootenay region with its energetic and inventive programming, contributing, no doubt, to its recognition as one of the top small art towns. Nelson would have ranked fourth if included in the U.S. town rankings.

Performing arts are presented in a setting that includes a visual arts exhibition space dedicated to local artists, a film center that shows foreign and art-house flicks, and an education center that offers classes in the visual and performing arts for adults and kids. The Capitol is by far the preferred venue for the Nelson Overture Concerts Society's series of four performances by top Canadian classical musicians, the wildly popular performances of the Nelson Little Theatre community theater, and an inventive children's theater series called Kootenay Youth Drama Sessions. The Capitol Theatre is itself a presenter organization that brings in touring artists from across Canada for drama, contemporary dance, jazz, gospel, and folk music shows.

People who live here have no cause to feel cut off from the nation's cultural mainstream. Canadian International College, a Japanese language institute, presents a performance series in the 150-seat setting of its Subpub that tends toward jazz and folk music with some poetry readings, and independent promoters occasionally bring "name" rock and country music acts into the Nelson Civic Center. Nelson is also the home of the Selkirk Music School, part of the town's community college, which attracts music students from across western British Columbia, some of whom also play in Nelson's bars and social clubs.

All Nelson needs for its visual arts scene to gain substantial exposure is a first-rate arts center, such as the West Kootenay National Exhibition Centre in Castlegar, a 30-minute drive west of Nelson. (There is talk of relocating this to the more sensible location of Nelson's historic downtown.) The Nelson Museum's Mildred Erb Gallery is a small visual arts exhibition space that does the best it can for the local arts scene, rotating monthly shows and holding opening receptions. The town's visual arts scene is largely in the hands of its commercial galleries. Although the one cooperative gallery, The Craft Connection, has 20 fine-craftspeople members. Nelson's seven commercial galleries are largely concentrated in the historic Baker Street district, but for most of the summer the town explodes into a visual arts heaven through a highly successful Artwalk program that runs from early July through late September.

Staged by the Nelson Arts Council for the past 17 years, Artwalk's three-month run draws so many tourists into town that many artists make most of their annual income from the event, with locally created art sold off the walls of galleries, restaurants, coffeehouses, medical offices, and bookstores. One of the most encouraging Artwalk-related benefits has been the development of a local art-collecting passion, so that now nearly everyone in town buys at least one item during Artwalk—it's become the social thing to do and to brag about. Each summer more locations become involved in Artwalk, and even places that don't sign on as official Artwalk sites hang regional art on their walls. It's the kind of event that fills restaurants, bars, and B&Bs, and it's something all Nelson supports proudly.

Alternatives

Each summer's Artwalk is a three-month alternative to Nelson's commercial gallery scene, and the event's success has led to art being exhibited year-round in local restaurants. All Seasons Café, Zocalo Café (love that name!), Wild Onion Café, and Up the Garden Path are a few of the many restaurants exhibiting Nelson art. The town's night scene happens at places like Studio 80 (jazzy), Civic Hotel (bluesy), All Seasons Café (folksy), and the Subpub (some of everything).

Arts Perspectives

Shawn Lamb, photographer, says "When we lost the Kootenay School of the Arts it was like a slap in the face for Nelson's arts community—but it also was the wake-up call that threw responsibility for what was going to happen in Nelson right back into the artists' laps. We were the ones who had to pick up the pieces, and now that the school's been restarted we all feel a tremendous sense of pride for what the artists have accomplished. It's taken us 12 years to do it, but now we have 12 great years (at least) to enjoy it."

Details

Population: 9,500

Important Arts Events: Musicfest in April; Artwalk in July, August, and September; Winter Crafts Market in December

Must-See Art Galleries: Artisans on Ward, Capitol Theatre, Craft Connection, Figments Gallery, Glass House Gallery, Hummingbird Gallery, Made in the Kootenays, Mildred Erb Gallery, Ward Street Gallery, White Buffalo Girls

Local Arts Agency: Nelson Arts Council
P.O. Box 422
Nelson, British Columbia
VIL 5R2
604/352-2402

Natural Foods Stores: Kootenay Country Coop and Nature's Path

Farmers Market: Saturday mornings at renovated Farmers Market building next to Cottonwood Falls Park

Canadian Broadcasting Company: CBC - 98.3 FM

Bookstores: Bookgarden Café, Oliver's, Hummingbird Gallery

Chamber of Commerce: 225 Hall Street
Nelson, British Columbia
VIL 5X4
604/352-3433

Salt Spring Island, British Columbia

Location

Western Canada's Gulf Islands are a group of nearly 200 forested isles scattered along the southeast coast of Vancouver Island. Similar in character to the San Juan Islands off the northwest tip of Washington, the Gulf Islands' largest land formation is Salt Spring Island. Many of its 9,500 residents are professional artists, fine craftspeople, musicians, writers, actors, and producers. To get anywhere from the island requires a ferry ride and drive, with the metropolis of Vancouver a 2½-hour haul across the Strait of Georgia.

Great Outdoors

Salt Spring Island's maritime climate means that its rolling landscape, soaked by nearly nonstop drizzle from October through April, stays a deep shade of green. The island's south end is its least populated, while Fulford Valley is filled with family farms. Many Vancouverites have built second homes on the northern end. Orcas are regular visitors to the island's shorelines, and British Columbia's waters abound with monster salmon, the local favorite for sportfishing. Mt. Maxwell Provincial Park and Ruckle Provincial Park are the island's best places for hiking and camping. Ski areas are about a three-hour ferry ride/drive off the island.

Lifestyle

Over the past decade, Salt Spring Island has attracted two types of arts professionals. First are the midcareer types, who appreciate the island's laid-back lifestyle. These tend to be busy folks who need access to Vancouver's airport, theaters, art galleries, and sound stages, but live here to add a measure of sanity to their lives. The second and larger group are artists who have "been there, done that." After having lived and worked all over Canada, the U.S., and Europe, these artists have settled on Salt Spring Island because it is a beautiful, supportive place in which they can comfortably put down roots. In the early 1980s when artists began arriving, an average-sized home cost less than $100,000. Today that same place costs $200,000. Summers double the resident population and bring in hordes of day tourists from Vancouver.

Local schools do a standard job of art education, managing to hang onto programs like their artist-in-residence courses, despite the provincial government's budget whacking. Many artists volunteer to teach at local schools. In addition, the Salt Spring Island School of Fine Arts offers summer art classes. Kids also have access to lots of performing arts groups, with many opportunities to sign up for after-school classes, especially in dance.

Arts Scene

Salt Spring Island's performing and visual artists will have their prayers answered in early 1997, when the community's new arts center, called ArtSpring, comes on board with its 265-seat performance hall and 5,200 square-foot visual arts exhibition and studio/classroom space. The island's other nonprofit visual art exhibit space is Mahon Hall, which is rented out for both visual and performing arts events. Salt Spring Island would have been slotted between Walla Walla, Washington, and Joseph, Oregon, in the U.S. town rankings.

Salt Spring Island artists prefer to deal directly with the public through the highly effective vehicle of studio tours. The studio tour operates weekly from late April through October, with nearly three dozen artists participating. Most open their home studios, which are scattered around the island's countryside; others operate from the town of Ganges in commercial building studios. During summer the Gulf Islands Community Arts Council coordinates ArtCraft, a three-month group exhibition that markets local artists' work in an auditorium setting. The island's 16 commercial galleries are very strong, and cultural tourists respect Salt Spring as a great place to buy art. Several galleries are especially worth taking a look at, including the Pegasus Gallery of Canadian Art, the Naikai Gallery, Vortex Gallery, Off the Waterfront Gallery, Stone Walrus Gallery, Thunderbird Gallery, and the studio/gallery of Adrian Town.

The island's performing arts scene is best described as eclectic. Some groups perform for awhile, disappear for awhile, and then return for another cycle. Others rent performance space in one of the island's many halls and stage their drama, contemporary dance, folk music, and choral performances where and when they can. But once ArtSpring is completed, it will see frequent use by theater companies like the Off-Centre Stage Society, the Theatre of the Norm, and Theatre Alive. The island has a year-round film series showing first-run and foreign films at Mahon Hall. Several pubs feature local musicians on the weekends. The main performing arts event on the island is the Festival of the Arts, which attracts many musicians, writers, poets, and ethnic dancers from Vancouver and Victoria for performances spread throughout July.

Alternatives

Several island restaurants hang local art, with rotating shows most popular at Alfresco Waterfront Café and Moby's Marine Pub.

Art Perspectives

Artist April Curtis says, "You become very islandized after moving here. People try keeping up their careers in Vancouver, and some try going into the city several times a week at first. But after you get tired of that, you just figure out the ways you can make a living by spending most of your time here on the island. Thankfully, there's always something to do."

Details

Population: 9,500

Important Arts Events: Erotica Festival in March, Artists Studio Tour from April to October, ArtCraft from June to September, Festival of the Arts in July

Must-See Art Galleries: ArtSpring, Off the Waterfront Gallery, Pegasus Gallery of Canadian Art, Vortex Gallery

Local Arts Agency: Gulf Islands Community Arts Council
114 Rainbow Road
Salt Spring Island, British Columbia
V8K 2V5
604/537-1678

Natural Food Store: Nature Works

Farmer's Market: Saturday mornings at Centennial Park

Canadian Broadcasting Company:
CBC - 690 AM

Bookstores: Etcetera, Volume Two

Chamber of Commerce: 121 Lower Ganges Road
Salt Spring Island, British Columbia
V8K 2T1
604/537-4223

Baie-St.-Paul, Quebec

Location

Baie-St.-Paul, a town of 7,500, rests in a beautiful setting at the end of a fjordlike cove along the St. Lawrence River. Directly to the southwest are Montreal, a three-hour drive, and Quebec City, an hour's ride along a winding cliffside highway that climbs high above the river.

Great Outdoors

Civilization has yet to make much of an imprint on this part of North America. Drive north out of Baie-St.-Paul and you'll soon end up in an uninhabited wilderness, a place traversed by dogsleds and caribou herds—and little else.

    One of Canada's best downhill ski resorts, Ski Massif, is just 20 minutes away, and a sophisticated cross-country ski resort, Le Genevrier, is right in town. Baie-St.-Paul is part of Quebec's Charlevoix, a spectacular region of mountains, fjords, cliffsides, rivers, and islands. The nearby wildlife management areas at Zec des Martre and Zec du Lac-au-Sable draw sport-fishers and hunters, who come for the speckled and red trout, moose, and bear. The mountainous provincial park at Grand Jardins (a 30-minute drive) is filled with hiking trails, rustic cabins, campgrounds, a nature center, and cross-country ski trails. At certain times of the year, Baie-St.-Paul turns into one of the world's premier destinations for whale watching, with belugas, finbacks, and even blue whales feeding right off its shores.

Lifestyle

The arts colony here was formed during the first half of the twentieth century when artists moved to Baie-St.-Paul to bask in the glory of master painter Clarence Gagnon, a charismatic leader who drew others into his inner circle. Rene Richard, another master painter, arrived in the 1940s and is credited with keeping the colony intact through some lean years.

    Today, having established its reputation among French, American, and Canadian art collectors, Baie-St.-Paul is a sterling example of cultural tourism. Hundreds of artists live and create here, fueling the many galleries marketing their work. There's even an internationally respected museum of contemporary art exhibiting local, regional, and international shows. Tourists swarm into Baie-St.-Paul from the Queen's Birthday (late May) through Thanksgiving (mid-October in Canada), many of them serious collectors from Montreal, Quebec, and Ottawa.

    The town also boasts some incredible food. Baie-St.-Paul is filled with European-style auberges (small, romantic hotels), many of which have outstanding French restaurants. More than a dozen mostly French restaurants have sprung up in this part of French-speaking Quebec. In fact, the Charlevoix is so very French that Baie-St.-Paul is home to a commercial snail ranch (OK, it's more like a farm) that cultivates the humongous sliders the Quebecois love slipping down their throats in between glasses of vin ordinaire.

Arts Scene

The visual arts are Baie-St.-Paul's economic driver, and the town would have come in at #32 had it been part of the U.S. ranking. The town's most prominent exhibition space is the Centre d'Exposition de Baie-St.-Paul with its adjoining Centre d'Art de Baie-St.-Paul, an enormous contemporary art museum/gallery complex originally built as a regional cultural center and converted to an arts center in the early 1980s. In the Centre's multitude of galleries, curator Françoise Labbe exhibits a breathtakingly diverse calendar of shows by international artists in the vanguard of the contemporary arts scene. The space also serves the local and regional arts community through its Centre d'Art, including a commercial sales gallery for visual artists and an exhibition gallery rotating local and regional one-artist shows and juried invitationals.

Baie-St.-Paul's commercial galleries are primarily concerned with the skilled, traditionalist landscape work that made this community famous, although one of them, Galerie Yvon Desgagnes, exhibits contemporary work too. Several galleries are seasonal, open only from May to October, but others remain open through the winter, doing strong business around the holidays. The year's biggest arts bash takes place during Reves d'Automne, a late September, two-weekend culinary and visual arts event which draws tens of thousands.

The town's performing arts are limited to summer community theater performances at the 150-seat community center and mainstage pop music at Au Café du P'tit Reveur, a Reves d'Automne performance space active only during the festival's two-week run. A summer festival of top names in Canadian classical, jazz, and pop happens at Domaine Forget in nearby Saint Irenee, and a summer theater festival is staged at Manoir Richelieu in nearby Pointe-au-Pic.

Alternatives

Most Baie-St.-Paul restaurants exhibit work by local artists, but you'll find the best examples at Le Mouton Noir and Les Deux Soeurs. The town does have nightlife, with Club O de la Maison Otis presenting Canadian folk music, and Bar l'Epicentre doing the country-western thing.

Art Perspectives

According to Françoise Labbe, director of Le Centre d'Art Baie-St.-Paul, "There have been artists here since the early part of the century, but the galleries didn't start catching on until the early 1970s. But once it started, many more galleries and artists started moving in. Most of them are in the middle of their careers and are very well known, so the quality of what's shown in the galleries tends to be very strong."

Details

Population: 7,500

Important Art Events: Young Painters Exposition in February/March, Festival International du Domaine Forget in summer, Panorama Exhibition in July/August, Reves d'Automne in September/October

Must-See Art Galleries: Atelier et Galerie d'Art Pierre Labrecque, Galerie d'Art Iris, Galerie l'Harmattan, Galerie Yvon Desgagnes

Local Arts Agency: Le Centre d'Art
4 et 23, rue Ambroise Fafard
Baie-St.-Paul, Quebec, G0A 1B0
418/435-3681

Farmer's Market: Saturday mornings at the marketplace in front of the Arena

Public Radio: CBC - 103.1 FM

Bookstore: La Librairie

Chamber of Commerce: 13 St. Jean Baptiste Street
Baie-St.-Paul, Quebec, G0A 1B0
418/435-3681

St. Jean-Port Joli, Quebec

Location

Quebec's Chaudiere-Appalaches region is densely forested land that runs from the south bank of the St. Lawrence River down to the far northern borders of Maine, Vermont, and New Hampshire. The town of St. Jean-Port Joli overlooks the river just an hour's drive northeast of Quebec City and is packed with talent and potential.

Great Outdoors

From St. Jean-Port Joli's perspective, nature's treasures should be enjoyed everyday. This 3,500-strong community of woodsmen is rapidly becoming a community of artists, making their crafts and earning their living from the forests on both sides of the St. Lawrence River.

The area's rivers and lakes are salmon spawning grounds. During the migration season, the town comes alive with American fishermen hungry for the local delicacy. The locals, however, keep many fishing spots to themselves. Old logging roads and lakes south of St. Jean-Port Joli serve as biking trails and waterskiing sites in the summer, and cross-country trails and ice fishing sites in the winter. The Appalachian Mountains of eastern Canada are the Chaudiere-Appalaches's best spots for camping and back-country hiking, especially at Parc Regional du Massif du Sud, less than an hour's drive southwest of St. Jean-Port Joli. The closest downhill ski areas are in the Laurentian Mountains two hours north of Quebec City.

Lifestyle

Rural, French-speaking St. Jean-Port Joli is so outgoing and friendly it makes you wish the French took their cues from the Quebecois. But then, St. Jean-Port Joli has a lot to be happy about. From a forestry-dependent economy, the town has diversified to capitalize on the potential of cultural tourism. St. Jean-Port Joli is on the verge of a phenomenon that catapulted Loveland, Colorado, into the top ranks of North America's small art towns.

St. Jean-Port Joli has always had a strong tradition of wood craftsmanship and carving. For decades, the shops along historic Place de l'Eglise have carried locally created carvings alongside the other work they sell. Artists living in St. Jean-Port Joli have developed a strong reputation for the quality and originality of their work. As commissions for larger pieces started arriving on artists' doorsteps, the artists themselves began experimenting with their sculpture, creating new artistic challenges for themselves. In recent years, sharp-eyed art collectors from Quebec City, Montreal, and Ottawa started snapping up art work in town. Sculptors have found markets for both contemporary and traditional work. Some have received commissions to create monumental works for Quebec public buildings.

This has led to two interesting developments for St. Jean-Port Joli artists. First, travelers throughout the province are noticing that astounding sculpture created in this small art town has been installed in public buildings all over Quebec. When they find out where the sculpture is made, they make a point of putting the town on their travel itineraries—a cultural tourism phenomenon.

Second, as other eastern Canadian sculptors have seen St. Jean-Port Joli artists excel in three-dimensional media, they have started moving into town to be part of the renaissance. Many contemporary sculptors now living and working in St. Jean-Port Joli don't sell through the local art market; their expensive work is shipped out of town to galleries in Montreal, Toronto, and Vancouver.

Arts Scene

Despite St. Jean-Port Joli's need for an arts space capable of accommodating monumental sculpture, it would have fit nicely between Quincy, Illinois, and Moscow, Idaho, in the U.S. rankings. And the town's business, government, and arts leaders are already planning such a project. Until then, the best nonprofit art exhibition space is Centre Municipal. The town hasn't yet attracted a contemporary art gallery, but nearly a dozen commercial galleries and studios exhibit traditional sculpture. A sculpture park at Domaine de Gaspé Village has nearly 20 public works of art donated to the town through its annual Fête Internationale de la Sculpture, which takes place each June along the St. Lawrence. The event features sculpture-carving teams from different nations and four from St. Jean-Port Joli. The town also has a school that teaches both traditional and contemporary styles of sculpture.

The town's performing arts resources are surprisingly diverse, with a contemporary dance and education center—the Academe Evonne Boyce Music School—the Theatre Populaire Drama School, and two theater companies.

Alternatives

Most of the cafés and restaurants on St. Jean-Port Joli's charming Place de l'Eglise exhibit the work of local artists.

Art Perspectives

Claude Blanchette, St. Jean-Port Joli's Director of Tourism, notes, "Our main goal right now is to develop a strategy for the future of our sculpture community. We're starting to build a regional reputation as a cultural tourism destination, but we need more specific events that people can focus on. We don't have the funding that a place like Banff has access to, so we largely have to do this ourselves   and it takes time "

Details

Population: 3,500

Important Arts Events: Fête Internationale de la Sculpture in late June, summer theater season at La Roche a Veillon

Must-See Art Galleries: Centre d'Art Animalier Faunart, Centre de Sculpture Est-Nord-Est, Galerie d'Art Port Joli

Arts Agency: Alliart
555 Avenue de Gaspe Est
St. Jean-Port Joli
Quebec, G0R 3G0
418/598-7262

Farmer's market: Place de l'Eglise (on Saturday mornings)

National Public Radio: Canadian Broadcasting Company (CBC) - 98.1 FM

Bookstore: Salon des Livres

Chamber of Commerce: 7 Place de l'Eglise
St. Jean-Port Joli, Quebec,
G0R 3G0
418/598-9465

The Top 100 Small Art Towns in the United States

Towns are listed in ranking order.

1 ✓	Eureka, California		✓35	Telluride, Colorado
2	Northampton, Massachusetts		36	Lanesboro, Minnesota
3 ✓	Taos, New Mexico		37	Beaufort, South Carolina
4 ✓	Durango, Colorado		38	Coupeville, Washington
5	Deer Isle, Maine		✓39	Woodbury, Tennessee
6	Panama City, Florida		40	Springville, Utah
7	Burlington, Vermont		41	Salida, Colorado
8 ✓	Newport, Oregon		42	Peterborough, New Hampshire
9	Asheville, North Carolina		43	Cape May, New Jersey
10	Belfast, Maine		✓44	Carson City, Nevada
11	Olympia, Washington		45	Blowing Rock, North Carolina
12	Middlebury, Vermont		46	Albany, Texas
13	Nantucket, Massachusetts		47	Johnson, Vermont
14 ✓	Ashland, Oregon		48	Rockport, Texas
15 ✓	Lawrence, Kansas		49	Alpine, Texas
16	Loveland, Colorado		50	Bigfork, Montana
17	Lahaina, Hawaii		51	Clarksdale, Mississippi
18 ✓	Berea, Kentucky		52	Hot Springs, Arkansas
19 ✓	Moab, Utah		53	Easton, Maryland
20	Fish Creek, Wisconsin		54	Kerrville, Texas
21	Jamestown, New York		55	Berkeley Springs, West Virginia
22	Walla Walla, Washington		56	Columbus, Indiana
23 ✓	Joseph, Oregon		57	Quincy, Illinois
24	New Harmony, Indiana		58	Moscow, Idaho
25	La Pointe, Wisconsin		59	Sandpoint, Idaho
26	Woodstock, Vermont		60	New Smyrna Beach, Florida
27 ✓	Cedar Falls, Iowa		61	Peekskill, New York
28	Elkins, West Virginia		62	Oxford, Mississippi
29	Abingdon, Virginia		63	Helena, Montana
30	Bisbee, Arizona		64	Fredericksburg, Virginia
31	Charlottesville, Virginia		65	Anacortes, Washington
32	Corning, New York		66	Dillon, Montana
33	Round Top, Texas		67	Amery, Wisconsin
34	New York Mills, Minnesota		68	Arrowrock, Missouri

69	Spencer, Iowa	85	Salisbury, Maryland
70	Hancock, Michigan	86	Ketchikan, Alaska
71	Sheridan, Wyoming	87	Fayetteville, Arkansas
72	Scottsbluff, Nebraska	88	Lancaster, Ohio
73	Homer Alaska	89	Salisbury, North Carolina
✓ 74	Virginia City, Nevada	90	Lewiston, Maine
75	Red Bank, New Jersey	✓ 91	Raton, New Mexico
76	Mitchell, South Dakota	92	Litchfield, Connecticut
77	Rehoboth Beach, Delaware	93	Easton, Pennsylvania
78	Salina, Kansas	94	Brunswick, Georgia
79	Westerly Rhode Island	95	Guthrie, Oklahoma
80	Shelburne Falls, Massachusetts	✓ 96	Madrid, New Mexico
81	Metaline Falls, Washington	✓ 97	Mariposa, California
82	Alfred, New York	98	Hannibal, Missouri
83	Newburyport, Massachusetts	99	Carnegie, Pennsylvania
84	Galena Illinois	100	Lewes, Delaware

The Top Small Art Towns in Canada

1   Nelson, British Columbia
2   Banff, Alberta
3   Salt Spring Island, British Columbia
4   Baie-St.-Paul, Quebec
5   Chemainus, British Columbia
6   St. Jean-Port Joli Quebec

Index

Other Books from John Muir Publications

Rick Steves' Books

Asia Through the Back Door, 400 pp., $17.95
Europe 101: History and Art for the Traveler, 352 pp., $17.95
Mona Winks: Self-Guided Tours of Europe's Top Museums, 432 pp., $18.95
Rick Steves' Baltics & Russia, 144 pp., $9.95
Rick Steves' Europe, 528 pp., $17.95
Rick Steves' France, Belgium & the Netherlands, 256 pp., $13.95
Rick Steves' Germany, Austria & Switzerland, 256 pp., $13.95
Rick Steves' Great Britain, 240 pp., $13.95
Rick Steves' Italy, 224 pp., $13.95
Rick Steves' Scandinavia, 192 pp., $13.95
Rick Steves' Spain & Portugal, 208 pp., $13.95
Rick Steves' Europe Through the Back Door, 480 pp., $18.95
Rick Steves' French Phrase Book, 176 pp., $5.95
Rick Steves' German Phrase Book, 176 pp., $5.95
Rick Steves' Italian Phrase Book, 176 pp., $5.95
Rick Steves' Spanish & Portuguese Phrase Book, 304 pp., $6.95
Rick Steves' French/ German/Italian Phrase Book, 320 pp., $7.95

A Natural Destination Series

Belize: A Natural Destination, 344 pp., $16.95
Costa Rica: A Natural Destination, 380 pp., $18.95
Guatemala: A Natural Destination, 360 pp., $16.95

City·Smart™ Guidebook Series

City·Smart™ Guidebook: Denver, 224 pp., $14.95 (avail. 9/96)
City·Smart™ Guidebook: Minneapolis/St. Paul, 224 pp., $14.95 (avail. 10/96)
City·Smart™ Guidebook: Portland, 224 pp., $14.95 (avail. 8/96)

Kids Go! Series

Kids Go!™ Denver, 144 pp., $7.95 (avail. 9/96)
Kids Go!™ Minneapolis/St. Paul, 144 pp., $7.95 (avail. 10/96)
Kids Go!™ San Francisco, 144 pp., $7.95 (avail. 10/96)
Kids Go!™ Seattle, 144 pp., $7.95 (avail. 9/96)